EXPLORING America's HIGHWAYS

Minnesota

Trip Trivia

compiled by

Michael Heim

T.O.N.E. Publishing
Travel Organization Network Exchange, Inc.
Wabasha, Minnesota
2004

Cover and graphic design by Toby Mikle at tmcreations.com
Special thanks to Val Courter, of Grinnell, Iowa for her assistance proofreading.

Printed in the United States
ISBN 0-9744358-1-3

Special Thanks
to my lifetime travel buddies

This book is dedicated to my long time traveling companions -
my wonderful wife Cindy, and our beautiful children, Robbie and Sara.
Without their patience, encouragement and wonderful company,
this book would not have been possible, or nearly as much fun.

I offer a heartfelt "thank you," and I look forward to our
continued travels...wherever they may take us.

Turn Your Next Trip
into an Entertaining Adventure!

Exploring America's Highway: Minnesota Trip Trivia is much more than a travel guide - it turns trips into fun, educational and interesting ventures. Unlike any other book or product on the market, Exploring America's Highways enables you to quickly and easily find information to enhance your trip, turning going from "Point A to Point B" into an entertaining adventure.

Wherever you're going in Minnesota, you can find your route. Then follow along to learn fascinating historical facts, local landmarks, prominent people, geographical insights, industry, inventions, as well as plain old fun trivia.

The cities and towns are arranged conveniently in your route order. You don't have to waste time looking back and forth throughout the book; we've laid it all out for you!

With travel details for 18 interstates and highways, easy-to-follow maps, and point-by-point descriptions, you trip will become as much fun as the destination!

What you'll find along your route:

Place Names	• Fascinating backgrounds of the names of cities and towns
Historical Significance	• Overview of significant local events throughout history
Local Landmarks	• Noteworthy points of interest from man-made to natural, unusual or just plain interesting.
Prominent People	• "Hometown" people who've gone on to achieve fame or importance in some way.
Geological	• Explanations of why we see what we see.
Industry	• What towns and areas produce what, how things are made, who makes them ... and why.
Inventions	• Interesting anecdotes of where things are created.

We all know every town has a story, and every road crosses paths with history. Now, Minnesota is yours to explore. With Exploring America's Highway: Minnesota Trip Trivia you will find the journey as enjoyable as the destination!

Happy Traveling!

Michael Heim

Michael Heim

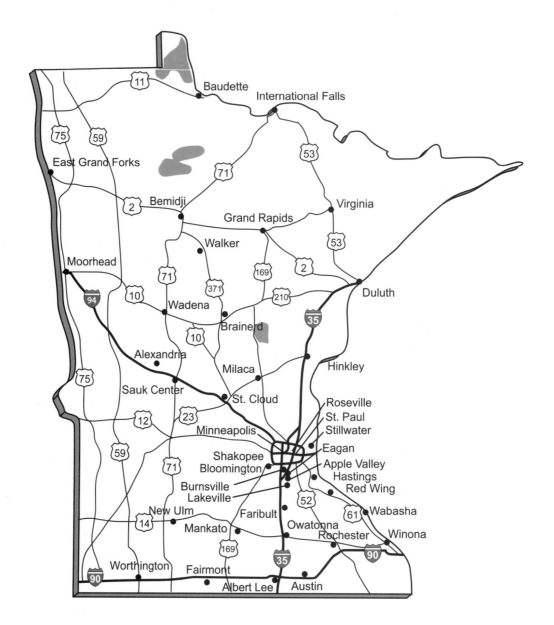

Table of Contents

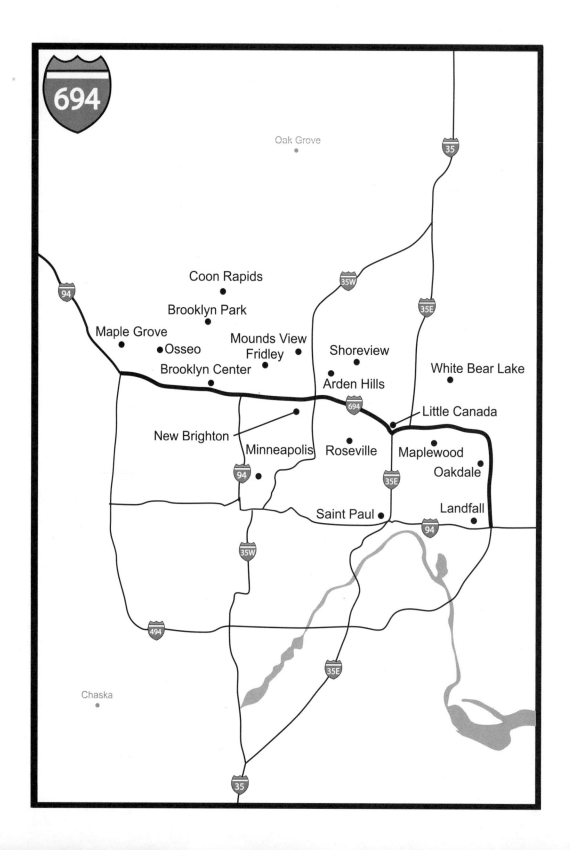

Landfall

Historical Significance

This town was started as a private trailer park that was developed by the Washington County Housing and Redevelopment Authority which enhance the manufactured home concept by including a school, community center and city hall.

Saint Paul
(See I-94 - page 34)

Oakdale

Place Name

Oakdale was named by Arthur Stephen, who served as Justice, Chair of the Board of Supervisors, and Postmaster for the area. The name was selected because of the many patches of oaks located in the surrounding valleys.

Maplewood

Place Name

Originally called St. Agnes, this town was renamed for the sugar maple trees found throughout the wooded areas around the state.

White Bear Lake

Place Name

The city got its name from the lake that it rests on. The area as a whole got its name from Native Americans who believed the shorelines were haunted by a White Bear who supposedly attempted to kill a brave's beloved. However, the brave killed the bear before it attacked his lover.

Local Landmark

The Erd-Geist Gazebo was built on the Lake in 1883 by Thomas Erd in

 White Bear Lake was the first city in the United States to ban cigarette vending machines.

3

honor of his daughter Annie and her husband Emil Geist. Erd died only two years after the construction of the Gazebo, but it certainly tells a fine story of a warm-hearted father-daughter relationship.

> Other notables that took shelter in the area include F. Scott Fitzgerald, Ma Barker and Baby Face Nelson.

General Trivia

The name "White Bear Lake" might ring a bell for readers of Mark Twain's "Life on the Mississippi". Twain explained the lake as having healing powers in that book.

Prominent People

Adventurer Gerry Spiess built a ten-foot sailboat christened the Yankee Girl, in his garage in White Bear Lake. Departing from Chesapeake Bay he made a solo voyage across the Atlantic, arriving in Falmouth, England on July 24, 1979.

Vadnais Heights

Place Name

The township was given the name of the lake where, French Canadian, Jean Vadnais, settled on the southeastern shores.

Little Canada

Place Name

Farmer voyageur and trader Benjamin Gervaise was one of the first of many French Canadians to settle in the township named after their homeland

Roseville

Place Name

Named after Isaac Rose, one of the first white settlers, who conducted the area survey.

Historical Significance

Roseville stands on land that was once home to the Dakota and Ojibway Natives. The Dakota believed their land was superior because it was located at the juncture of the Minnesota and Mississippi Rivers, which they poetically claimed was immediately over the center of the earth and beneath the center of heaven.

Many years later in 1940, Ramsey County Surveyors bolstered this claim when they placed a boulder on the spot they determined was exactly one-half the distance between the equator and the North Pole. This spot was just north of Roselawn Avenue in Roseville.

The first non-native settled in the Roseville area in 1843, six years before Minnesota became a territory.

In 1850 Rose Township was established, including the areas now known as Roseville, Lauderdale, and Falcon Heights, as well as parts of present day St. Paul and Minneapolis.

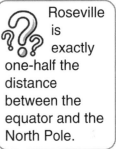

Roseville is exactly one-half the distance between the equator and the North Pole.

Farms and nurseries dominated the area until the 1930s when commercial development arrived, attracted by the wide-open space, convenient location, and the railroad. At the same time, people began leaving the inner cities for the more spacious, less congested lifestyle of the suburbs.

By 1948 the township form of government could no longer accommodate the area's rapid growth. Roseville incorporated as a village in May of 1948, followed by Falcon Heights and Lauderdale; and Rose Township ceased to exist.

Roseville's population and commercial development grew dramatically during the 1950s and the 1960s. The city then turned its focus from planning to redevelopment and preservation. Today Roseville is a mixed land-use community with a strong residential base and vibrant retail.

Prominent People

The first north-to-south bicycle ride across Africa was accomplished by Roseville natives Dan and Steve Buettner. Starting with their rear tires in the Mediterranean Sea, they ended the 272 days, 11,836 mile trek by rolling their front wheels into the Indian Ocean. Throughout their journey they encountered the challenges of the Sahara Desert, jungles and mountains as well as facing malaria, a civil war and thieves.

Shoreview

Place Name

The town was named in reference for the numerous lakes.

Historical Significance

The Dakota and Ojibwa Indians once inhabited the area that is now Shoreview.

Note: Indian mounds containing human bone fragments, arrowheads, pieces of pottery and bits of charcoal have been found on Rice Creek near the north shore of Long Lake.

Socrates A. Thompson was the first person to settle on the land in 1850. He was looking for land to do farming on. He left St. Paul accompanied by an Indian friend to find land. He eventually filed a claim for land near the Eastern Shore of Turtle Lake. He named this lake because of the large turtle he had captured in its waters.

Shoreview was first named Mounds View Township, which was named for the range of

hills running through the center of the township. It was organized on May 11, 1858, the day that Minnesota became a state. The township included cities of Shoreview, Arden Hills, New Brighton, Mounds View and parts of North Oaks and St. Anthony.

Shoreview became a city in 1975 through an act of the State Legislature.

In 1906 Joseph Hackey, a State Senator and millionaire, built a hobby farm called Arden Farms. This farm and the terrain eventually formed the basis for the City's name.

Historical Significance

The Sioux often used Lake Johanna as a resting point on their journey to Rice Lake for the fall wild-rice harvest.

* * * *

In 1850, Charles Perry became the first settler by breaking ground and planting potatoes on three acres adjacent to Lake Johanna. At that time, the land was part of Mounds View Township.

Place Name

The city was named after Brighton, Massachusetts, a cattle center serving the Boston area, which in turn was most likely named after the famed Brighton, England resort city.

Historical Significance

As with most towns in Minnesota, New Brighton and the surrounding area was first inhabited by Native Americans. The Dakota (also referred to as the Sioux) and the Ojibway (commonly known as the Chippewa) came through the area on rice harvesting treks, eventually locating near Long Lake at Rice Creek. Many artifacts have been found at this location including bones, pieces of pottery, pipes, and arrows.

In the mid 1800s came French and English settlers looking for land to homestead. As the number of settlers increased they recognized the need for an organized settlement. In 1858, a settlement was established which included a general store, school and mission church. A government with elected officers was also formed.

The most significant point in the history which led to the founding of New Brighton was the formation of the Minneapolis Stockyards and Packing Company in 1888. The company, which was located in what would be known as New Brighton, was formed to supply home demands and to claim a share of the growing trade.

Around that same time, New Brighton not yet officially a city was given its name by the predominately English founders.

One year before New Brighton became incorporated the first church was erected. The white wooden building with its tall spire was a distinctive landmark perched on the hillside on Cleveland Avenue. The church served as a center of worship as well as social activity.

The Village of New Brighton was incorporated on January 20, 1891. At that time fourteen passenger trains passed daily through the newly incorporated village.

New Brighton's first mayor was John T. Davies who bore the title of President (the title continued well into the 20th century). Davies was a Welshman who owned the Transit House Hotel on what is now the southwest corner of 10th Street and 5th Avenue. A firm saloon man, he refused to sell liquor to customers whom he judged had drunk their limit. He was one of the most esteemed people in the community and known as a sensitive gentleman and humanitarian.

As one can tell from reading New Brighton's early history, the presence of the stockyards transformed a sparsely populated piece of land into a thriving community. It is for this reason the citizens of New Brighton annually celebrate "Stockyard Days" in appreciation of the industry that gave the city its beginning.

Place Name

The one thing that brought residents to the area was the strange and awesome mounds of sand and gravel in its northwest corner, high enough to be seen from almost anywhere in the township and from much of Anoka County.

Today the mounds are nearly gone, sacrificed to the ravages of nature, the needs of this country during World War II when this area became an important small arms arsenal, and the thousands of loads of sand and gravel have since been removed. Only a few small battered hills remain to remind us of our name.

Historical Significance

The first landowners in the area remained stable until 1936. There were a few scattered farms, roads and large areas of wooded and brush land. The land had been overlooked by most real estate developers because it was too far north of Minneapolis and St. Paul, five miles beyond the city limits and city transportation.

In 1938, developers began to realize the possibilities of suburban housing in Mounds View Township. In 1951 the township began to change with the break off of over 6,120 acres and 2,000 people to form the Village of Arden Hills. For the next several years, portions of Mounds View Township would be annexed into surrounding communities. By early 1957, plans began to incorporate the balance of Mounds View Township. On April 22, 1958, Mounds View Township became a village.

The Township of Mounds View was created in the extreme northwest corner of Ramsey County on May 11, 1858, the day Minnesota became a state.

7

Fridley

Place Name

This town's name recognizes Abram McCormick Fridley, who was an agent for the Winnebago Indians, local farmer and a representative in the legislature.

Historical Significance

Before 1847, John Banfill became the first settler proprietor of Manomin, now Fridley. He was a territorial senator and became Minnesota's first State Auditor. Banfill built a tavern where Rice Creek flows into the Mississippi River.

This was a popular place for sawmills and lumber camps as well as wagons to stop on their long travel between St. Paul and the Dakotas on the Red River Ox Cart Trail. Now East River Road.

In 1847 the two story Greek Revival style house named Banfill Tavern and Wayside Inn, was built for soldiers and fur traders who traveled the course of the Red River Trail. This trail was also named the first Territorial Road.

In 1851-52 Banfill later opened a general store and post office. He sold the property in 1857. The building had several owners until 1912 when the Locke family purchased the land and ran a dairy farm, later using the house for a summer home. Anoka County bought the land in 1967 and operated it as the Anoka County Historical Society. Today, the Banfill-Locke Center for the Arts is used for local artists, patrons and art lovers to promote public awareness and appreciation of the arts and provides artists to exhibit, teach, market and perform their work.

* * * *

In 1856 Alexander Ramsey, Minnesota's first governor bought property in Fridley.

Mighty Duck and Mighty Ducks II were filmed at the Columbia Ice Arena.

General Trivia

In 1971 Fridley issued one of the nation's first television franchises.

Prominent People

Emily Trempe attended Totino Grace High School, in Fridley, Minnesota. She appeared in the tv show JAG, as well as in the movie Tar Beach and The Sisters Club.

Minneapolis
(See I-94 - page 38)

Coon Rapids
(See Hwy 169 - page 139)

Brooklyn Center

Place Name

Brooklyn Center was not named after Brooklyn, New York. It came from "Brooklyn Township" which was named by settlers in the Osseo area after they arrived from Brooklyn, Michigan.

Local Landmark

Although this site is known today as the Earl Brown farm, it originally belonged to Captain John Martin, who was involved in steamboating, lumbering, banking, flour milling and railroading. In the mid-1880s, he purchased 420 acres of rich Hennepin County farmland. Martin sold the farm to his grandson, Earle Brown in 1901. Brown gradually increased the size of the farm to about 750 acres.

Aspiring to be a gentlemen farmer, Brown initially used the land to breed award-winning Belgian Horses. But the farm was destined to become famous for activities unrelated to agriculture. In 1911, the village of Brooklyn Center was formed at a meeting held at the Brown farm.

As the nation became interested in aviation during World War I, Brown offered his farm and its buildings as a training field for U.S. military aviators. Though this offer was declined, the Brown farm did become the first commercial flying field in Minnesota in the summer of 1918, when hangars were erected and pilots began using the site as a training facility and airport. Although planes had previously landed on Minnesota lakes and at the Parade (grounds) near Dunwoody Institute, no formal air fields had been constructed.

In 1920 Brown was elected Hennepin County sheriff, a position he held twice, from 1920-1929 and then from 1943-1947. In 1929 he organized the Minnesota Highway Patrol, which used the farm as a training facility.

In 1932 he unsuccessfully ran for state governor, and lost to Floyd Olson. Brown lived on the Brooklyn Farm until his death in 1963, raising horses and collecting carriages.

In 1949 Brown willed the farm to the University of Minnesota, hoping that it would become the University's Agricultural Extension Center upon his death. After Brown died, however, the University sold the land and used the income to build the Earle Brown Continuing Education Center of the St. Paul Campus.

In 1985 the City of Brooklyn Center acquired the buildings and the property of the original homestead. Preserved for the people of Minnesota, it is a tangible link to the agricultural

> During World War I, Brown offered his farm and its buildings as a training field for U.S. military aviators. Though this offer was declined, the Brown farm did become the first commercial flying field in Minnesota in the summer of 1918.

9

heritage of what is now an urban area. It is also a memorial to an important figure in Minnesota history.

<u>(Historical marker located at Earle Brown Drive in Brooklyn Center)</u>

* * * *

The history of Brooklyn Center United Methodist Church dates back to 1854, making it the oldest congregation in Brooklyn Center.

The first Brooklyn Baptist Church was built in 1866.

Brooklyn Park is the hometown of former actor and professional wrestler, Jessie "The Body" Ventura. Ventura was also elected governor of Minnesota in 1998.

Place Name

In late 1853 and early 1854, settlers from Michigan staked claim to this area and named it Brooklyn Township, after their home territory of Brooklyn, Michigan.

Historical Significance

Brooklyn Park was part of the Fort Snelling Reserve in the early 19th Century, under the protection of the treaty with the Dakota Indians.

Early pioneers begin settling the territory west of the Mississippi River in 1852 after the government opened up the territory to homesteading. The territorial legislature set in motion the law that organized Hennepin County. That spring the first claims to the new territory would become Brooklyn Township.

General Trivia

Brooklyn Park was known for its potatoes and celebrates with the Tater Daze festival each year. Potato farming was a major industry for Brooklyn Park, nearly 40 growers were cultivating between 2,000 – 3,000 acres of potatoes a year.

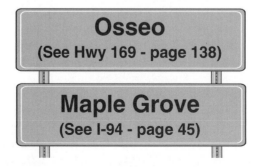

Osseo
(See Hwy 169 - page 138)

Maple Grove
(See I-94 - page 45)

10

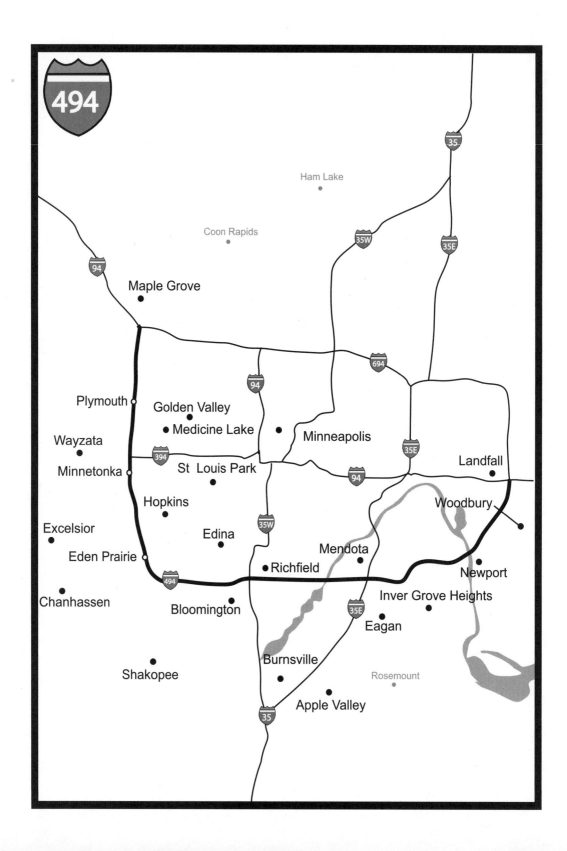

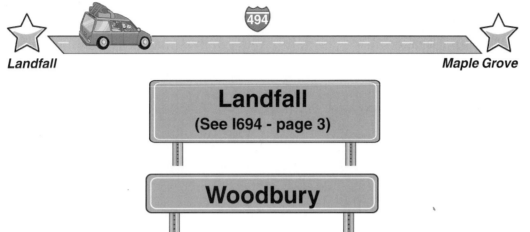

Landfall
(See I694 - page 3)

Woodbury

Place Name

Originally named Red Rock, after a sacred stone supposedly painted by the famous Dakota Chief Little Crow, the town was renamed in 1859 when the state legislature discovered another Red Rock Township in Minnesota. Woodbury was named after Judge Levi Woodbury of New Hampshire, a friend of the first town board chairman.

Local Industry

For the past several years, Woodbury has been one of Minnesota's fastest-growing cities. The rapid growth and development the city has experienced were anticipated in carefully crafted plans created many years ago by elected officials, citizen advisory boards, planning professionals and city staff.

Historical Significance

The first settlers came to Woodbury in 1844. Most of the area's early settlers migrated from the eastern states and from Germany. Immigrants also came from Ireland, Sweden, Switzerland, Scotland and Denmark. Over the years the people of Woodbury have contributed in many ways to the rich heritage that the city enjoys today.

In 1844 the town was largely covered with timber. Clearing the land for farming required considerable time and labor. Wheat was the principal crop grown, as well as barley, corn, and potatoes; and later soybeans became a crop of major importance. Generally the land was rolling and very fertile, which was particularly conducive to dairy farming.

The 1950s introduced a new phase in agriculture. Farming technology resulted in agriculture being an even greater contributor to the local economy. In 1955 the first housing development, Woodbury Heights, was started. By the 1960s, urban development spread out into the community and began to replace the farmland.

As Woodbury has grown from the status of township and village to the present-day city, many new schools and educational facilities have been added. The schools, which the pioneers worked so hard to promote, laid the foundation for the excellent schools in Woodbury today.

> Most of the area's early settlers migrated from the eastern states and from Germany. Immigrants also came from Ireland, Sweden, Switzerland, Scotland and Denmark.

Newport

Place Name

Mrs. James Hugunin suggested the name similar to other town of the same name in Rhode Island, Kentucky and in 30 other states.

St. Paul
(See I94 - page 34)

Inver Grove Heights

Place Name

Attracted by the area's rolling green hills of the countryside and the close proximity to the Mississippi River, early pioneers staked claims here by establishing a community.

Settlers from Germany laid claim to the wooded farmland in the northwest portion of the community, clearing and cultivating fields from among the area lakes. Other settlers from France and England built homes along the river.

Hundreds of settlers were attracted to the township that was named after an Irish fishing village, "Inver" and commemorating the homeland of the German settlers, "Grove".

Eagan

The first settlers to Eagan were the Mdewakanton Sioux Indians. They named Eagan "Magayateshne" meaning "People who do not eat geese".

Place Name

When the Irish settlers came, they named the 32-square miles near the Nicols and Wescott train stations "Eagan" in honor of the town's first council member, Patrick Eagan, an Irish immigrant from Tipperary.

Local Landmarks

From its earliest days, the Lone Oak Tree was the town's center for communication. Farmers stored milk cans ready for market under its branches. Official notices were posted on the trunk for residents to read. The tree succumbed to the city's rapid development when Highway 55 was reconstructed. The Lone Oak Tree city icon epitomizes the economic strength and solid growth of the community today.

Industry

At the turn of the 20th century, farmers in the townships of Eagan and Mendota were introduced to onion growing. Soon crops of onions led to the title of the "Onion Capital of the United States". The average yield was 10 tons per acre. By the 1920s, cities in other states replaced Eagan in successful onion production.

Historical Significance

Located along the Minnesota River, just south of Fort Snelling and the confluence of the Minnesota and Mississippi rivers, Eagan was attainable from Minneapolis and St. Paul via the old Cedar Avenue Bridge. The bridge, which still stands today, was built for horse drawn vehicles and cattle.

A new, modern freeway bridge was constructed in the 1980s. This paved the way for new construction and development south of the Minnesota River, making Eagan the largest city in Dakota County.

Corporations recognized Eagan's premier location, and took advantage of it.

Thousands of pilots from around the world train at the Flight Academy in Eagan. Flight simulators operate 20 hours a day, shutting down for 4 hours of maintenance each day.

* * * *

Eagan was the site of two plane crashes in the summer of 1921. Neither of these crashes occurred at the Lexington-Diffley airport site.

An airmail plane piloted by Mickey Eversole crashed on the Walter Sell farm near Lemay Lake, near the present bulk mail facility. The twin engine DeHaviland aircraft plummeted to the ground, but Mickey Eversole was able to parachute to safety.

A week later a twin seat-training plane crashed in the northwest corner of Eagan.

Mendota

Place Name

The name of this town is the Sioux word that means "meeting of the waters". This is a fitting name then, when one considers that the town lies by both the Mississippi and Minnesota Rivers.

Historical Significance

The Dakota people lived on these prairie lands by the 1700s. They knew this place as Mdo'-te or "the junction of one river with another". French explorers and traders who were here in the late 1600s named the Minnesota river Sans Pierres because the river was silty but had few rocks. British explorers and traders who arrived a few years later misunderstood the French name, calling the river Saint Peter's. In 1852, the territorial legislature changed the name of the river to Minnesota, a version of its Dakota name.

The American military arrived here in 1805 when Lieutenant Zebulon Pike signed a treaty with the Dakota, purchasing a parcel of land that included the river valleys and the high bluffs

across the river on which Fort Snelling was built.

What had been a meeting spot for the Dakota became a trading hub for the entire region when the American Fur Company opened a post at Mendota. Alexis Bailly took charge in 1826, followed by Henry Hastings Sibley in 1834. Sibley replaced the log buildings at the post with several permanent structures and others were added later. Four major structures remain today: a limestone company storehouse (1834); Sibley's limestone dwelling and store (1836); the limestone and sandstone house (1839) of trader Jean Baptiste Faribault; and, up the hill, a brick house (1854), of trader Hypolite DuPuis.

Trade ended here in 1851, when the Treaties of Traverse des Sioux and Mendota resulted in the removal of the Dakota to a reservation in the upper Minnesota Valley. Henry Sibley resided here until 1862 and led an active political career, serving as Minnesota Territory's first delegate to Congress (1849-53) and the state's first governor (1859-1860).

(Historical marker located on Hwy 13)

Local Landmark

> Mendota became the key point of fur trade for the American, Columbia and Fort Factory Fur Trading Companies.

Henry Hastings Sibley built the first stone house in Minnesota here in 1835. He was a factor for the American Fur Company, and through his influence the settlement became a pioneer center of business and cultural activities. In fact, the settlement became the key point of fur trade for the American, Columbia and Fort Factory Fur Trading Companies.

* * * *

Here at Mendota (where the rivers meet) missionaries ministered to both Indians and settlers, enduring the hardships of a sprawling wilderness that was the Minnesota country. In 1842, Father Lucien Galtiers built a small, log chapel with only two windows, where the Catholics of St. Peter's Parish worshipped for nearly eleven years.

In 1844 Father Augustin Ravoux, who had already spent three years in the area, arrived at Mendota to assist Father Galtier. When Father Galtier left to serve another parish in the fall of that year, Father Ravoux assumed full responsibility for ministering to the thriving Mendota community, which was the American Fur Company's chief trading center with the Dakota (Sioux) Indians in the Minnesota territory.

Father Ravoux had St. Peter's church constructed in 1853. Built of limestone quarried nearby and roofed with hand-split pine shingles, the entire structure measures only 35 x 75 feet, and the rear portion was originally used as living quarters for the pastor.

The steeple has been twice replaced. The original cross that topped the spire now hangs over the inside door. While alterations have changed the interior, the exterior remains much as it was in 1853.

(Historical marker located on Hwy 13)

Burnsville
(See I35 - page 105)

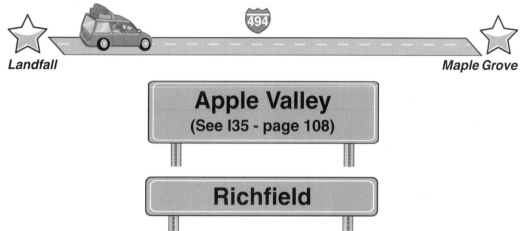

Apple Valley
(See I35 - page 108)

Richfield

Place Name

The people in the area voted choosing the name of Richfield, describing the fertile lands.

Local Landmark

The Minneapolis-St. Paul International Airport is built on much of Wold-Chamberland Field; named for Ernest Groves Wold and Cyrus Foss Chamberland, two Minneapolis airmen killed in France during World War I. The main terminal building is named after Minnesota native Charles Lindbergh.

Originally this area was developed as an automobile racetrack in 1914, with the first airplane hangar being built six years later in 1920.'

Bloomington

Place Name

The area was home to a band of the Dakota, "those of Good Road and Man of the Clouds", who lived on the bluffs of the Mississippi River.

The name of the town was given by early settlers from Illinois, perhaps after the town in their home state.

Local Industry

Today Bloomington's main attraction is the "Mall of America". The mall includes retail stores, outlet stores, gift shops, sports bars, restaurants, miniature golf, a movie theater, a LEGO factory with about 6,000 square feet of models, and even an amusement park. In the mall, one can find Underwater World, a large aquarium as well.

The Mall of America is the largest fully enclosed retail and entertainment complex in the United States

General Trivia

In the past, one could go to Met Stadium and see the Minnesota Vikings or the Minnesota Twins. Another option would have been to go to the Met Center to watch the North Stars.

These teams have now moved to other arenas, the Vikings and Twins play in the Metrodome in downtown Minneapolis; and in one case, such as the North Stars, to another state, Texas.

17

* * * *

Numerous movies were filmed in the Bloomington area including: The Mighty Ducks, Jingle All the Way, and Ice Castles.

Prominent People

Two brothers from Bloomington, Brennan and Scott Olson, invented rollerblades in 1980.

Two brothers from Bloomington, Brennan and Scott Olson, invented rollerblades in 1980. The two former high-school hockey players thought of the idea as a means to train for winter hockey all summer long. Putting the four wheels in a line, they started making their Rollerblades in a garage and selling them to other hockey players in the area.

* * * *

Actor Chad Bell, appeared in the TV episode of Matlock, Drexell's Class, and The Watcher before appearing in the films, Columbo, and the Murder of a Rock Star, Missing Parents, and Performance Anxiety.

* * * *

Professional hockey player Ronald Docken was born in Bloomington. A goal tender for the Johnstown Jets from 1973-1977. He starred in the movie Slap Show, which is the movie based upon his real life team.

Edina

Place Name

The town's name was derived from the local flour mill owners, named in honor of Andrew and John Craik's boyhood home near Edinburg, England.

Prominent People

Edina poet Barbara Ebensen works, Words with Wrinkled Knees and Cold Stars and Fireflies was chosen in 1984 as one of the hundred best books by the Library of Congress.

* * * *

Edina native David Bloom, worked in television stations in La Crosse, Wisconsin; Wichita, Kansas; and Miami, before joining NBC News in 1993, and later becoming their White House correspondent.

While traveling in an armored vehicle, the United States Army's Third Infantry Division, Second Brigade, he was traveling with came under Iraqi fire as the camera rolled. Bloom would later die on April 6, 2003 of a pulmonary embolism near Baghdad, Iraq.

* * * *

Mattie Shaw, mother of singer Prince, was a longtime social worker in the Minneapolis public school system.

Landfall   **Maple Grove**

* * * *

Local native Brandon Shiffman was the set production assistant for the movies Spider Man II, S.W.A.T., and Red Dragon.

Shakopee was founded in 1851 and named after the Dakota tribe's Chief Shakopee.

Local Landmark

This town is home to Valleyfair, a large amusement park. The park is 68 acres large with over 50 different rides to choose from, plus an IMAX theater and specialty shows.

Nearby Murphy's Landing is a re-creation of a 1890s village, complete with interpreters costumed for the period.

* * * *

Shakopee is also home to one of the most popular attractions in the state, the Minnesota Renaissance Festival. Here, bards and scoops, kings and queens, gather to dance or sing songs at many gift and food shops to entertain visitors in a medieval setting.

Prominent People

President Richard M. Nixon's secretary of commerce, Maurice H. Stans was born in Shakopee.

Place Name

Mrs. Elliot named the village in admiration of the beautiful natural prairie, describing it as an Eden Prairie.

Place Name

This city's founders named this community Chanhassen because the word meant "sugar maple" in the Dakota language.

Local Landmark

The University of Minnesota Landscape Arboretum houses more than 4,000 species in a 900-acre area.

* * * *

Landfall   **Maple Grove**

Prince built his ten million dollar multimedia Paisley Park studio in Chanhassen.

Minneapolis native Prince Nelson, known as Prince, swept the Grammy Awards with his soundtrack to Purple Rain, which won awards for best soundtrack, best rock performance and best R & B song. Prince built his ten million dollar multimedia Paisley Park studio located in Chanhassen.

Place Name

This town owes its beginning to a colony, known as the Excelsior Pioneer Association, which was formed in New York City in 1852. They named their new settlement in allusion to Henry W. Longfellow's world-famous short poem, "Excelsior" which Longfellow wrote in 1841.

Prominent People

Christmas Lake is named for Charles Christmas, the first county surveyor of Hennepin County elected in 1852, who platted the original town site of Minneapolis for John H. Stevens and Franklin Steele. (Historical marker located on Hwy 7)

In 1853, Peter Miller Gideon and his wife Wealthy, arrived in Minnesota from Ohio and settled on the shores of Lake Minnetonka. Long interested in fruit growing, Peter Gideon determined to satisfy the craving of pioneer families for apples and other fruits thought all previous efforts to grow them had failed.

In 1854 he recorded that he planted one bushel of apple seed and a peck of peach seed. For fourteen years he planted, seeded, and grafted more than 10,000 apple, cherry, peach, pear, plum, and quince trees; but hard winters, blight, grasshopper plagues, and other reverses prevailed. Each year he had to start anew.

From one seed he obtained from Maine, a seedling grew that withstood the hard Minnesota winters and produced in 1868 the celebrated Wealthy apple, which was named for his wife and hailed as the "best apple produced since Adam and Eve left the Garden of Eden". From this flourished the Northwest's fruit growing industries.

(Historical marker located on County Road 19)

Geological

Like most lakes in Minnesota, Lake Minnetonka was formed during the Ice Age of the last two million years. During several separate glacial periods, ice advanced along different routes across the state. The glaciers, along with large volumes of sediment (clay, silt, sand, gravel, and boulders) trapped in the ice, altered the pre-existing terrain and created the landscape we see today.

Before glacial action, the surface of this region consisted of sandstones and limestones which formed from sediments deposited in seas that covered the area 300 to 500 million years ago. After the seas retreated, rivers carved a valley system into the sedimentary bedrock.

This ancient valley system had provided southward drainage through the region. The bedrock floor of a principal valley of that ancient system now lies as much as 122 meters below the surface of Lake Minnetonka.

About 25,000 years ago, at the peak of the last glacial period, or Wisconsin glaciation, an advancing glacier, which was passing over the ancient river valley that now lies beneath Lake Minnetonka, filled the valley with ice. Sediment that melted out of the overriding glacier then buried the ice trapped in the valley. The glacial ice and sediment from more recent glacial advances. As a result, when glaciers last receded from Minnesota 10,000 years ago, large blocks of ice were buried deep in the ancient valley under thick piles of sediment. When the ice blocks melted, the overlying sediment collapsed and created numerous depressions that filled with water, which are called kettle lakes. At Lake Minnetonka, the ice blocks were so big and close together that the depressions coalesced to form the large, composite kettle lake that we see today.

<u>(Historical marker located on Lake Street in Excelsior)</u>

Place Name

This town name was changed from West Minneapolis to Hopkins to honor the former adventurer and gold prospector, Harley Hopkins, who settled in the area.

Place Name

A group of local business developers from Minneapolis formed the St. Louis Park Improvement Company, naming their company after the Minneapolis and St. Louis Railroad.

Place Name

"Minne" means water and "tonka" means big.

Historical Significance

Minnetonka was still a part of the Spanish territory that was included in the Louisiana Purchase in 1803 when the colonists on the Atlantic coast declared their independence from Great Britain.

The first recorded exploration of the area by European settlers was in 1822, when a group from newly constructed Fort Snelling made its way up

> Dakota and Ojibway Indians believed the land around Lake Minnetonka was the legendary home of an extinct race.

21

Minnehaha Creek (then known as Brown'sCreek or Falls Creek) to the lake.

Settlement in the Minnetonka area was encouraged by local, eastern and even foreign newspapers. Most of the earliest settlers were from New England and other eastern and central states. Later, the Irish settled in northern Minnetonka.

In the 1860s Scandinavians came where the climate and terrain reminded them of their native land.

Immigrants from Czechoslovakia settled in the southern part of Minnetonka from 1854 to 1871. They contributed greatly to the professional, business and agricultural segments of the population. The raspberries they grew in Minnetonka for sale in Hopkins prompted Hopkins to call itself "The Raspberry Capital of the World".

General Trivia

In 1852 a claim was staked on Minnehaha Creek near McGinty Road, resulting in several firsts.

The sawmill that was constructed was the first privately operated mill in Minnesota west of the Mississippi River.

The settlement of Minnetonka Mills that grew up around the mill was the first permanent European-American settlement west of Minneapolis in Hennepin County.

Oak timbers from this mill were used to build the first suspension bridge across the Mississippi River at St. Anthony/Minneapolis in 1853. A few houses still stand in the Minnetonka Mills area that were built with lumber from this mill.

Prominent People

Charity Hill attended Hopkins High School in Minnetonka, Minnesota. She started her stage career at age 10 in Minneapolis, Minnesota with the world renowned Children's Theater Company.

Charity began her television career with over 15 national commercials under her belt as well as a Miss Teen America title, while also performing with music sensations Prince, M.C. Hammer, and LL Cool J.

Minnetonka is where the Tonka Trucks were developed and manufactured.

She appeared in the TV episodes of Smart Guy, Sister Sister, The Jamie Foxx Show, and Martial Law.   Other performances include the Ovation Award-winning hit pop opera, 'Bare'. (Voted Best Musical of the year)

* * * *

Nancy Parsons, was born in Lake Minnetonka. She garnered a Family Film Award for Best Actress in Porky's Revenge (1985), an Academy of Science Fiction & Fantasy nomination for Best Supporting Actress in Motel Hell (1980), a Dramalogue Award for the play, 'Dead End At Sunset'.

Wayzata

Place Name

The name comes from the Dakota word, Waziyata, meaning at the pines, or the north. The early settlers chose the name in reference to its location on the north side of the east end of Lake Minnetonka and not for the scarcely found pine trees in the area.

Historical Significance

Wayzata was originally a small farming village that was blessed with the arrival of the railroad. James Hill laid his St. Paul and Pacific Railroad here, but it blocked off the town's access to the Twin Cities. The townspeople were so mad that they threatened to sue Hill if he didn't move it. An annoyed Hill moved it all right. He moved it a mile out of town in spite so that the townspeople would have to walk quite far to catch a train. This inconvenience angered the citizens even more. They pleaded, they negotiated, and finally, they got their way.

In 1906, Hill moved the railroad back into town to a better location. The current Wayzata Depot is a national historic landmark.

Kris Kamm, who played "Stuart" on the television sitcom "Coach", attended high school in Wayzata.

Prominent People

Grace Carter Lindley is from Wayzata. She is hailed in the National Ski Hall of Fame for her championship slalom ski runs.

Minneapolis
(See I94 - page 38)

Golden Valley

Place Name

The beautiful valley surrounded by sparkling lakes resulted in the descript naming of this town.

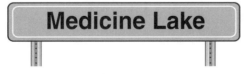

Medicine Lake

Place Name

This community was established on a peninsula on the southern end of Medicine Lake, and thus the name.

Plymouth

Historical Significance

⭐ Like many towns across the country with the same name, it commemorates the city of Plymouth in Deveonshire, England at the mouth of the River Plym; or the world renowned boulder called Plymouth Rock, the site where the Pilgrims sailing aboard the Mayflower in 1620 landed.

Plymouth's history can be traced back to 1400-1500 AD. The original inhabitants were the Wahpeton Sioux (Dakota). Their encampment was at the north end of Medicine Lake.

Medicine Lake is derived from the Native American word "Mdewakan," meaning "Lake of the Spirit". The Dakota named it after a warrior who overturned his canoe. His body was never recovered.

Antoine LeCounte, a guide and explorer, was the first settler to this area. He arrived in 1848, but did not settle until 1852. He carried mail from the Red River country to the south, trading goods to Native Americans for horses on his way. LeCounte built the first cabin at what is now East Medicine Lake Blvd. at 29th Ave. N.

Plymouth's beginning as a town occurred in 1855 on the northwest shores of what is now known as Parkers Lake. A gristmill and other structures were built in the area. In the spring of 1857, when Parkers Lake flooded, the mill was taken down and moved to Freeport, Minnesota, which is now called Wayzata.

The settlers of Plymouth formed a militia in 1862, during the conflict between white settlers and the Dakota at Fort Ridgeley. When the Civil War started, Plymouth paid its volunteers $25 to enlist. At about this time, Plymouth's growth began to take on a new look. Schools and churches were built and a post office was located in Plymouth. By 1863, hotels were being built.

More changes occurred after the Civil War. By 1880, Plymouth boasted a population of 1,074, and reaped $667 in annual taxes. Farming became the trade of most settlers. Roads were built across Plymouth, making access to other towns possible.

Industry

The K-Tel sell records primarily via television.

Medina

Prominent People

Medina is the hometown of Tour de France winner, Greg LeMond.

Landfall

494

Maple Grove

Maple Grove
(See I94 - page 45)

INTERSTATE

94

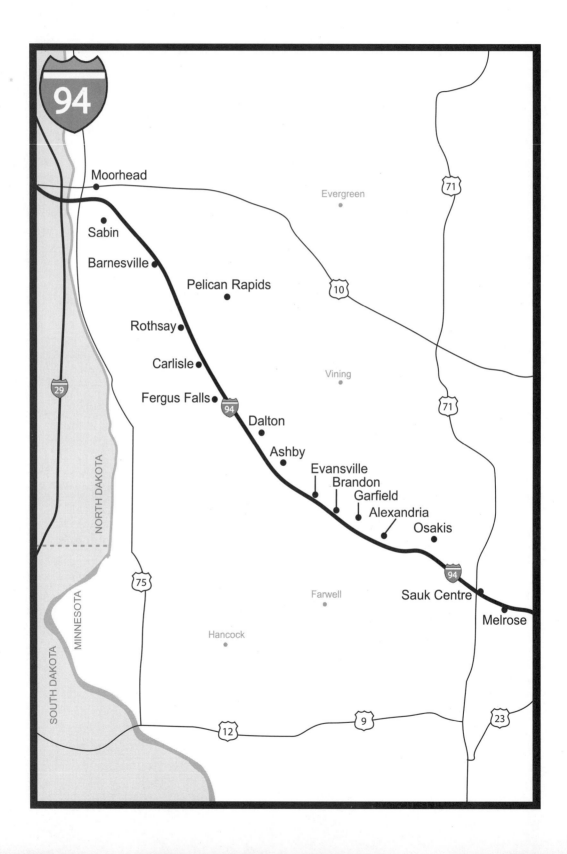

94

Moorhead

Evergreen

71

Sabin

Barnesville

Pelican Rapids

10

Rothsay

Carlisle

Vining

71

Fergus Falls

94

Dalton

Ashby

Evansville

Brandon

Garfield

Alexandria

Osakis

NORTH DAKOTA

29

Farwell

75

Sauk Centre

94

Melrose

MINNESOTA

SOUTH DAKOTA

Hancock

12

9

23

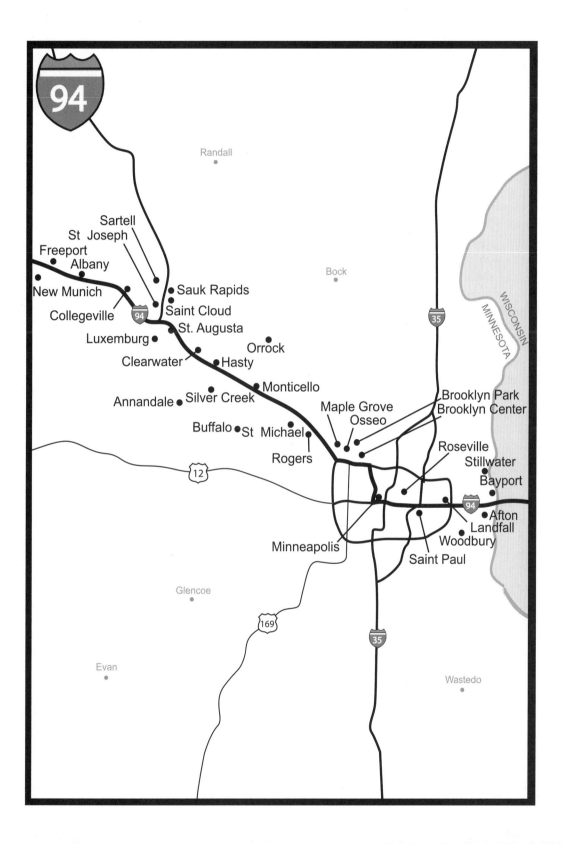

Bayport

Place Name

Baytown was one of the first permanent establishments that developed in this area of eastern Minnesota, platted by mill owner Socrates Nelson and others.

In 1922 Bangor, Baytown, and Middletown combined to form what is now Bayport.

Historical Significance

Forming a large stretch of the border between Minnesota and Wisconsin, the St. Croix is one of America's most scenic Wild Rivers. Its valley is sometimes referred to as the "New England of the West".

The Minnesota territory had been organized and named just two years earlier in a convention at the river town of Stillwater, the "Birthplace of Minnesota".

Along with the Brule River in northern Wisconsin, the St. Croix forms a water passageway between Lake Superior and the upper Mississippi River that was well known to the Dakota and Ojibway people and became a highway of the early fur traders. In the first half of the 19th century lumbermen found the river useful for transporting logs and lumber in huge drives from the white pine forests of the north to the booming markets of the growing Midwest.

Swedish novelist Fredrika Bremer saw the St. Croix valley as "just the country for new Scandinavia", and the first of many Swedish settlers in Minnesota built their homes near here in 1850. The Minnesota territory had been organized and named just two years earlier in a convention at the river town of Stillwater, the "Birthplace of Minnesota".

In the 20th century the St. Croix valley had become an important recreation area for residents of the Twin Cities. Interstate Park was established in 1895 as a joint enterprise of Wisconsin and Minnesota. It was the first such cooperative state park in the United States. Several other parks and forest reserves now occupy much of the land on both sides of "America's Rhine", and thousands enjoy its beauty year round.

(Historical marker located at west bound rest area on I-94)

Industry

The Andersen Corporation is the largest industry in this community. It was established by Hans Jacob Andersen in 1912 as a lumber company, and today it is famous for its window making facilities and fine corporate reputation.

One of the main accomplishments of the Andersen Corporation was the standardizing of the dimensions of many of the windows. This allowed mass production and vast growth for the company. Today, Andersen is the most recognized brand name in the window and patio door industry.

Local Landmark

The Minnesota State Prison is also in Bayport. It includes twenty-two enclosed acres as

well as 1,000 acres of farmland.

Farm machinery and twine are manufactured within the prison and sold on the open market. As a result of this and efficient management, the prison is self-supporting. All net profit goes to the State treasury.

Lying on the St. Croix River, this town is named after the smooth waters of Lake St. Croix.

Historical Significance

In the middle of the 1800s, the city was the center of the logging industry after the Chippewa granted permission to begin cutting.

Stillwater was a convenient location for logging, not only for the lumber, but also because logs could be sent to ports far down the Mississippi.

* * * *

One of Minnesota's first major industries was born here on August 24, 1839, when the slow, cumbersome up-and-down saw of the Marine Lumber Company cut the first commercial lumber in the state from trees felled in the rich white pine forests of the St. Croix Valley. The mill was built by a group of settlers from Marine, Illinois, at a site slected a year earlier by David Hone and Lewis S. Judd.

During the winter of 1839-40, the saw at Marine produced about 5,000 board feet of lumber a day. From this modest beginning, the much rebuilt and enlarged mills of the Walker, Judd and Veazie Lumber Company was by 1877 turning out two million board feet of lumber, 500,000 shingles, and 200,000 laths a year with an average daily work crew of fourteen men.

Financial depression, a huge log jam that prevented logs from reaching the mill, extensive tornado damage and a low-water summer combined to cause failure of the business in 1885. By 1895, after a few years of intermittent operation in the hands of other companies, the mill closed forever, and the extensive frame buildings were torn down. Only the ruins of the mill's engine house serves as a reminder of Minnesota's magnificent pine forests and the profitable lumber industry that built the towns and cities of an expanding nineteenth-century mid-America.

<u>(Historical marker located on Hwy 4)</u>

Local Landmark

Brick and limestone buildings are scattered down the bluffs. Among these buildings are the Warden's House and the Washington County Courthouse, which were all constructed in the early to mid 1800s.

In 1849, The Governor of the new Territory of Minnesota, Alexander Ramsey, urged the Territorial Legislature to provide for a "proper and safe place of confinement" for prisoners of the territory. Because of Ramsey's request, the Legislature appropriated $20,000 for the erection of a penitentiary.

The site chosen for the penitentiary was in a ravine at the north end of Stillwater. This ravine is known as "Battle Hollow" because of the battle fought there in July of 1839 between the Dakota and the Ojibwe. It was a good location for a prison because natural cliffs bound the ravine on three sides.

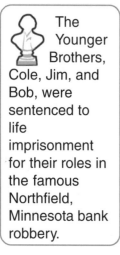

The Younger Brothers, Cole, Jim, and Bob, were sentenced to life imprisonment for their roles in the famous Northfield, Minnesota bank robbery.

In May 1851, the territory chose the firm of Jesse Taylor & Company to construct the prison building out of stone. By early 1853, the three-story prison building was completed. It contained six cells and two dungeons for solitary confinement, a workshop and an office. The Warden's House, which sits outside this ravine, was completed at this time also.

Francis R. Delano, the first warden, assumed office, and moved into the house on April 4, 1853. A total of thirteen wardens administered over the prison until 1914, when the last of the prisoners were moved into new facilities.

In November 1876, three notorious convicts entered the Minnesota Prison. The Younger Brothers, Cole, Jim, and Bob, were sentenced to life imprisonment for their roles in the famous Northfield, Minnesota bank robbery in which several people were killed and others wounded.

After the prison was moved south of Stillwater, the old warden's home housed deputy wardens.

(Historical marker located at 602 N. Main Street)

* * * *

Minnesota's first courthouse, a three-room frame structure erected at the corner of 4th and Chestnut Streets in Stillwater in 1849, had become inadequate by 1866. On November 6 of that year, Washington County voters approved funds for the construction of a new building.

For the magnificent sum of $5, Socrates Nelson, a prominent Stillwater lumberman, and Mrs. Elizabeth M. Churchill offered the city a block of property high on "Zion's Hill". By the time ground-breaking ceremonies were held in April, 1867, Augustus F. Knight, St. Paul's first resident architect, had been commissioned to design the building. His unique design reflects the Italianate style then so popular. Constructed of native sandstone faced with red brick, the courthouse features a projecting portico with two tiers of ten rounded arches.

Two local contractors, George M. Seymour and William M. May, supervised the construction which was completed during the winter and spring of 1869-70, despite the seemingly insurmountable difficulty of laying the imported English floor tiles in the correct pattern. The courthouse stands today as "an ornament to the city" and "a credit to the county".

(Historical marker located at corner of Fourth and Chestnut Streets)

* * * *

On exhibit in the Carnegie Public Library is a bottle of wine over fifty years old, and the minutes of the annual meetings the Last Man's Club of Company B, First Minnesota Volunteer Infantry. Formed here on July 1, 1884, these were the veterans of the Civil War.

There is a nice story that accompanies these exhibits. There was a pact made by the group that they would set aside the bottle of wine, and the last surviving member was to

drink it. Charles Lockwood was this man, but he never drank the wine because of the sentiments that he had for his dead comrades. He died in 1935.

General Trivia

Stillwater has also had a history of some strange sightings. On August 17, 1961 five people claimed to have seen a group of UFO's arranged in a V formation. On March 22, 1978 Dean Andrie claimed to have experienced a close encounter of the first kind.

The patent for a pop-up toaster was applied for in 1919 by Charles Strite for use in his Stillwater company's cafeteria.

Afton

Place Name

This community was settled by the French in the late 1830s, and was platted in 1855. It was named after the Robert Burns' poem "Afton Water".

Historical Significance

Many settlers from the New England area later settled here. When they came, they brought with them some of their good taste for architecture. A good example of this New England style architecture is the Mackey House, which was built in 1855. The doorway details and porch columns are built in the Greek Revival style. There is also a long porch of the Connecticut type built at an angle into the house.

Prominent People

Among the early settlers in Afton was Joseph Haskell, one of the state's first farmers.

Local Landmarks

An example of architecture unique to Afton is The Little Red House. Once a two-room log cabin in the 1850s, this serves as a good example of how early settlers added on extra rooms when needed.

The original owner of the house was Reverend Putnam, a Baptist minister who served as a chaplain in the Civil War.

* * * * *

The Historic Afton House Inn has been operating since 1867. Its architecture fits in perfectly with the New England-style surroundings, and its location next to the St. Croix River.

Woodbury
(See I494 - pg 13)

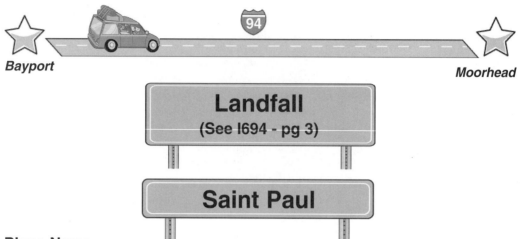

Bayport

Moorhead

Landfall
(See I694 - pg 3)

Saint Paul

Place Name

Located on the banks of the Mississippi River, Saint Paul is the bustling capital of Minnesota. When settlers originally founded Saint Paul, they called it "Pig's Eye". The name came from one of the founders who had a deformed eye that was injured in a fight. When Roman Catholic Priest, Father Galtier built a log cabin church in the town, he renamed the city "Saint Paul's Landing". Eventually, the word Landing was dropped, and the present name was decided upon.

Historical Significance

The city's strategic placement on the Mississippi River allowed for its rapid growth. In its early development, Saint Paul became known as the Boston of the West. The reason for having such an honorable nickname was because businessmen and educators flocked to the city in herds, thereby eliminating other struggling frontiers. German and Irish immigrants were the dominant ethnic groups that lived in the city at this time.

Local Landmarks

The developer of the Great Northern Railway, James Hill, was born in southern Canada in 1838 and began his career in transportation as a 17-year-old "mud clerk" on the bustling Saint Paul levee. He spent 20 years in the shipping business on the Mississippi and Red rivers, and in 1878 along with several other investors he purchased the nearly bankrupt Saint Paul and Pacific Railroad. Hill toiled ceaselessly during the next two decades to push the line north to Canada and west across the Great Plains and Rocky Mountains to the Pacific Ocean. "When we are all dead and gone," Hill declared of the renamed Great Northern Railway, "the sun will shine, the rain will fall, and this railroad will run as usual".

James Hill, built his house in Saint Paul. The house contains 32 rooms, 13 bathrooms, and 22 fireplaces.

"Empire Builder" Hill pursued a vast network of related businesses: coal and iron mining, electric and water power development, Great Lakes and Pacific Ocean shipping, agriculture and milling, banking and finance.

Hill supported many educational institutions and built the Saint Paul Public Library along with the reference library that bears his name.

He spoke at countless county fairs and civic organizations on scientific agriculture and sound business practices.

Presidents sought his financial support and economic advice on national and international concerns.

Bayport   *Moorhead*

After amassing a personal fortune of $63 million, James J .Hill died in his Summit Avenue Home on May 29, 1916, one of the wealthiest and most powerful figures of America's gilded age.

<u>(Historical marker located at 240 Summit Avenue)</u>

* * * *

Historic Fort Snelling served a valuable purpose by keeping the peace, protecting trade, and implementing policy for the United States government.

Fort Snelling was the only Minnesota army post to remain in active service through the Spanish American War, World War I and World War II.

* * * *

Appointed by President Zachery Taylor in 1849, Alexander Ramsey came to Minnesota as the territory's first governor. Ramsey stayed in Minnesota for his remaining fifty-four years and, during a successful political career as a Whig and then a Republican, served as mayor of Saint Paul, state governor, United States Senator, and Secretary of War in the cabinet of Rutherford B. Hayes. When the Civil War broke out in 1861, Ramsey was the first Union governor to offer troops to President Abraham Lincoln.

 The famous Civil Rights Dred Scott case had its origin at Fort Snelling.

The fifteen room Ramsey house of native limestone, typical of the elegant late Victorian period, was designed in a French Renaissance style by Saint Paul architect Monroe Sheire. It had been under construction for four years by 1872, when Alexander and Anna Ramsey moved in. A focus for the political, cultural and social life of Minnesota for nearly a century, the house was occupied by three generations of Ramsey's, all of whom affectionately preserved the structure and its furnishings.

<u>(Historical marker located at 265 South Exchange Street)</u>

* * * *

The Minnesota State Capital is a towering mass of granite and marble, symbolizing the growth and development of the state.

Architect Cass Gilbert, who modeled the structure after the Italian Renaissance style, designed the building.

 Completed in 1904, the Minnesota State Capital has the largest unsupported marble dome in the world

* * * *

Saint Paul is also home to Indian Mounds Park. The park has ancient Hopewell Indian burial mounds that are believed to have been around for more than 2,000 years.

* * * *

The home of Minnesota's first newspaper is Saint Paul. James Madison Goodhue was a journalist from New Hampshire who established the paper. He named it the Minnesota Pioneer. Originally, he had hoped to name the paper The Epistle of Saint Paul, but many in the newspaper business talked him out of it. The Saint Paul Pioneer Press descends directly from Goodhue.

* * * *

The "Vision of Peace" is a 55-ton carved onyx sculpture created by Carl Milles. The thing that makes the "Vision of Peace" unique is that it was dedicated in 1936 and cost approximately $75,000 to construct. Saint Paul residents were furious that such a large sum of money was spent in the midst of the Great Depression. However, the figure, which depicts an Indian God offering peace, is considered one of Milles' finest works. Today, the people of Saint Paul appreciate this work of art quite a bit more than they did back then.

Invention

Did you ever wonder who was the mastermind behind those ingenious little yellow sticky notes? Well, the answer lies in Saint Paul.

Art Fry was an employee of 3M. He knew they encouraged the development of new products based on employee input.

Art always had problems keeping his place in his choir hymnal. He used scraps of paper and other odd materials but nothing seemed to work.

He then remembered an earlier invention by 3M employee, Dr. Spencer Silver. Silver created an adhesive that stuck but could also be removed with ease. He worked at perfecting the little notes until he finally brought them to the marketing department. Their response was far from ecstatic, yet they agreed to sell them anyway. Lucky for them that they did. Today, post-it-notes bring in millions and are used throughout the world.

Native American Chief Sitting Bull was the target of an assassination attempt in Saint Paul's Grand Opera House in 1884.

* * * *

Richard Drew of St. Paul developed and patented transparent cellophane tape for 3M in 1930. Known as Scotch Tape, he created the product from a pressure-sensitive masking tape that was used as a border when repainting cars.

* * * *

Another fun piece of history originates from Saint Paul native, DeWitt Wallace. Wallace was injured in World War I. As he sat at home recovering, he became frustrated at the long length of magazine articles. He attempted condensing them and hoped to publish shorter articles.

Wallace marketed the idea to Lila Bell Acheson, whom he later married. The Wallaces received the Medal of Freedom for their invention, a new kind of magazine with a household name. It's called Readers Digest.

General Trivia

The city of Saint Paul also contains the world's largest river port in the upper Midwest.

* * * *

The first full-time professional chamber orchestra in the United States was also established here. It was the Saint Paul Philharmonic. Today it's called the Saint Paul Chamber Orchestra.

* * * *

The Saint Paul Winter Carnival was started in 1886. In 1888, the carnival palace was the largest ice structure ever built, over 55,000 ice blocks.

Prominent People

The first woman to reach the North Pole was from St. Paul. Anne Bancroft and six others battled the cool Arctic weather and spine-tingling winds in hopes of reaching the Earth's most northern point. Averaging twenty miles per day in their 500-mile trip, the team finally reached the North Pole on May 22, 1986.

* * * *

Charles Schulz comic strip, under the original name "Li'l Folks" first appeared in the Saint Paul Pioneer Press in 1947. A syndicate who renamed it Peanuts then purchased the strip. Schulz was never really thrilled about the name change, but he accepted it. Coincidentally, Charlie Brown was named after one of Schulz's friends from art school.

> Good grief! Legendary cartoonist Charles Schulz comes from Saint Paul.

* * * *

Melvin Calvin, who was born in St. Paul in 1911, won the Nobel Prize for Chemistry in 1961. His studies and research traced the complex processes of photosynthesis for the first time.

* * * *

Sculptor Paul Manship originates from the Saint Paul region as well. His sculptures are world-renowned. Manship was the first American to have his work displayed in Tate Gallery in London.

* * * *

Famous novelist, F. Scott Fitzgerald was born in Saint Paul in September of 1896. His works' include Tales of the Jazz Age, The Great Gatsby, and This Side of Paradise. Scott died at the young age of 44. He coined the term the "Jazz Age". When he died he probably never knew how widely read his writings would be.

> Bert Reynolds ex-wife, Loni Anderson, was born in Saint Paul. She gained fame for her role on the television series WKRP in Cincinnati.

* * * *

William Colby, director of the CIA (Central Intelligence Agency) for Presidents Richard Nixon and Gerald Ford from 1973 to 1976 was born in Saint Paul.

* * * *

Wendell Anderson was born in St. Paul. He was a member of the 1956 U.S. Olympic ice hockey which won the silver medal. Following his hockey career he became a lawyer served as a legislator in both the House and Senate before becoming Governor. He ended his career by appointing himself to fill Walter Mondale's U.S. Senate seat when Mondale was elected as vice president in November 1976.

* * * *

Author and Hollywood screenwriter Max Shulman was born in Saint Paul. He is known for creating Dobie Gillis, the character in short stories, novels and a television show.

* * * *

Saint Paul native Melvin Calvin was awarded the Nobel Prize in Chemistry in 1961 for the discovery of the details of the photosynthesis process.

* * * *

After the daytime soap opera, The Doctors, was taken off the air, St. Paul native, Julia Duffy, would go on to fame as the sometime self-infatuated maid on Newhart.

* * * *

Other famous names that are associated with Saint Paul include Linda Kelsey, who played Billie Neuman on The Lou Grant Show, and Supreme Court Justice Harry Blackmun who wrote the historic Roe v. Wade decision.

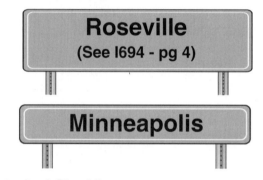

Roseville
(See I694 - pg 4)

Minneapolis

Historical Significance

> The word Minneapolis derives from a combination of the Dakota word for water (minne), and the Greek word for city (polis).

Although this is the official name of the city, it also has many nicknames. It has been called The City in Touch with Tomorrow, The Sawdust City, and The City of Flour. Prior names of the city have been All Saints, Hennepin, Lowell, Brooklyn, and Albion.

It has been called the City of Flour mainly because of its fame in the late 1800s. In 1880, the Washburn Crosby Company was recognized nationally by the Miller's International Exhibition out of Cincinnati as having the best flour displayed at the Exhibition.

The first explorers to visit this region were the French. Father Louis Hennepin discovered adjacent St. Anthony falls soon after in 1680. By 1800, a sawmill and a flourmill were constructed near the falls. By the 1840s, the village of St. Anthony was established on the east bank of the Mississippi and the village of Minneapolis was established on the West Bank. A suspension bridge later linked the two communities together. In the year 1872, Minneapolis and St. Anthony were united to form one city under the present name.

* * * *

Minneapolis was actually the second of the Twin Cities to develop. The growth of Minneapolis was sparked after the Civil War, when Scandinavians entered the city in ever increasing numbers. They can be held directly responsible for the commercial, economic, and social growth of the city. They set up shops of all trades, including such occupations as lawyers, tailors, doctors, and bankers.

Three time periods in particular encouraged the growth of the city. In the late 1880s, the idea of laissez faire resulted in the construction of several buildings. These buildings clustered themselves into separate groups. For example, the retail stores all clustered in a similar area, as did manufacturing plants and public buildings.

> The first explorers to visit this region were the French. Father Louis Hennepin discovered adjacent St. Anthony

By 1906, a "City Beautiful" plan was developed by architect John Jager. He was stirred by the Chicago Worlds Fair City Beautiful Movement. Eventually, the 1920s witnessed the construction of a skyline with the building of the Rand Tower, the Northwestern Bell Telephone Company, and other skyscrapers. The buildings certainly gave Minneapolis the "look" of a big city.

The last developmental boom that occurred in Minneapolis is still being felt today. The boom began following the Second World War. After coming out of the war, the country as a whole was ready for change and expansion. The people of Minnesota were concerned about their future. They made their plans for it with an optimistic outlook. Perhaps one of the greatest developments of this time was the Nicollet Mall, which added significance, attraction, and value to the downtown area. These three time periods successfully developed Minneapolis into a genuinely unique urban area.

Local Landmarks

Although Minneapolis is a very urban area, it does have a large number of parks and recreational areas. Charles Loring, who is known as the father of Minneapolis Parks, realized that Minneapolis' natural beauty would go to waste if the areas were not preserved as parks. He lobbied the Legislature to create a Park Board. Thankfully, they created one. The result has been the development of many recreational areas for people to enjoy.

> Minnehaha Falls inspired William Longbellow's poem "Song of Hiawatha", Life-sized statues of the mystical lovers, Hiawatha and Minnehaha, are located above the falls.

* * * *

Minnehaha Park and Minnehaha Falls have been known for its natural beauty ever since it was discovered. William Longfellow's poem, "Song of Hiawatha", was inspired by this graceful area. Life-sized statues of the mystical lovers, Hiawatha and Minnehaha, are located above the falls. It is perhaps the story of these two lovers that blanket the park and the falls with a romantic air.

10,000 years ago, melt water from the Wisconsin glacier was discharged through the Mississippi River and plunged over a ledge of Platteville limestone into a gorge cut chiefly in the white St. Peter sandstone. The undercutting action in the soft sandstone caused the limestone ledge to

break off with a vertical face, thus maintaining the falls, while causing them to retreat upstream. When the falls in the main channel passed the upper end of the island, the entire flow in the river was diverted to the main gorge and the falls in the west channel were abandoned. This unique and unusual geological feature, an abandoned waterfall, is located at the north end of the former west channel.

The cataract in the Mississippi has migrated to St. Anthonys and Minnehaha has retreated from the abandoned channel to its present location, where the undercutting action responsible for the migration is apparent.

<u>(Historical marker located in Minnehaha Park)</u>

* * * *

The statue and home of Colonel John Stevens, who claimed the first area of land in the region, is located just south of the Minnehaha Falls.

* * * *

St. Anthony Falls is credited as the origin of Minneapolis. The Falls located on the Mississippi River are about 16 feet high and hundreds of yards wide. This waterfall was responsible fo powering the first hydroelectric central station in the U.S. and is still used to generate electricity.

The falls can be seen viewed from the Upper Lock situated near the waterfall. The Upper Lock is the last of the 29 locks and dams that make up the waterway from St. Louis to Minneapolis.

* * * *

With the outbreak of the Civil War in 1861, Fort Snelling expanded beyond its limestone walls, formerly a part of the U.S. Indian Agency. As the frontier moved west following the war, the fort, as Headquarters of the Department of Dakota, administered and supplied dozens of western posts.

 The historic ground of Fort Snelling was a pivotal place in the development of the Northwest.

The military played an increasing world role after 1898, and the fort continued to grow. Handsome brick buildings lined Taylor Avenue, a hospital, offices, barracks and officer's quarters. Opposite the extensive parade grounds were the support facilities, such as stables, workshops and warehouses.

During World War I the fort was enlarged to a total of some 400 structures. Here Minnesota's recruits for both world wars first entered the service. Many others served between the wars in the Third Infantry and other units long associated with what was then known as the "Country Club of the Army". Fort Snelling closed in 1946, but it remains a fond memory for many who played a part in its long history.

<u>(Historical marker located on Hwy 55)</u>

* * * *

Completed in 1883, the Stone Arch Bridge is a 2,100 ft. long bridge similar in structure to a Roman viaduct. This bridge is made of limestone and is the only stone arch bridge to cross the mighty Mississippi.

40

* * * *

The 57 story IDS Center building located downtown took more than 1,000 workers laboring together a total of 370,000 days to build the massive tower that is forcefully enclosed by glass and steel. The skyscraper is unique in that it has a ceiling made entirely of glass.

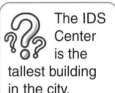

The IDS Center is the tallest building in the city.

* * * *

Nicollet Mall is an attraction that is part of the park system within the city. Cars are not allowed in the mall because the streets are reserved solely for pedestrians and bikers. Visitors can find a variety of restaurants and alluring stores in the mall area.

The Nicollet Mall's popularity is partly due to its national debut in the "Mary Tyler Moore Show", as well as the sight for the filming of several other films. This includes "Purple Rain", "Old Explorers", "Drop Dead Fred", and "Ice Castles."

* * * *

The Minneapolis City Hall contains some very significant features. Built in 1891, the 30,000 ton, four-faced clock tower used to be the largest working clock tower in the world. Above the clock there are fourteen chiming bells.

Starting in 1912, a man by the name of Joseph Auld climbed up all 447 steps to the top for 50 years to ring the bells for holidays and various other occasions.

* * * *

The Kenwood Neighborhood stretches from the Lake of the Isles to Loring Park. The beauty of the area has gained national attention because it was the place that Mary Tyler Moore lived in her television show.

The Mary Tyler Moore television show took place in the Kenwood Neighborhood area.

* * * *

Minneapolis is home to the largest university in Minnesota. In fact, The University of Minnesota is so big, that it has its own bus system, police and government. U of M has excelled historically in both academics and athletics. The athletic teams are members of the Big Ten conference, and therefore, put up with some of the toughest competition in the country.

Famous people who've attended the University of Minnesota include:

- Actor Henry Fonda.

- 1984 Democratic presidential nominee Walter Mondale

- Actor Robert Vaughn

- Science fiction writer Poul Anderson

- Seymour Cray, built the first supercomputer.

* * * *

The University is famous for its many medical accomplishments. Dr. Stuart Jamieson performed Minnesota's first heart-lung transplant in 1986 and the Midwest's first double-lung transplant in 1988. Doctors Robert Good and Richard Hong also performed the world's first successful bone marrow transplant here in 1968. The world's first successful open-heart surgery was performed here on a five year old named Jackie Johnson in 1952 by F. John Lewis and C. Walton Lillehei.

The University was also one of the first in the nation to include condoms in snack vending machines.

Sports Trivia

The Hubert H. Humphrey Metrodome spans 60 million cubic feet and takes 250,000 cubic feet of air pressure a minute to keep the dome inflated. It cost 55 million dollars to build.

The Minnesota Twins became the first team in baseball history to win the American League West after coming in dead last the year before. The Twins were also the first American League team to host three million fans in one season. That happened in 1988. The longest ball ever hit in the Metrodome was 480 feet long. The holder of this record was their first baseman, Kent Hrbek. The Twins were originally the Washington Senators, but became the Twins in 1961. They have won two World Series.

Note: the first official hit in the Metrodome was in a preseason game by Pete Rose of the Cincinnati Reds.

* * * *

The Minnesota Vikings have a long and storied NFL history. Some of the famous names that have donned the purple and gold are Ahmad Rashad, Fran Tarkenton, Chris Doleman, and Chris Carter. The Vikings have been to the NFL Superbowl four different times, but have lost each game.

* * * *

If you prefer basketball, the Minnesota Timberwolves can also be seen in action in Minneapolis. Of course, this isn't the first professional basketball team Minnesota has had. The Minneapolis Lakers once played here before moving to Los Angeles in 1960. They were lead by George Mikan, one of the first four men selected into the Basketball Hall of Fame.

The Timberwolves play at the Target Center. There are also many concerts that take place at the Target Center.

Geological

Like the rest of Minnesota, Minneapolis gets cold and a large amount of snow. The state on average, gets about twenty inches of snow in the winter. However, on November 1, 1991, which is fairly early in the winter season, Minneapolis got 24 inches of snow in 24 hours. It literally took days for people to clean up this white, fluffy mess.

This was not the only incident involving a large amount of snowfall in a short amount of time. In 1940, 16.2 inches of snow fell on the city in only 14 hours.

Prominent People

In 1880, a Minneapolis Doctor by the name of H.S. Tanner tried to attempt an incredible biblical feat. He fasted for 40 days. Dr. Tanner believed that the fast would prove that the only function that the stomach served was that it was annoying. His first meal after his forty-day hiatus from eating was milk and watermelon. He didn't prove his theory, but he did get more press after his invention for the electric light bulb. Tanner died at the age of 87, and still hung on to the belief that the stomach's only function is to be a nuisance.

* * * *

Minneapolis native George Munsing can be credited with making underwear much more comfortable. Munsing's innovative idea entailed covering wool thread with silk. This young entrepreneur enjoyed the underwear business. He eventually patented on-piece underwear, known as union suits. Union suits were used to keep warm. In 1978, the name of these cozy undergarments was changed to the ever-popular Long Johns.

* * * *

Former presidential candidate, Hubert Humphrey used to be the mayor of Minneapolis in 1945. Although he didn't win the election against President Nixon, Humphrey served as an outstanding Senator in the United States Congress. He is known as the "elder statesman of liberalism".

* * * *

The plaintiff in the famous U.S. Supreme Court case Bakke vs. University of California calls Minneapolis home. Allan Paul Bakke was refused admission to the University of California Medical School twice. Bakke sued on the grounds of reverse discrimination and won by a narrow Supreme Court vote. The decision influenced the use of quotas throughout the nation.

* * * *

James Arness and his brother Peter Graves, who both changed their names, both made it big in Hollywood. Arness was the infamous marshal Matt Dillon on "Gunsmoke" for twenty years. Graves, on the other hand, served as a new anchor here in the Cities, until he moved on to star in "Mission Impossible".

> James Arness was the infamous marshal Matt Dillon on "Gunsmoke".

* * * *

Astronaut Robert Cabana is also from Minneapolis. After serving in the Marines, Cabana was selected to pilot the 1990 mission into space.

* * * *

Born in Minneapolis in 1908, Lew Ayres was a talented musician and actor. His most famous role was "All Quiet on the Western Front". Because of his continual protests to World War II, Ayres lost his popularity quickly and no longer acted in movies.

* * * *

Famous film musician, George Stoll was born in Minneapolis as well. His scores include

"For me and my Gal", "Meet me in St. Louis", "Babes in Arms", and lastly, "Anchor's Aweigh", for which he won an Oscar in 1945.

* * * *

Engineers from the Honeywell's firm in Minneapolis assisted Hollywood director Stanley Kubrick in designing the film "2001: A Space Odyssey". Their creative ideas made it to the big screen and brought some popularity to the firm.

* * * *

The artist formerly known as Prince, or Prince Rogers Nelson, to be more specific, was born in town in 1958.

Talented Jazz performer, Oscar Pettiford was also Minneapolis-born. Pettiford was nationally known for his phenomenal music and played with every major jazz group in the mid 1900s.

* * * *

The movie "Purple Rain" was filmed in Minneapolis, and is an autobiography describing the life and times of this 1980s musical legend. His songs hit the top of the charts on several occasions and his music is still widely listened to and appreciated.

* * * *

Minneapolis is also the hometown of Richard Dean Anderson. Anderson played Dr. Jeff Webberin the daytime soap opera, "General Hospital". But he is even better known for playing the intelligent and adventurous "MacGyver".

Before making it in Hollywood, Anderson made a bicycle trip by himself from Minneapolis to Alaska and back, traveling 5,600 miles.

* * * *

Known as "America's Wartime Sweethearts", Minneapolis' born Andrew Sisters (Maxene, Patty and Laverne) are famous for their 1941 hit "Boogie Woogie Bugle Boy".

* * * *

Oscar winning movie producer Mike Todd (aka Avrom Hirsch Goldborgen was born in Minneapolis), won best picture in 1956 for Around the World in Eighty Days.

* * * *

North America's 1988 Scrabble championship was won by Minneapolis resident, Bob Watson.

* * * *

Minneapolis native Bernie Leadon, got his start as a guitarist with Linda Ronstadt's band. He left the band when she formed a new backup band consisting of Don Henley, Glen Frey and Randy Meisner. Leadon would return one night to join the group which made such a good sound, that Ronstadt tried to keep them all together. Unfortunately for her, Leadon and the others went off on their own. As the Eagles they won a Grammy in 1972 for their hit, "Lyin' Eyes".

* * * *

44

Minneapolis born actor Ed Flanders won a Tony and Emmy for A Moon for the Misbegotten before going on to star in the Emmy-winning role of Dr. Westphal on "St. Elsewhere" in 1982.

Inventions

The McGraw Electric Company marked the first automatic pop-up toaster under the name Toastmaster in June 1926 at a retail price of $13.50.

During his career with the RCA Corporation, Minneapolis native Elmer Engstrom would be instrumental in the development of the color television.

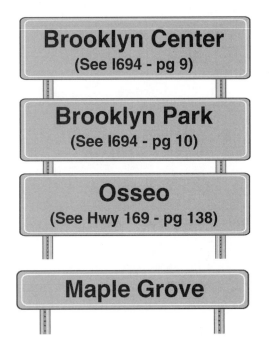

Brooklyn Center
(See I694 - pg 9)

Brooklyn Park
(See I694 - pg 10)

Osseo
(See Hwy 169 - pg 138)

Maple Grove

Place Name

An abundance of the hard or sugar maples in the forest around the village gives it its name.

Historical Significance

The Winnebago Indians were the only inhabitants of the Maple Grove area until 1851 when Louis Gervais settled in the area.

Prominent People

The Polynesian family band, The Jets, comes from Maple Grove.

* * * *

National champion drag racer, Tom Hoover, is also from Maple Grove.

Bayport   **Moorhead**

Rogers

Place Name
Officers of the Great Northern Railway Company named the village.

St. Michael

Place Name
This town was given the name of the Catholic Church built here in 1856.

St. Augusta

In 2000 St. Augusta incorporated and tried to change the name to Ventura, in honor of Minnesota Governor Jess Ventura. However, due to popular vote the name remained St. Augusta.

Place Name
Father Pierz named the first church in the area St. Augusta, which later became the name of the township.

Some believe that the village was named for Augusta Wilson's daughter who passed away at an early age.

Buffalo

Place Name
Lake Pulaski and Buffalo Lake encompass the town of Buffalo. The town was named for the unusually large amount of buffalo fish in the Buffalo Lake.

Historical Significance
The early settlers survived by selling ginseng, which was abundant in the area. Ginseng is in high demand by the Chinese, who use it for medicinal purposes. The settlers, therefore, profited heavily from selling it.

Local Landmark
The town's courthouse has an interesting financial history. The building was constructed in 1877at the price of $26,000. However, payments were delayed on it and the final price tag ended up being more than $100,000, which was an extremely large sum of money at the time.

Prominent People

As far as fame in Buffalo goes, writer Margaret Culkin Banning was born in the city in 1891.

Place Name

Thomas Jefferson's home in Charlottesville, Virginia bore the name Monticello, which was given to this town and 22 others throughout the country.

Historical Significance

Before its incorporation, Monticello saw a notorious murder scheme in 1859. H.A. Wallace was allegedly murdered by his neighbor, Oscar Johnson. He was tried and acquitted but soon after he was supposedly lynched by Emery Moore. Then Moore was arrested, but he too was soon released after a mini-battle between the lynchers and the authorities occurred.

Everything turned out all right in the end, though. The authorities arrested all of the lynchers and finally put the whole fiasco to rest.

* * * *

This is not the only tragedy faced by Monticello. In 1971, the Northern States Power Company's nuclear reactor in Monticello spilled 50,000 gallons of radioactive water. The water contaminated parts of the Mississippi River and St. Paul's water supply.

Place Name

The town is named in honor of Scottish immigrant Robert Orrock, who came to America in 1831, settling as a farmer here in 1856.

Local Landmark

The community of Orrock lies in the middle of the Sherburne National Wildlife Refuge and the Sand Dunes State Forest. The Sand Dunes State Forest is a wooded area that shows signs of the final stages of glacial activity in central Minnesota. As the glaciers melted, wind and water eroded the ground, creating the Mississippi River Sand Plains. With more than 30,000 acres of forest, the Sherburne National Wildlife Refuge is a unique combination of grasslands, wetlands and woodlands.

 The Sand Dunes State Forest is a wooded area that shows signs of the final stages of glacial activity in central Minnesota.

Silver Creek

Place Name

Named for Silver Creek where the first New Englanders settled in the early 1850s.

Historical Significance

In 1854, more than thirty settlers from Amsterdam also arrived. They purchased eighty acres of land and built a house that was only 50 x 70 feet. That may seem fairly big, but it wasn't big enough for all 30 of them. Within two years, more than two-thirds of the group left. Most of the community can still trace its ancestry back to Amsterdam today.

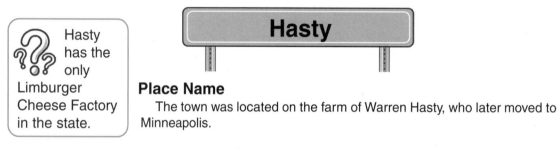

 Hasty has the only Limburger Cheese Factory in the state.

Hasty

Place Name

The town was located on the farm of Warren Hasty, who later moved to Minneapolis.

Clearwater

Place Name

This town receives its name from the Clearwater Lake and River, which is a tributary to the Mississippi River.

Annandale

Place Name

The town's name has a number of arguable origins. First, it was supposedly named by a politician after an actress named Lizzie Annandale. Upon visiting the town, the politician saw posters of the actress throughout Minnesota and wanted the town to represent his respect for the actress. Others argue that the town was named for a Scotland seaport or for the Annan River. Yet, no one really knows for sure.

Luxemburg

Place Name

Named by the German settlers who came to the area for the province and city in western Germany.

Local Landmark

St. Wendelin's Catholic Church stands out in this town. The church was built in the 1880s and is made of rough stone walls. The scenery around the church makes visitors feel like they are in nineteenth century Minnesota.

Saint Cloud

Historical Significance

St. Cloud began as three separate settlements founded by three distinctively different gentlemen. One settlement was founded by Sylvanus B. Lowry, a political figure interested in fur trade and a former southern slave owner. John L. Wilson, a native of Maine who was interested in a sawmill, founded another settlement. The third settlement was founded by George P. Brott, a professional town-site promoter.

> The name of the town is in reference to Napoleon's residence at St. Cloud, France.

The three settlements, founded between 1853-1855, were located on the west bank of the Mississippi River near the Sauk River. The settlements were as varied as their founders. Lowry's settlement was inhabited by southerners who kept slaves; Wilson's settlement contained Catholics from Germany, and Brott's settlement had anti-slavery Protestants.

The demand for protection from the varied hardships of pioneer life forced the three settlements to merge into one city. In 1856, the city of St. Cloud was incorporated. This name was chosen due to the domination of Wilson's settlement and a strong liking for Napoleon's residence at St. Cloud, France.

The stormy life of a pioneer community during the Civil War marked St. Cloud in many ways. The slavery issue caused repeated flare-ups in the city, and Native-American warfare continued to press the pioneers together for protection.

During the 1860s and 1870s, the city of St. Cloud grew rapidly in both population and economic activity. The city was the head of navigation on the Mississippi River and the southern terminus of overland routes to the forts, settlements and trading posts in the northwest. Ox carts from the north no longer continued to St. Paul, but now traded at St. Cloud.

The discovery of colored granite deposits in 1868 began an important phase of St. Cloud's industrial growth. St. Cloud granite companies now make building stone and monuments that are shipped to every part of the country.

Industry

In the spring of 1868 the firm of Breen & Young opened the first commercial granite quarry in Minnesota on the site of what is now the St. Cloud Reformatory. Their first order was for stone for the corners, steps and trimmings of the U.S. Custom House and Post Office in St. Paul.

Nearly as old as the earth itself, granite is one of the strongest, most durable stones on the planet. In Minnesota substantial outcroppings of granite lie along the Minnesota River valley near Ortonville and Redwood Falls. It is also found in the St. Cloud area of eastern Stearns County and adjacent parts of Benton and Sherburne counties.

In the mid-1800s most of the commercial granite in the U.S. came from New Hampshire and other rocky areas of the East. The market for granite was relatively small in the sparsely settled Midwest, and transportation costs made it difficult for Minnesota companies to compete for work in faraway eastern cities. Many quarries failed, but others survived as new uses for granite were developed. Prosperity came to the St. Cloud area quarries in the 1890s when monument work began to replace paving, bridge and foundation blocks as their principal product.

The "busy, gritty, granite city," as St. Cloud came to call itself, continues to be a major supplier of granite. Prized now more for its beauty than its strength, granite quarried near here graces such state landmarks as the Capitol and the History Center in St. Paul.

(Historical marker located on Hwy 10)

Jodi Thelen, the actress who played Kate in The Wedding Singer was born in St. Cloud. She also appeared in the TV episodes of Grace Under Fire, Dawson's Creek and Touched by an Angel.

Prominent People

Science fiction writer Philip C. Jennings, the author of The Bug-Life Chronicles comes from St. Cloud.

★ ★ ★ ★

Joel Gretsch was born in St. Cloud. He is married to William Shatner's daughter, Melanie.

Following a number of appearances at the Guthrie Theatre in Minneapolis, he went on to appear in episodes of numerous TV shows including Saved by the Bell, Melrose Place, Friends and Pacific Blue.

★ ★ ★ ★

Actor Rod McCary also comes from Saint Cloud. He appeared in such TV shows as The Flinstones, Walker Texas Ranger, Team Knight Rider, and the Power Rangers.

Sauk Rapids

Place Name

Sauk Rapids was originally a chunk of land sought after by the Native

American Sac tribe. The Sac took refuge on this land after being forced to leave Wisconsin for attacking white settlers.

Historical Significance

Sauk Rapids served an important function in the early days of its existence. Since the town was the meeting point for rail and ox-cart traffic via the Northern Pacific and Great Northern Railways, the city of Sauk Rapids was significant to transporting goods.

However, in 1886, a tornado destroyed the city and killed 79 people. The only structure left from the town's boom days is the foundation of an old sawmill. Consequently, flour milling replaced transportation as the primary industry.

>  Sauk Rapids supplies some high-grade rock from its quarries. Probably the most famous function its granite has served was to construct the Civic Opera Building in Chicago.

Sartell

Place Name

Joseph Sartell, was one of the areas first farmers settling here in 1854.

Historical Significance

Sartell holds a great deal of Native American history. One example is the Indian boundary established by the Prairie du Chien Treaty of 1825, which crosses the Mississippi River in Sartell. There is a sign at the point at which it crosses that marks the boundaries. The Sioux were restricted to the southern part of the line, while the property to the north of the line was designated as Chippewa territory.

Saint Joseph

Place Name

This town was given the name of its church.

Historical Significance

Between 1854 and 1857 many Catholics came to the United States from Germany and settled in central Minnesota at St. Cloud and in the Sauk Valley; their religious and educational needs were met by the Benedictines.

The Benedictine Order and Rule were established at Monte Cassino, Italy, in 529, and spread far beyond. In the 1840s Boniface Wimmer, a monk at the Abbey of Metten in Bavaria, promoted mission work in the United States, established a monastery in Pennsylvania where he became the first American Benedictine abbot, and subsequently became an important figure in the creation of Saint John's Abbey and University.

In the 1850s Benedicta Riepp, a nun from Saint Walburg Abbey in Eichstatt, Bavaria,

Jerry and Patty Wetterling established a nonprofit foundation to focus national attention on missing children and their families. Their son, Jacob, was the eleven-year-old that was kidnapped from St. Joseph while riding his bike.

spearheaded the movement of Benedictine sisters from Saint Marys, Pennsylvania, to central Minnesota where they founded Saint Benedict's Monastery and eventually the College of St. Benedict.

Both the Benedictine monks and the nuns of the Order of Saint Benedict, originally from Bavaria, arrived in St. Cloud are from Pennsylvania in the 1850s. By the mid-1860s they had moved to their present locations, the nuns to Saint Joseph and the monks to Collegeville. These institutions have preserved excellent late 19th and early 20th century buildings which possess historic integrity and importance. Saint John's also preserves several buildings designed by internationally known architect Marcel Breuer, including the famous church.

The Benedictine of Minnesota have established high reputations through their many services to humanity for nearly a century and a half. They created important academies, schools for higher education, hospitals, orphanages, homes for the aged, and missions which extend beyond Minnesota to distant parts of the country and world.

In addition, they are pioneers in establishing public radio, the liturgical and ecumenical movements, pastoral work, educational publishing, arts and crafts, and the development of a world-renowned library.

(Historical marker located on I-94 east bound rest area)

Collegeville

Place Name

The town name is in reference to St. John's College, when the college was moved from St. Cloud to its present location.

Local Landmark

St. John's Abbey was founded in 1856 on the west bank of the Mississippi River near St. Cloud and permanently located in the Indianbush, now Collegeville, on the shore of Lake Sagatagan in 1866.

St. John's was the first Benedictine Abbey in the Upper Midwest, and from the beginning its monks were educators, ministers of the word, and artisans. Their first ministry was among the settlers and Indians throughout Minnesota and North Dakota during the frontier era. Subsequently abbeys and priories were founded in Washington, Saskatchewan, Kentucky, the Bahamas, Mexico, Puerto Rico and Japan.

St. John's University was chartered by the territorial legislature of Minnesota on March 6, 1857. The campus is also the site of St. John's Preparatory School, the Institute for Ecumenical and Cultural Research, the Liturgical Press, and the Monastic Manuscript Microfilm Library.

Several campus buildings, including the renowned Abbey Church, were designed by architect Marcel Breuer.

(Historical marker located off I-95 at St. John's University)

General Trivia

Minnesota Public Radio, originally started broadcasting as KSJR at St. John's University. Despite the rock 'n' roll era, KSJR, was devoted to classic music and the fine arts. It would become one of the country's largest and most successful public radio stations.

Place Name

Shares the same name as numerous townships, villages and cities in 17 other states named for the capitol of New York.

Place Name

This town is named by the early settlers who came to the area from Freeport, Illinois.

Local Landmark

Germanic heritage can be seen in the architecture throughout the town of Freeport. Two buildings that illustrate early 20th century style include the roller mill and the Gothic Revival Sacred Heart Roman Catholic Church.

Prominent People

Frank Benolken, who was from Johnsburg, Illinois, which is near Freeport, came to the area to work as a salesman for the St. Paul Harvester. He later went on to become a state legislator.

Place Name

A hunter, from Munich, Bavaria, who stayed with the first settler in the area for several years, is responsible for giving the city its name.

General Trivia

In its early days, New Munich held an old, annual ritual on Corpus Christi Day. This event is celebrated on the Thursday following the eighth Sunday after Easter.

After mass, the congregation would leave the church and follow young flower girls dressed in white, the priest, and the cross bearer. The worshipers would then proceed to four shrines, approximately one mile apart, where they would kneel to pray after a gunshot is fired, representing Jesus' death in the nearby fields.

Melrose

U.S. Air Force Captain James Gallagher,with a crew of thirteen completed the first nonstop flight around the world.

Place Name

The village of Melrose was settled in the mid 1850s, by Scottish immigrants who named their new home after the city of Melrose in their native homeland.

Otherwise it's possible they created the name by honoring two local daughters by the name of Melissa (Melvina) and Rose.

Prominent People

U.S. Air Force Captain James Gallagher, a native of Melrose, with a crew of thirteen completed the first nonstop flight around the world. The 43rd Bomb Group flying a B-50 bomber, Lucky Lady II, refueling four times in-flight completed the 23,452 mile trip in ninety-four hours and one minute.

Sauk Centre

Place Name

Sauk Centre was the boyhood home for talented novelist, Sinclair Lewis. Sinclair Lewis was the first American author to win the Nobel Prize for literature.

At the southern tip of Sauk Lake lies the city of Sauk Centre. The city is named for the Lake, which likewise was named for the small band of Sauk Indians who occupied this area of land.

Prominent People

When Harry Sinclair Lewis was born on a bitter cold February 7, 1885, Sauk Centre was a raw prairie town with an unpaved main street and five or six blocks of false fronts. A gawky, sensitive child who achieved little success in school and was the brunt of every crude piece of horseplay, "Red" Lewis spent most of his youth tagging after his adored older brother and doctor-father, and reading every book he could find. He began to write at age fifteen. Despite the years of lost jobs and false hopes that followed his graduation from Yale University in 1908, he persisted in his determination to be a writer.

With the publication of Main Street and Babbit Lewis became a successful

novelist and critic of American culture, winning the Nobel Prize for Literature in 1930. He returned frequently to Minnesota; never able to deny his underlying attachment to the Northern Middle West, he described it as "...the newest empire of the world... a land of dairy herds and exquisite lakes, of new automobiles and tar-paper shanties and silos like red towers, of clumsy speech and a hope that is boundless". Lewis's talent declined and he died alone in Italy on January 10, 1951. As he had requested, his ashes were brought home to Sauk Centre.

<u>(Historical marker located at 812 Sinclair Lewis Avenue)</u>

* * * *

Nearly every small town has a Main Street, a town center where residents gather to conduct their business, greet their neighbors and exchange news of the day.

Today the concept of main street is suffused in a nostalgic glow, as we remember the virtues and simplicity of small-town life. But it wasn't always so. The publication of Sinclair Lewis's novel Main Street in 1920 jolted Americans out of their sentimental view of their hometown.

Lewis set his novel in the fictional town of Gopher Prairie, whose residents he depicted in an unflattering light. Soon the term "Main Street" took on a negative meaning, becoming synonymous with narrow-minded, small-town provincialism.

Although Lewis intended Gopher Prairie to represent the American village in general, it quickly came to be associated with his own hometown of Sauk Centre. The local newspaper expressed its displeasure by waiting six months before acknowledging any connection to the nation's most talked-about novel. As the book gained popularity, however, Sauk Centre came to appreciate its celebrity status.

Gradually the phrase "Main Street" lost its negative meaning as American film makers and writers in the 1930s and 1940s returned to the glorification of small-town virtues. Sauk Centre's association with Lewis's novel, which had at first brought ridicule, eventually conferred on the town a special dignity.

Now Sauk Centre's Main Street stands as the living symbol of the American small town.

<u>(Historical marker located on I-94 westbound rest area)</u>

* * * *

Sauk Centre was also one of the eighteen small towns actress Jessica Lange lived in as a child.

Place Name

Although the name Osakis means "danger", there really is no immediate danger in the city of Osakis these days. However, this wasn't always the case. The town got its name because of the precarious encounters that often times occurred between the Sioux and Chippewa tribes in the area.

Historical Significance

Osakis was one of the stops on the Burbank Minnesota Stage Company line to the Red River, established in the spring of 1859 upon the opening of the Fort Abercrombie military road. During the Sioux Outbreak of 1862 the maintenance of this line of communication was vitally important, and the route was constantly patrolled by troops.

(Historical marker located on Hwy 27)

General Trivia

The lake with the same name is sometimes called the "Mother Walleye Lake" because of the numerous walleye that inhabit the waters. Not surprisingly, the lake is among the top ten fishing lakes in Minnesota.

Alexandria

Place Name

In 1866, the city of Alexandria was founded by Alexander Kincaid, for whom the town is named.

Historical Significance

Prior to its development, the city of Alexandria was dominated by Ojibwa and Sioux Indians. As a young city, and even today, the city prospers because of the rich farmland common in the area.

The city boasts a statue of Knute Nelson, the only American of Norwegian birth who is honored by a statue in Oslo, Norway as well.

Prominent People

Knute Nelson, who was known for his courage and common sense, served the people of Minnesota as a public office holder for over 50 years.

Born in Norway in 1843, he was elected to the Minnesota legislature and to two terms in the United States Congress before becoming the state's first foreign-born governor in 1893.

He then served with distinction for 28 years in the United States Senate, where he championed such causes as conservation, a federal income tax, and pure food and drug legislation.

(Historical marker located on South Nokomis Street)

* * * *

Graduate of Jefferson High School, John Hawkes won over audiences and critics alike with his soulful portrayal of "Bugsy", the lovelorn sailor in The Perfect Storm. He also starred opposite Keanu Reeves in Hardball as "Tricky", Reeves' best friend and business partner.

* * * *

56

The son of a high school English teacher (father), and a second grade teacher (mother), Peter Krause (pronounced KROW-zuh) was a pre-med student at Gustavus Adolphus College before switching to his final major of English Literature. His Hollywood acting career includes appearing in TV episodes of Caroline in the City, 3rd Rock from the Sun, Spin City; as well as the movie We Don't Live Here Anymore.

Local Landmark

Another big old statue in the area is the appropriately named "Big Ole Statue".The statue is 28 feet tall and weighs four tons. The statue is so impressive that it was displayed at the 1965 World's Fair in New York.

One of the most recognizable monuments in the state, the statue displays a Viking warrior with a spear, sword and armor.

Although arguable authentic, the 1362 Kensington Runestone was discovered in the area in 1898 by a Swedish farmer. Unaware of the value of the stone, the farmer used it primarily as a doorstop.

Garfield

Place Name

This town was named after the second martyred president, President James Garfield, who was shot by assassin Charles Guiteau on July 2, 1881.

Brandon

Place Name

The current name was given for Stephen Douglas's birthplace in Vermont. It was changed from its original name of Chippewa which referred to the rivers and lakes used by the Ojibwe as their roads to the Dakota country.

Evansville

Place Name

The name of this town honors the areas first mail carrier Albert Evans. Albert had a log cabin in the area where he could stay overnight when he was on his route between St. Cloud and Fort Abercrombie. Unfortunately Evans was killed in the Dakota War of 1862.

Local Landmark

Near the city of Evansville and Melby is neighboring Lake Christina. This area is home to the "seven sisters". These seven stately hills can be seen on the South shore of the Lake and range from 100 to 350 feet in height.

Ashby

Place Name
This town could have been named for Ashby, a town in England; or for the pioneer farmer from Norway, Gunder Ash.

Dalton

Place Name
Ole Dahl, was the original owner of the site where the town was built.

Fergus Falls

Place Name
Incorporated in 1872, this city is named after James Fergus. Fergus financed the expedition of Joseph Whitford, whose efforts led the city to being incorporated.

General Trivia
When the first post office was established soon after the city's incorporation, a German postmaster was hired. It is said that the postmaster couldn't read a word of English. So, how did he deliver the mail? Well, he didn't. In order to fulfill his job duties, he dumped all the mail into a pile on the floor and invited villagers to search through the pile for their mail.

* * * *

In 1919, a tornado hit the city, killing 60 people and destroying everything in its path. The area hospitals were practically the only buildings left standing. Surprisingly enough, the walls of an entire house were carried away, but the cupboards remained intact without breaking the fragile china inside.

 The Fergus Falls City Hall was designed after Independence Hall in Philadelphia.

Local Landmarks
Inspiration Peak, the second highest peak in Minnesota, is located within the city.

Carlisle

Place Name
Carlisle received the same name as a city in England, a Kentucky county and other cities across the country in eleven other states.

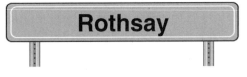

Rothsay

Place Name
Officials for the Great Northern Railroad gave this station the name of a seaport 30 miles west of Glasgow, Scotland. Incidentally this is the only town in the United States with this name.

Pelican Rapids

Place Name
Pelican Rapids got its name from the river that descends in the area with rapids drifting over boulders. The Ojibwa gave the river their name for pelican, spelled Shada in the Song of Hiawatha by Henry W. Longfellow.

General Trivia
A Minnesota woman, the skeleton of a girl about fifteen years of age, was discovered at this point in 1931 by a highway repair crew. Although the skeleton has not been dated exactly, based on the site geology scientists believe it to be perhaps 10,000 years old. This would make the Minnesota Woman America's oldest human skeleton.

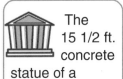

The 15 1/2 ft. concrete statue of a pelican built in 1957, is the largest in the world.

Two artifacts, a dagger of elk horn and a conch shell, were discovered with the bones. Archaeologists believe that the girl drowned in Glacial Lake Pelican, which adjoined Glacial Lake Agassiz, a huge body of water that covered much of northwestern Minnesota during the last ice age.

(Historical marker located on Hwy 59)

Barnesville

Place Name
This village was started by George Barnes in 1874. A farmer and wheat merchant, George owned and managed a rather large farm near Glyndon, 15 miles north of Barnesville.

He built the first store in the area, was president of the North Pacific Grain Company and was responsible for the construction of grain elevators along the Northern Pacific Railroad route from St. Paul to Tacoma, Washington.

Geological

Barnesville is located on the beach of the prehistoric Lake Agassiz. It is obvious to scientists that this lake was once a fertile forested land since tree remnants are often times recovered from beneath the lake deposit.

Place Name

Dwight May Sabin for whom the town is named for, was a Stillwater businessman who engaged in the lumber industry, and the manufacturing of machinery, engines and cars. He later became a state and U.S. senator.

Place Name

Moorhead was named in honor of Dr. William G. Moorhead who was director at the Northern Pacific Railway.

The railway connected with the town in 1871. Farming in the rich Red River Valley and the dominant railway industry transformed Moorhead into a boomtown.

Local Landmark

The Heritage Hjemkomst Interpretive Center tells the story of the Viking ship Hjemkomst and its voyage across the Atlantic.

St. John's Episcopal Church was designed on an Elizabethan model by the noted architect, Cass Gilbert, among whose other significant buildings is the present Minnesota State Capitol. Construction of St. John's began on August 1, 1898. On February 12, 1899, the church was consecrated and the first confirmation held.

Episcopal Church services in Moorhead date from 1872 when the Reverend James Gilfillan conducted a service in a Northern Pacific Railroad passenger coach. With the arrival of Benjamin F. Mackall, a licensed lay reader, regular services began on May 13, 1873. When the parish was organized in 1875, Mackall was elected Senior Warden, an office he held for 62 years. The movement to construct the present church was led by Mackall and W.H. Davey, who donated the land on which St. John's stands.

(Historical marker located on Hwy 75)

Prominent People

Born in Maine in 1842, Solomon G. Comstock worked on the family farm until he came of age and then followed the pioneers west. After reading law in Bangor, he studied at the

University of Michigan, then went to Omaha and Minneapolis. Finally, in the fall of 1871, "poor, but full of vigor, hope and talents," Comstock established a successful legal practice in Moorhead. His sound judgment and solid statesmanship won his appointment as Clay County attorney and then election to the state legislature as representative and senator and to the United States House of Representatives.

In the late 1870s, Comstock donated six acres of valuable city property for the establishment of a state normal school, later to become Moorhead State College. His belief in higher education was also reflected in the career of his daughter Ada Louise, who became a noted educator and third president of Radcliffe College.

Comstock built his imposing eleven-room frame house in 1883 for his wife Sarah and their children. One of the few remaining urban homes to boast the spacious grounds typical of the late 1800s, the house was donated to the Minnesota Historical Society for restoration and preservation in 1965.

(Historical marker located on Hwy 75)

Industry

The fertile areas along both banks of the Red River of the North were once the bed of a huge lake known to geologists as Glacial Lake Agassiz. When the last glacier retreated and the lake slowly drained some 9,000 years ago, the plain left behind contained some of the richest farmlands in North America.

The flat valley lands were well suited to the new farm machinery of the 1870s and 1880s. Settlers followed the railroads west and sent their huge wheat crops back to the growing flour mills in the Twin Cities. Many of the "bonanza" farms of the valley were more than 2,000 acres in size, and the largest was more than 30,000 acres.

Farm protest movements followed the wheat belt, because the single-cash-crop farmers with heavy machinery investment were especially vulnerable to price fixing by the railroads, grain buyers, and milling monopolies. The Farmers' Alliance, the cooperative marketing movement, the Nonpartisan League, and the Farmer-Labor Party in turn found strength in the Red River Valley.

Although wheat is still grown, sugar beets, sunflowers, and potatoes are today the staples of the valley agriculture, which is still characterized by large-scale operations, high capital investments, and the employment of seasonal workers.

(Historical marker located at the tourist information center on I-94)

INTERSTATE 90

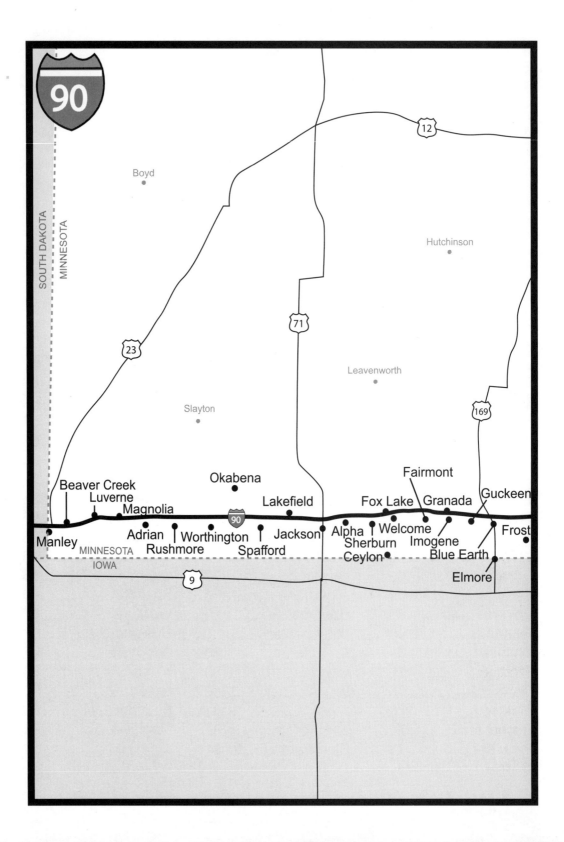

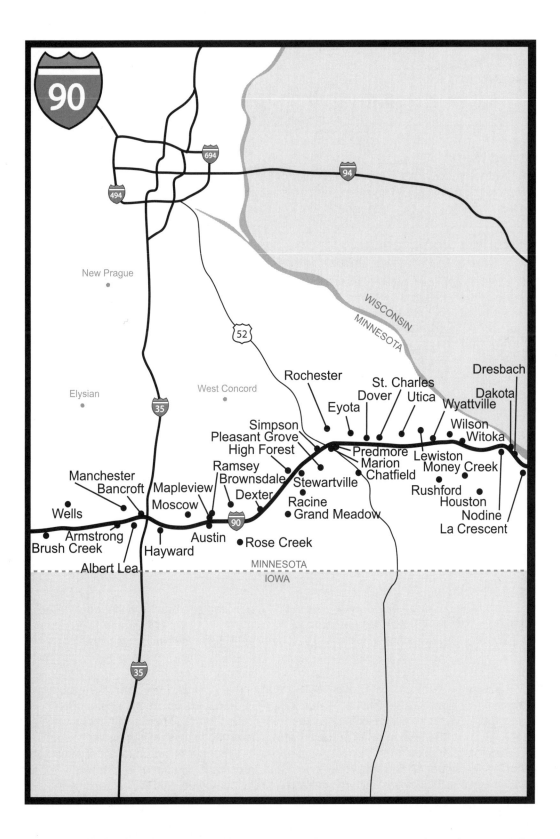

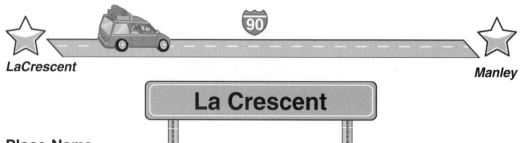

La Crescent

Place Name

Rivalry with LaCrosse, Wisconsin influenced the settlers to change the town's name from Manton to LaCrescent. This is the Mohammedan emblem, and the town name was changed to this under the mistaken conviction that LaCrosse was named for the crusaders' symbol.

Historical Significance

The town's earliest settler and a fur trader, Peter Cameron, arrived in 1851. He envisioned a metropolis here, and dug a canal to the Mississippi hoping to drain the lowlands. Part of his abandoned project is still visible in the city.

LaCrescent is known as the "Apple Capital of Minnesota."

General Trivia

LaCrescent is known as the "Apple Capital of Minnesota," and for good reason. John Harris came to the area around 1856 establishing an orchard on the western edge of town where the bluffs starts to rise. The sheltered river valley allowed him to successfully grow 20 different varieties even when skeptics didn't believe they could be grown in the cold climate of Minnesota. The most popular apple is the Haralson.

Dresbach

Place Name

The town of Dresbach is also located conveniently near the Mississippi River and is named in honor of George Dresbach.

Historical Significance

The area was first settled by a colony of French settlers, later purchased by George Dresbach who established a stone quarry.

Note: Winona travertine is a widely used limestone that is quarried in the area.

* * * *

In the years between 1835 and 1860, steamboats from St. Louis and the Illinois river towns of Rock Island and Galena carried hundreds of tourists up the Mississippi River past "a thousand bluffs which tower in countless fascinating forms". Their destinations were the frontier town of St. Paul and the famous Falls of St. Anthony in what is now Minneapolis.

Made popular in the east by panorama painters, writers, and lecturers, the "Fashionable Tour" of the upper Mississippi River combined the scenic "grandeur and majesty" of the west, a chance to glimpse real Indian villages along the shores, and the luxury and fine food provided by the big excursion boats.

By 1854 visitors could travel from New York City to Rock Island entirely by rail in about 48 hours, step onto a steamboat heading north, and experience the "tonic of wildness" in a comfortable four-day round trip to St. Paul, where boats docked at the rate of four or five a day during the summer months.

<u>(Historical marker located on I-90 at the tourist information center)</u>

Historical Significance

This river town was developed by Nathan Brown, who came to the area establishing a stockyard and ferry service across the Mississippi River to Wisconsin.

Place Name

The name was changed from Rose Hill, supposedly because two government surveyors couldn't find "no dining" place to eat.

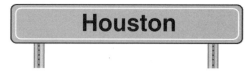

Place Name

Settlers were attracted to Houston, named for General Sam Houston of Texas, because of the hundreds of springs that exist here.

Place Name

This town is located in the Root River Valley, which indirectly is responsible for the town's name. It seems that one of the men got his pocketbook wet while in the creek. Spreading out the bank notes on a bush to dry, the wind blows sending the money back into the stream. Unfortunately some of it was never found. So as a result they named the stream, after which the town was named, Money Creek.

LaCrescent   *Manley*

Place Name
Witoka was captured by the Sac (Sauk) tribe near here. Her father, a Wabasha war chief, came to her daring rescue.

Place Name
The town was named for one of the areas first settlers, Warren Wilson.

Place Name
It was named by an unanimous vote by the nine settlers on Christmas Day after the Rush Creek tributary of the Root River. The Rush Creek was given the name in reference to the tall rushes that grew along its banks.

Local Landmark
"Buffalo Bill's Peak" is the name of the bluff above the site where Buffalo Bill rehearsed one of his Wild West shows.

Place Name
Hiram Wyatt was the area's postmaster and person the village is named after.

Place Name
S. J. Lewis, the area's first settler gives his name to the town.

Local Landmark
Lewiston was the first stagecoach stop in the Winona-Rochester area. Now a private entity, Ramer's Tavern is a relic of those busy days. Worn out travelers took a break from

their journeys here and took complete advantage of the tasty food and warm atmosphere for which the old town was famous.

Place Name

This township derives its name from the ancient city of Utica, founded by the Phoenicians in North Africa.

Historical Significance

St. Charles was founded in an interesting way. When the founders surveyed the area in 1854, they wanted to strategize a way to develop the town quickly. Their final decision was to give a free one-acre lot to every Christian democrat that agreed to settle here. This proved to be an attractive deal that was accepted by many settlers.

St. Charles is named in honor of St. Charles of Italy, who became cardinal of Milan and secretary to Pope Pius IV.

Place Name

The town and nearby river were named after Dover, New Hampshire, where many of its early settlers came from.

Place Name

Taken from the Dakota word, iyotan, meaning greatest or most.

Chatfield
(See Hwy 52 - pg 261)

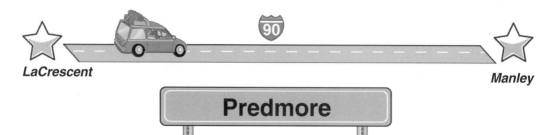

Place Name

Predmore is another town that takes the name of one of its earlier settlers, J.W. Predmore.

Seventeen states throughout the country have the same name as this village which honors the distinguished general in the Revolutionary War from South Carolina, Francis Marion.

Historical Significance

Marion was a horse-changing stop on the old St. Paul-Dubuque stagecoach route.

In 1856 it was the unsuccessful rival of Rochester for the county seat. The village slowly declined in population to a few families after being defeated in this attempt for the county seat, and was accordingly ignored by the railroads.

Place Name

Yorkshire, England native Thomas Simpson came to the United States with his parents where he grew up to be a surveyor for the U.S. government. He was responsible for running the meridian and parallel lines in the southeast part of the Minnesota Territory.

Rochester

Place Name

Rochester is the seat of Olmsted County and was established in 1854 as a crossroads campground for the immigrant wagon trains pouring into the area. George Head of Rochester, New York is credited as the father of Rochester.

Local Landmark

Rochester's fate was changed for the better when a certain young Englishman started working in a local chemist's shop. The same year the town was born, the English chemist became an American doctor, thus starting a career destined to make this settlement home to the world's most renowned privately owned Medical Center.

Dr. William W. Mayo, along with his sons William J. and Charles H., started a medical

practice during the pioneer days of medicine. Charles began his medical career at age nine, standing on a box to administer ether while his father operated. As the Mayo reputation flourished, the family practice eventually outgrew the family. The Mayo's asked other doctors to join them, thus possessing specialists in a variety of fields to complement their medical skills. People came from all around the country, and even from all around the world, to get help from the talented and innovative physicians at the Mayo Clinic in Rochester.

* * * *

Research is part of the way Mayo practices medicine. Research has grown from the laboratories of a couple physicians to programs that include over 250 scientists.

Research milestones include; the development of a high-altitude oxygen mask and anti-blackout suit to protect test pilots from the dangers of high altitudes and contributions to the development of the heart-lung machine. This technology allows medical teams to perform open-heart surgery.

Some of the more interesting research conducted through the clinic involves the use of computerized lasers to kill brain tumors and infusion of chemicals to dissolve gallstones, making surgery avoidable.

Today, over one-third of the members of the Mayo staff are involved in research, which has ultimately led to improved patient care and modern medical miracles.

* * * *

The first Mayo Clinic site was known as the "1914 Building", and it stood where the Siebens Building stands today.

The Mayo practice then moved to the Plummer Building in 1928. The building was named after and designed by Dr. Henry S. Plummer and has stone relief carvings integrated into the exterior, which depict Minnesota wildlife, medical symbols, and mythology. The stone at the corner of 1st Avenue shows Dr. Plummer studying the plans for the building. The large brass doors remain open at all times and have closed only 3 times, once for the assassination of John F. Kennedy and twice for the deaths of prominent Mayo physicians.

On top of the Plummer Building is a 56-bell carillon tower dedicated to American soldiers. This is the most complete carillon in North America, containing 56 bells. All the bells were forged in Europe, and cover 4 ½ octaves. One of the bells weighs four tons. The current Mayo building was built in 1955. In 1969 an additional 10 floors were added along with another 10-story building.

* * * *

The Mayo Clinic treats nearly 300,000 patients annually.

On a typical day, Mayo gets over 1,000 new patients, 148 admissions to the hospitals, 3,358 radiology procedures, 185 surgical procedures, 28,800 lab tests, 12,800 blood tests, 247 units of blood and blood components used and 580 electrocardiograms performed.

A great love of nature led Dr. Charles Horace Mayo, co-founder of the Mayo Clinic, and his wife Edith (Graham) Mayo to purchase a small red brick house and 340 acres in 1907. Their growing family and desire to preserve the natural beauty of the surrounding woodlands

led to the construction of two more houses and the accumulation of 3,300 acres. Ivy Lodge was built in 1908, and in 1910 "Dr. Charlie" himself designed and built the Big House on the hillside.

Unique in construction, the Big House reflects a variety of architectural styles and ideas gathered by the Mayos in their world travels. It is built of poured reinforced concrete, with outside walls over a foot thick enclosing an air space of hollow insulating tiles. Nevertheless it remains homelike rather than monumental. Antiques and art treasures blend in an atmosphere of informality and hospitality.

Ease of circulation and ample lighting through long rows of windows and large bays are among the additions made by Dr. and Mrs. Charles William Mayo, the second occupants.

Many notables, including President Franklin D. Roosevelt, Emperor Haile Salassie of Ethiopia, and the King and Queen of Nepal, have been entertained here.

In addition to its houses, the estate has a summer teahouse, a greenhouse, stables and barns.

<u>(Historical marker located at 3720 Mayowood Road SW)</u>

* * * *

The Silver Lake was created by the damming of the Zumbro River. Home to an estimated 30,000 Giant Canadian Geese, this is the world's largest winter concentration of this species.

In 1963 biologists identified the geese as "Branta Canadensis Maxima" (Giant Canada Geese). This subspecies of geese was believed to be extinct until Rochester's flock was discovered during a routine visit for banding and weighing.

The average Giant Canadian weighs more than 12-14 lbs with a wingspan of 69-71 inches. The Western Canadian weighs approximately 8 lbs. and has a wingspan of 66 inches.

* * * *

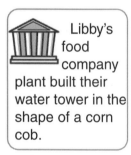

Libby's food company plant built their water tower in the shape of a corn cob.

Properly named, the Peace Fountain represents hope for peace throughout the world. In 1989, the City of Rochester commissioned Charles Eugene Gagnon, a local sculptor of international acclaim, to create the Peace Fountain.

It stands 12 feet high and is made of circular tier of interlocking bronze doves. There are 57 of the life-sized doves. They symbolize the 50 United States and the 7 major continents of the world. The 3 doves on top represent past, present and future.

* * * *

Rochester is the home to the first public junior college in the state. The college opened in 1915. Today, the University Center Rochester comprises Minnesota's two major public higher education systems and the campus houses Rochester Community and Technical College, Winona State University-Rochester Center and the University of Minnesota Rochester Center. Thus, The University Center Rochester is a unique model of integrated academic partnership.

Industry

IBM (International Business Machines) in Rochester is the largest IBM facility in the world

under one contiguous roof. The site's predominate mission is the development of software and hardware and the manufacturing of two of IBM's midrange servers, the RS/6000 and AS/400.

The Rochester laboratory is also involved in hardware development activities in IBM's Network Station and cross-platform software development of other IBM products.

IBM began operations in Rochester in 1956 with 174 employees working in a 50,000 square foot leased facility. This is now the Ability Building Center on Valleyhigh Drive. Today, IBM Rochester occupies about 3.6 million square feet of owned and leased space in Rochester. That's equivalent to about 78 football fields.

IBM introduced the first personal computers, designed in Rochester in 1981.

Prominent People

Supreme Court Justice Harry Blackmun lived in Rochester. He wrote the majority opinion for the landmark court case "Roe V. Wade". President Nixon appointed Blackmun in 1970 to the highest court in the nation.

* * * *

Actress Shirley O'Hare was born in Rochester. Her Hollywood career included numerous TV shows including a number of episodes on The Twilight Zone, The Outer Limits, Mannix, Marcus Welby, M.D., and others, along with starring in films such as Rocky.

General Trivia

When walking around Rochester, make sure you hold tightly to your hats. Rochester is the eighth windiest city in the United States.

Hollywood screenwriter and director Warren Skarren was born in Rochester. His writing credits include numerous screenplays such as Batman, Beetlejuice, Beverly Hills Cop II. Plus he was the associate producer of Top Gun.

Pleasant Grove

Place Name

The quaint town of Pleasant Grove is located in the dark green forests of southeastern Minnesota. These beautiful groves of oaks gives the community its name.

Stewartville

Place Name

Located on the banks of the Root River, the town of Stewartville was named for Charles Stewart. Stewart founded the town by establishing a mill there in 1858.

Richard Warren Sears is from Stewartville. He worked on the Stewartville Railway before selling watches that eventually lead to opening a watch store in Minneapolis and later his retail store in Chicago.

Prominent People

A famous Stewartville native was Richard Warren Sears. He worked on the Stewartville Railway. One day he received a misdirected shipment of watches and decided to sell them to passersby. Profits allowed him to open a watch store in Minneapolis and which he later moved to Chicago. He hired a young watch repairman, Alvah C. Roebuck who would eventually become his partner in the 1880s. Sears and Roebuck had huge successes in working together. Their efforts revolutionized the merchandising business.

Place Name

Established first as Pleasant Valley the name was changed to High Forest, in reference to its high location on the Root River surrounded by forests.

Place Name

Racine is the French name, meaning "root" of the nearby Hokah or Root River.

Place Name

The county commissioners gave their town the name Grand Meadow in allusion to its being an extensive prairie.

Place Name

Mahlon Parritt and his son Dexter, for whom the town is named, were two of the first settlers in the area.

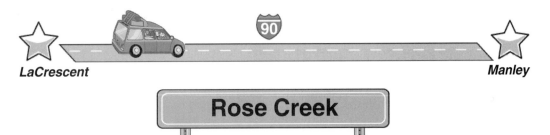

Rose Creek

Place Name

The small town of Rose Creek sits among flat grain fields. This town was named for the small stream that twists and turns throughout the town.

General Trivia

Rose Creek was actually on the first Route in Minnesota to be dedicated as a wildflower route. The state of Minnesota has attempted to set up a wildflower route system based on the beauty of the flowers illuminating from Rose Creek and surrounding areas.

Brownsdale

Place Name

Connecticut native Andrew Brown settled in Minnesota establishing a lumber and milling business. His brother Hosmer, an area farmer, would become a state legislature representative.

Ramsey

Place Name

Governor Alexander Ramsey is commemorated by the naming of this town.

Mapleview

Place Name

When the community was founded, the 100 families in the area named their new home after a row of hard maple trees growing on the west side.

Austin

Place Name

Founded in 1856, Austin sits on the banks of the Cedar River. It was named after its first settler, Austin Nicholas.

Historical Significance

Austin is also the county seat. The way that Austin became the county seat is an entertaining story.

The town of Frankfort was initially given the privilege of holding the seat; yet, no official site was built to serve as the Courthouse. Instead, a portable tin box was kept in town to keep important files and money.

In 1856, a meeting of county commissioners was held in Frankfort. Two members of the commission were from Austin. After the meeting, they decided to take the tin box home with them to Austin. They did this in hopes that the community would consider Austin the County Seat simply because the box would be held there.

Fleeing with the box caused too much trouble though. The two men ended up getting arrested in nearby High Forest. However, before their arrest, they pleaded with a local man to hide the box. He complied, and the whole fiasco resulted in a countywide election that finally gave Austin the much-wanted county seat.

Austin is home to a Hormel packing and Food Products Plant that makes SPAM®-an American icon.

Industry

SPAM® became prominent in world history due to the impact it made in feeding the troops in WWII not just Americans, but our allies as well. Hence, the town is sometimes referred to as "Spamtown, U.S.A".

The corporations evolution from a commodity meatpackers to a multinational meat and food processor has resulted in the development of contemporary, convenient and flavorful value-added consumer branded products such as Dinty Moore stew, Dubuque Plumpers and Jennie O Turkey to name just a few.

A century ago, Hormel Foods introduced Americans to another culture's cuisine with its line of Italian meats. In recent years, the Fortune 500 company has unveiled an array of additional ethnic foods from the Mediterranean, India, Asia and Mexico that include brands such as Herdez, House of Tsang, Marrakesh Express and Patak's.

Local Landmark

The Horace Austin State Park is an interesting historical site located in heavily wooded land atop the Cedar River bank. In the early to mid 1840s, many United States soldiers camped here, including Dred Scott.

General Trivia

Austin is home to the Miss Minnesota Pageant as well. The winner of this contest advances to the famous Miss U. S. A. pageant held in May.

Prominent People

The 1965 Pulitzer Prize for poetry went to Austin native Richard Eberhart.

* * * *

Professional Golfers Association players Tom Lehman and Lee Janzen were born in Austin.

* * * *

One of the most famous baseball players associated with Austin is William "Moose" Skowron, Jr. He had a successful 14 year career playing with the New York Yankees and other major league teams winning seven pennants and were in seven World Series, winning five titles.

* * * *

The novel Going After Cacciato, about the Vietnam War written by Tim O'Brien of Austin received the National Book Award in 1979.

* * * *

Josh Braaten comes from Austin. His acting career includes appearances in Spin City, Less than Perfect and the movie Dumb and Dumberer: When Harry Met Lloyd.

* * * *

Actor Jay Christianson's TV appearances include Law and Order, The Sopranos, and Without a Trace. Christianson comes from Austin.

> Football great John Madden is also from Austin. His success as a coach for the Oakland Raiders included seven division championships, an AFC cup, and finally a Super Bowl win.

Place Name
Prior to the town's establishment, a fire was set during the dry season burning the area timber. The town's name was given for the resemblance of the devastating scenes in Russia under the great Napoleon.

Place Name
When David Hayward moved back from Iowa, he was one of the first settlers in the area.

Historical Significance
Like immigrants from many other countries, Mexicans were drawn to the United States by the promise of work. They began arriving in Minnesota in large numbers during the 1900s. Recruited from Mexico and the southwestern U.S., they found jobs at farms in southern Minnesota, the Minnesota River Valley and the Red River Valley.

At first most of the Mexicans and Mexican Americans in Minnesota were migrant or seasonal workers, staying only for the few months they were needed in the fields of vegetables and especially sugar beets. Gradually, more and more of them "settled out", remaining over the winter to become permanent residents of the state. The story of Minnesota's Mexican community is the story of these two groups, year-round residents and migrant workers.

Many of those who stayed migrated to St. Paul, where thriving Mexican neighborhoods began to emerge. As this community grew, residents turned for support to their churches and other organizations like the West Side's Neighborhood House, which offered citizenship classes, athletics and job training. By the 1940s many resident Mexican Americans had shifted away from field work to industrial jobs in the cities, many at meat packing plants and canning factories.

Migrant workers in rural areas had fewer opportunities. Though missionaries started summer schools and some companies built housing, the workers faced many hardships, poor health care, crowded living conditions and long work days. Despite the difficulties, migrants continued to come to Minnesota for seasonal agricultural work, mostly from Texas. Conditions have slowly improved for them as Minnesotans have come to understand their needs in job placement, education and health services.

As with all immigrant groups, Mexicans in Minnesota experienced pressure to adopt new ways of living. But in the 1970s a trend emerged that continues today, preservation by the Mexican-American community of their culture and Spanish language.

(Historical marker located on I-90 east bound rest area)

Albert Lea

Place Name

Albert Lea was founded in 1855 after construction of a dam to power a water mill. It is named for Col. Albert Lea who first surveyed the area in the early 1800s.

Historical Significance

Austin and Itasca challenged each other to a horse race to decide whom the County Seat would go to.

One interesting story about this city is set back in the earlier days of the community. Both Albert Lea and neighboring Itasca were battling each other for the county seat. The competition was so fierce that the towns challenged each other to a horse race to decide whom the seat would go to.

In fact, the town of Albert Lea was so concerned about winning that they actually kidnapped Itasca's horse. They then raced Itasca's horse against their horse for practice. Albert Lea's horse dominated the trial runs.

Feeling good about the race, the town of Albert Lea returned the Itasca's horse the following day for the actual challenge. Much like the practice, Albert Lea's horse was victorious, and Albert Lea was granted the county seat.

This race seemed to be a turning point for both towns. Itasca is now, more or less, a ghost town. Albert Lea, on the other hand, has turned into a prosperous, recreational area.

* * * *

Early in the 1890s, even before the automobile age, bicycling Minnesotans and those interested in improved mail delivery and farm marketing were clamoring for better roads. But

Minnesota's constitution, adopted with statehood in 1858, expressly prohibited the state from engaging in "works in internal improvements".

The few roads of that era were secondary importance to the river highways that had carried most early settlers into the region, and after 1865 attention was focused on the fast-growing railroad and streetcar systems.

Counties and townships built the few roads and bridges that their residents petitioned for, financed by property taxes and a requirement that all able-bodied men of 21 to 50 years of age work three days each year on the roads.

It was the automobile that finally brought good roads to Minnesota.

In 1902 Minneapolis recorded its first automobile speeding arrest, and a new law the following year required autos to be licensed by the state boiler inspectors.

In 1909, 7,000 cars and 4,000 motorcycles were registered, but road construction lagged until 1920, when there were over 330,000 licensed vehicles and a constitutional amendment was finally passed to "get Minnesota out of the mud". It allowed the state to construct a trunk highway system of 70 numbered routes financed by vehicle taxes. Today's I-35 follows a portion of the route of Minnesota Constitutional Road Number 1 from Albert Lea to Duluth.

<u>(Historical marker located at tourist information center on I-35)</u>

Prominent People

Albert Lea was home of actress Marion Ross who has played the mother on both "Happy Days" and the "Drew Carrey Show".

She appeared on Broadway in 1987 with Jean Stapleton in a revival of "Arsenic and Old Lace". Marion appeared in numerous TV series including a number of episodes on Gilmore Girls, Touched by an Angel, and even as Grandma on SpongeBob SquarePants.

Albert Lea was home of actress Marion Ross who has played the mother on "Happy Days."

* * * *

Born Edward Ray Cochran on October 3, 1938 in Albert Lea, Minnesota. Eddie moved with his parents when he was 14 to Bell Gardens, California where he began playing the guitar.

In 1954, Eddie joined up with songwriter Hank Cochran to form a little band with Eddie performing as the second vocalist. Even though Eddie and Hank were not related, the group became known as the Cochran Brothers.

Albert lea is the home of rock singer Eddie Cochran.

In 1956, Eddie and an old friend, Jerry Capehart, who was also a songwriter, landed a recording contract with Crest Records, a small label in Hollywood, California.

An executive at Liberty Records, heard Eddie's singing and thought he could make Eddie into Liberty's answer to Elvis. To help launch Eddie's career, Si Warmoker arranged for him to have a cameo role as himself singing the song "Twenty Flight Rock" in the 1956 movie The Girl Can't Help It, starring Jayne Mansfield.

Eddie eventually had the hit record titled "Summertime Blues" in 1958. "Summertime Blues" scored top with the teenage listeners and Eddie became one of Liberty's biggest successes.

* * * *

Native Milton Reynolds would become a millionaire in the 1940s with the development and marketing of a new type of ball-point pen.

Place Name

George Bancroft is the person honored by the city's name. Bancroft was the founder of the Naval Academy and a minister to Great Britain and Berlin.

Place Name

The town was first named Buckeye, but quickly changed to Liberty. It was renamed a few months later after a town in Illinois by Mathias Anderson.

Place Name

The town is named for state senator, Thomas Henry Armstrong, who built a grain elevator here.

Place Name

More commonly known as "Bully Wells," the name acquired for the town is for James Wells, a local fur trader and farmer.

Place Name

The town was named for the small creek it was located on, which takes its name for the thick brush of vegetation, from small trees and thickets growing along its banks.

Frost

Place Name

This town receives its name for Chicago architect, Charles Frost.

Elmore

Place Name

The original settlers in Elmore, Minnesota were attracted to the area once again because of the excellent farmland it provided. Settlers flocked to the area from Iowa led by Crawford Wilson.

Originally, the town was called Dobson, however, in 1862, the city's name was changed to Elmore after Andrew Elmore of Wisconsin. The reason for this was because Andrew was a good friend of many of the early settlers.

Blue Earth

Place Name

The unique city of Blue Earth got its name from the river it lays next to.

Historical Significance

Since its territorial days in the mid-19th century, Minnesota's identity has been rooted in agriculture. With acres of prairies and woodlands to turn into farms, the state proved attractive to waves of settlers from eastern states and other nations.

At first, family farms grew crops and raised animals for their own use. As transportation and farming methods improved, farmers began growing crops to sell. In the 1870s and 1880s, wheat was the main crop. Gradually farmers diversified, switching to other, more profitable crops. Today, Minnesota is a leader in the production of sugar beets, turkeys, soybeans, oats, flax, sunflowers, peas and corn.

The Native Americans who lived in the area named both the town and the river, Mahkota meaning Blue Earth. They dug up bluish-green clay from the rocks of the river gorge.

So central is agriculture to the state's economy that it has given rise to many related industries. In the late 19th and early 20th centuries, Minnesota was the flour milling capital of the world, due largely to local advancements in milling technology. Since then the state has remained in the forefront of the food processing and food science industries. Home to such corporate giants as General Mills, Pillsbury, Cargill and Hormel, Minnesota is not just an agricultural state but an agribusiness center.

Agriculture has played a role in shaping the state's cultural and political life as well. No Minnesota summer would be complete without a visit to a county fair or the Minnesota State

Fair, one of the largest in the country. Two leading farm organizations, the National Grange of the Patrons of Husbandry (the Grange) and the cooperative movement (the Co-op), were formed here. Agriculture has even spawned Minnesota's unique brand of the Democratic Party - the Democratic-Farmer-Labor Party.

In recent decades Minnesota's agricultural landscape has changed. Now dotting the countryside are large, consolidated farms where crops and animals can be raised more cost-effectively. What once was the backbone of the state's farm economy, the small family farm, is gradually becoming less common.

(Historical marker located at westbound rest area on I-90)

* * * *

With the Louisiana Purchase in 1803, the United States acquired a vast area west of the Mississippi River. Eager for information about its new territory, the government dispatched a series of explorers to learn more about the land and the native people who lived there.

Expedition leaders recorded their observations, in words, on maps, and in pictures. Each built on the work of earlier explorers until, together, their findings put Minnesota on the map.

The first to conduct a U.S. expedition from Ft. Snelling to the west was Major Stephen H. Long in 1823. Traveling with him through the Minnesota and Red River valleys were scientists, a landscape painter and an interpreter.

In 1835 the government sent English geologist G.W. Featherstonhaugh to further explore the remote region. He kept detailed journals of the expedition and later published his account. It is an important eyewitness record of a frontier in transition, as traders, missionaries, and the military gradually forced the Dakota out of their tribal lands and traditional way of life.

Another witness to those changes was the artist/author George Catlin, who traveled throughout North America making a complete pictorial record of American Indians before their culture was forever altered. In 1836 he recorded the Pipestone Quarry in what became southwestern Minnesota. His panoramic pictures of the site recorded the religious rites of the Indians as they quarried the stone at this sacred site for carving and trading throughout native North America.

No other explorer did more to increase our knowledge of this region than French map-maker Joseph Nicollet. Commissioned by the U.S. Army in 1836, Nicollet and his assistant John Fremont led two surveying expeditions into the triangle of land between the Missouri and the Mississippi rivers. Nicollet's map of the area, extraordinarily accurate for its day, remains a monument to the achievements of western explorers.

(Historical marker located at the east bound rest area on I-90)

Local Landmark

On the interstate near Blue Earth lies a golden colored slab of concrete. This place symbolizes a link that connects the east coast to the west coast.

* * * *

Minnesota's first stained glass window is displayed at the historic Episcopal Church.

> Blue Earth has the world's largest statue of the Jolly Green Giant. This Jolly Green Giant actually wears a size 78 shoe! He is 55.5 ft. tall (including the base) and cost $43,000 to build.

Invention

Ward Cosgrove brought a new kind of pea from England that was unlike anything people have ever seen. The long, wrinkled, vegetable was called the "green giant" by the Minnesota Valley Canning Company.

The company was unable to patent the "green giant" because descriptive words were not patent able. In 1925 they added a giant as the company symbol which they were able to patent; and later colored green to symbolize the growing of green things. "Jolly" was added in 1935, along with a nice leaf outfit and a big grin that is known today.

The world famous ice cream sandwich also originates from Blue Earth.

Guckeen

Place Name

After the post office declined the town's original name of Derby because of another town with a similar name, they named it after the person whose land the town was built on, Patrick Guckeen.

Granada

Place Name

Granada is taken for the name of a medieval Moorish city in Spain.

Imogene

Place Name

The residents didn't like the original Spanish name of their town, Cardona. So, they renamed it Imogene after the daughter of Cymbeline from one of Shakespeare's plays.

Fairmont

★ This community was originally called Fair Mount because of the fine view across the lakes and adjoining countryside. The name changed slightly describing the rolling hills in the area.

Geological

The city is situated among a chain of 18 crystal clear lakes. The lakes themselves tell a story of glacial existence in the area. The strange distribution of the lakes show that there may have possibly been a stream flowing through the land before the development of the glaciers. The glaciers stopped the stream from flowing which prevented all of the lakes from being connected by streams today.

Historical Significance

The 1870s brought a four-year grasshopper plague to Fairmont. The community was almost completely destroyed, but began to flourish again with the arrival of English farmers. Unfortunately, locusts again destroyed a large portion of the crop. Yet, the English men, many of whom were Oxford and Cambridge graduates, used their intelligence, and moved on. In fact, the men introduced fox hunting to the state. They became known as the "Fairmont Sportsmen" by fellow Minnesota residents. The arrival of the railroad in 1878 caused Fairmont to prosper even more.

Local Landmark

The historic opera house was built in 1901. It is also one of the few opera houses remaining in the Midwest.

* * * *

Fort Fairmount, known also as the Chain of Lakes post, was a substantial log stockade on the present Martin County courthouse grounds. It was built in September 1862 for defense against the Sioux and was garrisoned by volunteers and troops of the 25th Wisconsin.
(Historical marker located on Lake Avenue)

Prominent People

Dale A. Garner was born in Fairmont in 1948. Gardner joined NASA in the late 1970s and has since flown extensive 6 and 8-day missions in both 1983 and 1984 respectively.

* * * *

Paul Willson appeared on "Cheers" during its first season as bar patron, Tom, before starting his recurring role of Paul in 1991. He also made guest appearances on Malcolm in the Middle, Frasier, and Boston Public.

* * * *

Native Kevin Von Felt was an assistant on Close Encounters of the Third Kind. He spent his summers in Logan, Iowa with his grandparents. Both his and Johnny Carson's grandfathers

were at one time mayors of Logan.

In 1994 he produced, directed and adapted a staged production of "A Christmas Carol" in Los Angeles with John Gielgud, Brian Keith, Shirley Jones and Kevin McCarthy.

Place Name

While the town is named for Alfred Welcome, whose farmland was located on the southwest side of the town, the citizens of Welcome are unusually hospitable to strangers. They must be eager to justify the town's name.

Place Name

Railroad officers called the town site, Tenhassen. However, since that name was already in use, a group of men sitting in Tom Sahr's general store suggested Ceylon, for the boxes of Ceylon tea on the shelves.

Walter "Fritz" Mondale, the U.S. Senator would represent Minnesota before serving as Jimmy Carter's vice-president. His run for president against Ronald Reagan was unsuccessful.

Place Name

The small town of Fox Lake is named after the lake that it is located on.

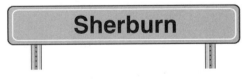

Place Name

The town's name may be in honor of two people with ties to the railroad. The first is in honor of an officer's wife of the Chicago, Milwaukee and St. Paul Railroad from McGregor, Iowa or otherwise in honor of Sherburne S. Merrill, an official of the Southern Minnesota Railroad.

Place Name

Alpha takes its name from the letter A in the Greek alphabet, which is formed from the first and second Greek letters.

Place Name

In the valley of the Des Moines River lies the town of Jackson. The city was named for pioneer merchant, Henry Jackson.

Prominent People

Tom Tangen was born in Jackson, Minnesota. His debut film was "Purple Rain".

Place Name

Lakefield is a small community located in the woods and fields near South Heron Lake.

Place Name

Okabena is a Native American word meaning "the resting-place of herons". This name is appropriate since the town lies on the western bank of Heron Lake.

Spafford

Place Name

Ontario, Canada born John Spafford was a local farmer and storekeeper. Sometime the name is spelled with an "o" rather than the "a" which is an older English version.

Worthington

Place Name

Dr. A.P. Miller along with Ransom F. Humiston formed the National Colony Company, were the founders of Worthington. His wife, Mary Dorman Miller, suggested using the maiden name of her mother for the town's name. Incidentally, Mary's grandfather was the brother of Thomas Worthington, a former governor of Ohio.

Historical Significance

Established in 1871, Worthington was originally a prohibition colony called Okabena, which was the Dakota name for the nesting place of herons.

Prohibition was a passionate issue at one time in this town. One local story tells of a few men who didn't take prohibition quite as seriously as some in the community did, and they ended up literally paying for it!

A storekeeper once bootlegged a crock of whiskey into town. He dispensed it as an extra moneymaking scheme to complement his regular business.

Two patrons who bought the liquor knew that the storekeeper only had five gallons available for sale. However, the patrons added up their consumption over time and found out that they drank more than 40 gallons of whiskey in one winter.

Confused, the two men confronted the storekeeper. The storekeeper admitted to replacing the whiskey with rainwater.

Prominent People

Worthington's most famous lady is Mary L. Davis. Davis was born in 1935 and grew up to be a successful children's writer.

 The Nobles County Pioneer Village depicts pioneer life in the late 19th and early 20th centuries. The village displays close to 40 restored structures from the pioneer era including a hospital, railroad station, saloon and a general store.

Rushmore

Place Name

This town bears the name of S. M. Rushmore, an early merchant from the area.

Adrian

Place Name

The town was named for Adrian Iselin, the mother of Adrian C. Iselin, a St. Paul and Sioux City Railroad director.

Geological

> Blue Mound can appear bluish from a distance, but it is actually composed of a reddish-pink-to-whitish rock called quartzite. The bluish appearance may be caused, in part, by the lichens that cover the quartzite outcrops.

The landscape along Interstate 90 between Austin and Adrian varies from a flat to a gentle rolling plain. This topography was shaped beneath a thick lobe of glacial ice. About 14,000 years ago, glacial ice advancing through the Manitoba region followed the lowlands of the Red River valley and the Minnesota River valley and reached south into central Iowa. At its maximum, the ice lobe's western margin deposited glacial sediment (clay, silt, sand, gravel, and boulders) as it melted, producing a broad belt of low hills called a moraine, which extends to the northwest. Streams to the east of this moraine drain into the Mississippi River system, whereas streams to the west, like Kanaranzi Creek just south of here, drain into the Missouri River system. Thus, the moraine is now a drainage divide.

Farther westward and just north of Luverne, there is a bedrock upland called Blue Mounds. This quartzite formed from a quartz sand whose grains, over time, were cemented by silica and partially recrystallized, making a solid, hard rock that is resistant to erosion. The color shades of the quartzite are due to iron oxides that exist as thin films around and between the quartz grains. The quartzite of Blue Mound has probably been a high point on the landscape for much of the time since its formation 1.7 billion years ago. It was an island when shallow seas covered this area 97 million years ago. The surrounding rocks contain fossils of animals that lived in these waters: sharks, turtles, sponges, and even mosasaurs - large fish-eating lizards related to the modern monitor lizard.

The area west of here was also glaciated, but much earlier, at last a half million years ago. Blue Mound was not high enough to escape the great thickness of ice that covered this region at that time. The hard quartzite bears the scratches left by those passing glaciers.

<u>(Historical marker located on I-90 at west bound rest area)</u>

* * * *

When the wind blew it looked like waves upon the sea. This was the sight that greeted the explorers and then later settlers to southwestern Minnesota. Home for centuries to American Indians, this was a unique sight to people from the forested eastern United States. Stretching from Illinois to the Rocky Mountains was grass growing up to six feet high, broken with scattered trees near lakes and streams, this land lay waiting to be tilled.

Called the prairie, which is a French word for meadow, this expanse is duplicated in few other parts of the world, including the pampas of Argentina and the Black Earth Belt of Russia. There are three types of prairie, the short grass, the mixed grass and the tall grass prairie. It was the tall grass prairie that covered southwestern Minnesota where three grasses dominated. They were the Big Bluesteam (Andropogon gerardi), Indian Grass (Sorghastrum natans) and Switch Grass (Panicum virgatum).

Pollen records appear to indicate that prairies were established following the retreat of the Wisconsin Glacier some 18,000 years ago. The pattern of grass was maintained over the

following years by moisture or lack thereof, fires, and the fact that once a prairie sod is established it is hard for other seedlings to compete. Today the prairie remains only in small patches in reserves or untillable areas. Most of the trees you see were planted as shelter belts by the homesteaders and later farmers. Although the prairie disappeared after nourishing the buffalo (bison) for years, it still continues to nourish. The rich farmlands of the corn belt that help feed the nation are the direct result of thousands of years of rotted grass roots.

(Historical marker located on I-90 at west bound rest area)

Historical Significance

As the state was explored and settled by Euro Americans, it became necessary to connect one place of settlement to another. The Native Americans had numerous trails that they used, some of which had developed from animal paths. The fur traders and the oxcarts that traveled between Winnipeg and St. Paul created other networks of trails, but as settlements increased there was a need for better maintained roadways.

Early roads established by the federal government were built to "facilitate the business of government". Establishing routes between military posts was the first order of business.

Early roads established by the federal government were built to "facilitate the business of government". Establishing routes between military posts was the first order of business. In 1820 efforts were made to establish a road between Fort Snelling and Camp Missouri (located near present day Omaha, Nebraska), but surveys did not find a good route. In 1836 the U.S. Congress appropriated $100,000 to fund a road to connect the Red River of the North with Arkansas. Captain Nathan Boone arrived at Fort Snelling to begin the survey work in 1838, but it was never completed.

Not until the 1850s were the first military roads built. A law requiring the Secretary of War to construct certain roads in the Territory of Minnesota was passed on July 18, 1850. They were as follows: the Mendota-Wabasha Road, the Point Douglas-St. Louis River Road, the Point Douglas-Fort Ripley Road and the Red River Addition, the Swan River-Long Prairie Road and the Mendota-Big Sioux River Road. The last, which would have connected Fort Snelling to Fort Leavenworth, Kansas, was only completed to Mankato. Of the original 560 miles of military roads only small portions are still in use, as county and township roads. But those five roads formed the framework of the statewide network of roads that followed.

(Historical marker located on I-90 at east bound rest area)

Place Name

Philo Hawes suggested the name after the Rock County, Wisconsin village he used to live in prior to coming to the area.

Luverne

Place Name
The towns name honors the areas first settlers, Phil Hawes's daughter, Eva Luverne.

Historical Significance
This city was first explored by Joseph Nicollet in 1839. Yet, the Natives that occupied this territory at the time were hostile to new settlers. As a result, the territory remained unoccupied by settlers for another 30 years.

Prominent People
United Nations diplomat and newspaper editor J.R. Wiggins was born in Luverne in 1903.

Beaver Creek

Place Name
James Comar, a local homesteader suggested the town take the name of the local creek; which was given for the abundance of beaver in the area.

Historical Significance
Scattered throughout the rich farmland of southwestern Minnesota are large outcroppings of a hard red-to-pink rock known as Sioux quartzite. These rocks were formed from sand, silt, and shells deposited by shifting seas that advanced and retreated over this land more than a billion and a half years ago. In a few locations, the ripple marks of ancient shorelines are still clearly visible in the rocks themselves.

South-western Minnesota has large outcroppings of a hard red-to-pink rock known as Sioux quartzite.

Within the quartzite deposits are smaller layers of a dark red stone known as pipestone or Catlinite, named for the well-known nineteenth century artist George Catlin. For centuries Indians from many different tribes quarried the soft red stone at what is now Pipestone National Monument. From the precious rock they fashioned beautiful pipes and other ceremonial objects.

On many of the quartzite surfaces in this region are carved drawings of buffalo, turtles, thunderbirds, weapons, and human stick figures. Some of these mysterious works of art, called petroglyphs, are believed to be more than 5,000 years old and probably played a part in ceremonies to assure good hunting.

(Historical marker located at tourist information center on I-90)

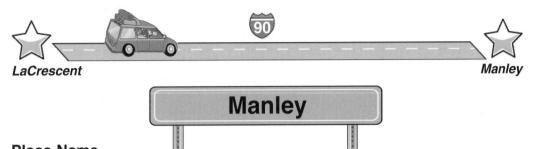

LaCrescent

Manley

Manley

Place Name

Named for one of the leading stockholders of the Sioux City and Northern Railway, W.P. Manley. He also was the Security National Bank of Sioux City, Iowa cashier.

INTERSTATE
35

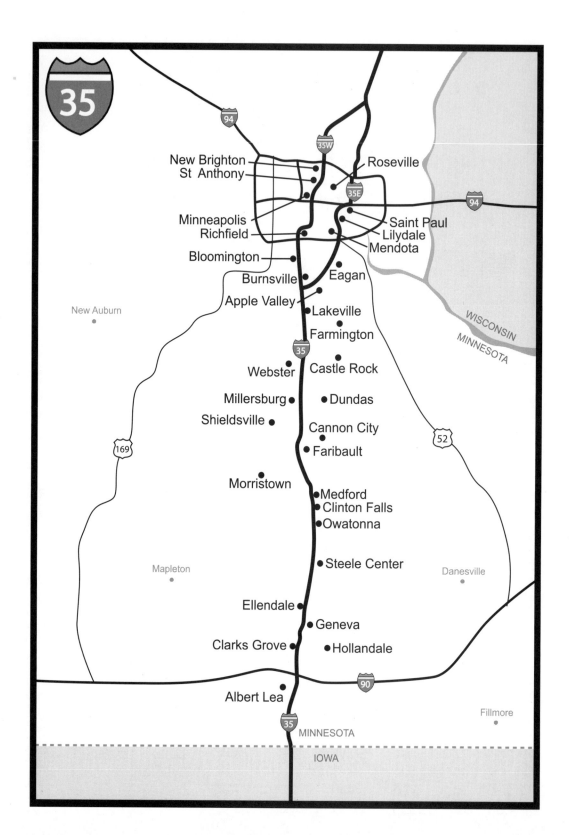

94

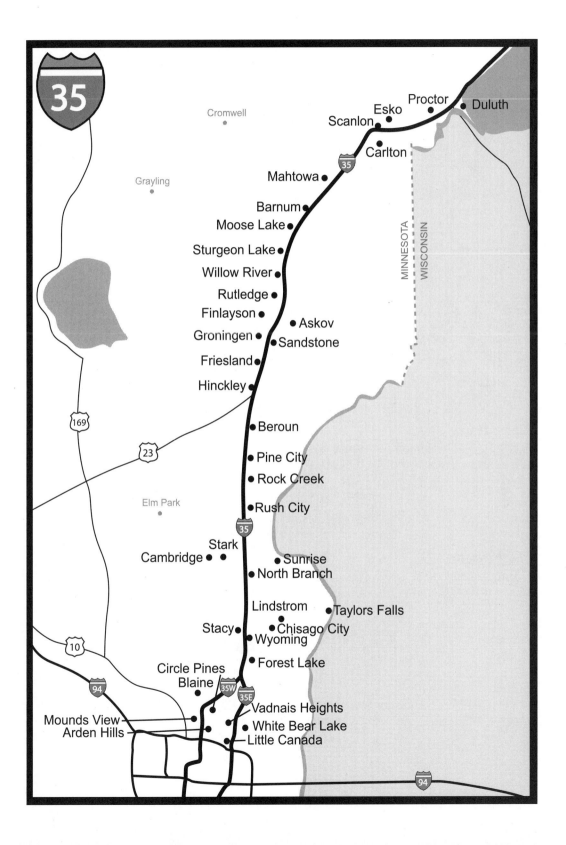

Cromwell

Grayling

Proctor • Duluth
Esko
Scanlon
Carlton
35
Mahtowa •
Barnum •
Moose Lake •
Sturgeon Lake •
Willow River •
Rutledge •
Finlayson •
• Askov
Groningen • • Sandstone
Friesland •
Hinckley •

169

23

• Beroun

• Pine City

• Rock Creek

Elm Park
• Rush City

35
Stark
Cambridge • •
• Sunrise
• North Branch
Lindstrom
• Taylors Falls
Stacy • Chisago City
• Wyoming
Circle Pines
• Forest Lake
Blaine
35W
94
35E
Mounds View Vadnais Heights
Arden Hills White Bear Lake
Little Canada

10

MINNESOTA WISCONSIN

94

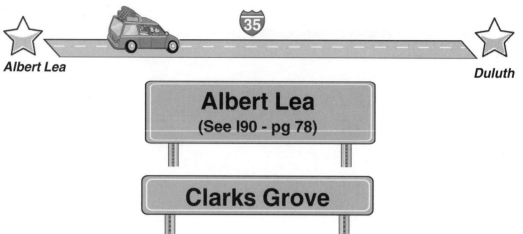

Albert Lea   Duluth

Albert Lea
(See I90 - pg 78)

Clarks Grove

Place Name
This town get its name from John Mead Clark's grove located just east of the village.

Industry
Minnesota's first creamery was established in Clarks Grove in the 1890s. The organization of this dairy cooperative led to the development of the state's Land O' Lakes Association.

Hollandale

Place Name
The Payne Investment Company purchased 15,000 acres of swampland draining it for development. Families of Dutch descent established farms.

Geneva

Place Name
The first postmaster, Edwin Stacy, who was also the probate judge for the county, suggested the name after Geneva, New York.

Ellendale

Place Name
Ellendale was named for the kindness Mrs. C.J. (Ellen) Ives shown through her good deeds of kindness to the many working men in the area.

Steele Center

Historical Significance

During its first session in 1858 the Minnesota State Legislature established the first of several schools for the training and care of citizens who suffered mental and physical disabilities and for children who were unable to care for themselves. The first school opened in Fairbault in 1863, after five years of delay due to lack of funds. Called an "Asylum", later an "Institute", and now an "Academy", its students were those who were blind and deaf. Separate schools were later established here for the blind, the deaf and the mentally deficient. In 1885, a State School for Dependent and Neglected Children opened in Owatonna. While it closed in 1970, the Faribault schools continue to function.

The schools are similar in both style and plan to buildings found at Minnesota state hospitals and correctional facilities. A typical complex included separate buildings for admissions, classrooms, gymnasium, a hospital, a laundry, and farm buildings. The farms allowed the schools to be partially self-sufficient. The schools were established by law to provide the students with activities and training, while protecting them from the "slights and rebuffs" of the outside world.

The first clinical psychologist to be employed in a mental retardation institute in the United States was at the Faribault State School. A.R.T. Wylie was that pioneer in the field of mental health research.

(Historical marker located on I-35 at north bound rest area)

> The town and county were named in honor of Pennsylvanian Frank Steele who was instrumental in the growth of the lumbering industries in the Twin Cities (Minneapolis and St. Paul) area.

Industry

Early settlers grew bumper wheat crops in southern Minnesota's fertile prairies, land that today supplies produce for a thriving 270-million-dollar-a-year canning industry.

Sweet corn canneries opened in Austin and Mankato in the early 1880s, followed soon after by similar factories in Faribault, Owatonna, and LeSueur. Soon Minnesota's canners were experimenting with new technologies and new products, and in 1903 the automated Big Stone Cannery Company founded by F.W. Douthitt changed the industry nationwide. Douthitt's plant in Ortonville had a conveyor system, mechanical corn husking machines, and a power driven cutter that produced the first whole kernel canned corn. The Green Giant Company, also founded in 1903 as the Minnesota Valley Canning Company, introduced golden cream-style corn in 1924 and the first vacuum packed corn in 1929.

Corn is still the major canning crop in Minnesota. The state's more than thirty plants also freeze and can peas, beans, carrots, tomatoes, pork, beef, chicken products, and such unusual items as rutabagas. Mankato was the site of the nation's first carp cannery in 1946.

(Historical marker located on I-35 at south bound rest area)

Owatonna

Place Name

Legend says the town is named after a young Native girl named Owatonna. Chief Wadena of the Dakota tribe moved his entire village to this place in order for his sick daughter to be able to drink from its mineral spring, which is rich in iron and sulphur. The daughter recovered very quickly after this.

However, the name is more likely in reference to the fact that for hundreds of years before the arrival of the first white settlers, Native Americans camped on the banks of a river they called "Ouitunya," which means straight. And today the name of the major river in Steele County.

Industry

Some excellent commercial enterprises are situated in Owatonna. In 1897, the Gainey family established the highly reputable international manufacturer, "Jostens".

The headquarters for Federated Insurance are also located in the heart of the town. Wenger Corporation, Owatonna Tool, and Truth hardware are among the other corporations that influence the industrial success of this town. These industries also contribute to the city's wealth, allowing it to have one of the highest per capita income statistics.

Local Landmarks

Banker Carl Bennett wanted more than a prominent new building to house his family's business. He wanted a work of art. Bennett's search for an architect led him in 1906 to Louis

Louis Sullivan, one of the country's most inventive designers created a magnificent home for the National Farmers' Bank

Sullivan, one of the country's most inventive designers. Together they created a magnificent home for the National Farmers' Bank in the heart of downtown Owatonna. This brilliant collaboration of patron and architect produced what many consider the finest small-town bank in America.

After helping to make Chicago the country's architectural capital in the 1890s, Sullivan came through with a bank design for Owatonna unlike any other. Believing that function and form of a building should complement one another, he conceived a structure resembling a treasure chest, a fitting image for a bank that housed people's savings.

Sullivan chose for his bank a theme he used often, a arch within a square, then attached to it a rectangular office building. He combined those simple, monumental shapes with complex ornamental details that brings the building to life. Set in sandstone-and-brick walls are two huge stained-glass windows, each framed by a wide band of terra cotta, a hard, molded clay, accented by a narrow band of glass mosaic.

The architect did not create this masterpiece alone. His sketches were completed by his draftsmen, George Elmslie, who designed much of the ornamentation and went on to become a noted Minnesota architect. Joining them were a team of skilled craftsmen who created the ornate interior, a "color symphony" of painted plaster, stained glass, and huge cast-iron

chandeliers. The finished bank was dedicated in 1908.

Remodeling has altered some of the interior features. But much of the original splendor of Louis Sullivan's bank remains. In 1976 it was designated a National Historic Landmark.

<u>(Historical marker located at 110 North Cedar Street)</u>

The former Owatonna train depot houses the famous 1880 "Old 201" locomotive was once driven by the famous engineer, Casey Jones.

* * * *

The Village of Yesteryear features a firehouse, schoolhouse, church, railroad station, general store and several other 19th century buildings that were relocated to show what frontier life was like in the past.

* * * *

Thirteen original buildings remain at Minnesota State School Orphanage. It was the only orphanage in the state's history with nearly 13,000 dependent and neglected children entering the institution from 1886 to 1945.

Prominent People

Edda Gunnar Marshall was born in Owatonna in 1910. He was a Broadway and movie star until he began his hot television series, "The Defenders". Marshall won two Emmy's in 1962 and 1963 for the talented role he played as the father in the father and son team of lawyers in the series.

* * * *

Otto Josten started it all in 1897 when he purchased a small watch and jewelry business in Owatonna. Not long after, he began producing pins, medals and rings to commemorate special events. The jewelry his company produced was finely crafted from quality materials and often made to customer specification. Zip forward more than 100 years and you'll see Jostens today as a national celebration company providing many high school students with their class rings.

* * * *

The youngest of five children born to Walter and Virginia Wynkoop. Joel D. Wynkoop was born in Owatonna, Minnesota on August 24th, 1960. He currently lives in southern Florida, where many of his films are shot on location including Lost Faith (1992).

Place Name

The town was named after the nearby falls on the Straight River. Both the river and the town commemorate New York governors, George and DeWitt Clinton. DeWitt was also influential in the building of the Erie Canal.

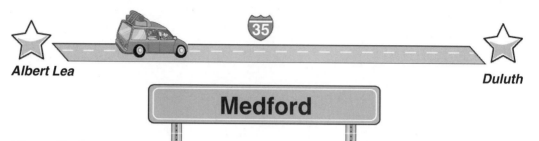
Medford

Place Name

Englishman William Colling is responsible for the naming of this township. After homesteading in the area for awhile, he returned to his home in England aboard the ship Medford. His son was born on the ship and would be named after it. Colling suggested naming the township after his son, Medford.

Morristown

Place Name

Reverend Jonathan Morris was a minister in Indiana and Ohio for 25 years with a denomination called Christians or Disciples. He moved to Minnesota settling in the area in 1855.

Faribault

 The city got its name from Alexander Faribault, a trader who built a fairly large trading post in town.

Local Landmark

Alexander Faribault was the son of fur trader Jean Baptiste Faribault and his wife, Pelagie. Alexander first entered the area in 1826 to establish a trading post for the American Fur Company on Cannon Lake. He moved the post a few miles east in 1835 and in 1844 finally established it at the present site of the city of Faribault.

Like many of the traders, Faribault wielded great influence over the local Dakota Indians with whom he did business. He played a part in persuading them to sign treaties in 1851, opening most of their land in Minnesota to white settlement and assigning some of their treaty money toward the payment of fur trade debts.

With his fur trade and treaty profits, Alexander Faribault built his house in 1853. One of the first frame houses in the newly opened land, it served for many years as a community center, chapel, polling place, and meeting hall.

(Historical marker located at 12 N.E. First Avenue)

* * * *

The Seabury Divinity School was one of several schools comprising the Bishop Seabury Mission founded in the frontier community of Faribault in 1858 by the Rev. James Lloyd Breck. Both the mission and seminary were named in honor of Samuel Seabury, America's first Episcopal bishop. Establishment of the mission in Faribault was a key factor in the

Albert Lea   **Duluth**

community's designation in 1860 as See of the Diocese of Minnesota by Bishop Henry Whippel. The Faribault schools flourished under Whippel's direction from 1860 to 1901, educating area children and training clergy for missionary work in the West.

The Divinity School shared a common campus with the Shattuck Grammar School until 1873, when the continued growth of both schools brought a decision to move the seminary to a site on the outskirts of town.

The seminary remained a vital component of the Diocese's educational work in Faribault until 1933, when it merged with Western Theological Seminary of Chicago to form Seabury-Western Theological Seminary located in Evanston, Illinois.

(Historical marker located on First Street S.E.)

* * * *

Elected first bishop of the Episcopal Diocese of Minnesota in 1858 at the age of thirty-seven, Whipple soon became known as "Straight Tongue" by the Dakota and Ojibway Indians whose rights he worked to secure through the reform of U.S. Indian policies and an active Indian mission program. Speaking almost alone, it was Whipple who persuaded Abraham Lincoln to commute most of the sentences of Dakota men condemned to death after the conflict of 1862.

The cathedral developed out of work begun in 1858 by James Lloyd Breck. The cornerstone was laid on July 16, 1862. James Renwick, architect of St. Patrick's Cathedral in New York City is credited with the design. Envisioned as a gathering place for the Parish of the Good Shepherd, Seabury Divinity School, Shattuck, and St. Mary's Hall, the Faribault Cathedral was consecrated on June 24, 1869. The tower, designed by Ralph Adams Cram, architect of St. John the Divine in New York City, was added as a memorial to Bishop Whipple after his death in 1901. Whipple is buried in a crypt beneath the chancel.

> Believed to be the first Episcopal cathedral built in the United States, the Cathedral of Our Merciful Savior is also a monument to Henry Benjamin Whipple.

In 1941, St. Mark's in Minneapolis became the diocesan cathedral. However, the "Bishop's Church in Faribault" remains the home of an active congregation and a place of pilgrimage in southern Minnesota.

(Historical marker located on Second Avenue)

Prominent People

Heisman Trophy winner and College Football Hall of Famer Boo Smith was a native of Faribault. He played for the University of Minnesota's "Golden Gophers" in college. As a professional, Smith played with the Green Bay Packers and the Los Angeles Rams.

Cannon City

Place Name

Cannon City is more a village than a city. Never-the-less it gets its name from the river that flows through "the city".

General Trivia

Edward Eggleston's popular 1873 novel The Mystery of Netropolisville was based on scenes from the area.

Shieldsville

Place Name

Ireland native James Shields introduced and persuaded his native colonists to take up farming in the area.

Shields a major general in the Mexican War, practiced law in Illinois where he would become a state legislature, auditor, judge and later a U.S. Senator.

Millersburg

Place Name

George Miller purchased 160 acres from James Fitzimmons where he built a mill and hotel. He platted the remaining acreage to establish the town site.

Dundas

Place Name

The town is named for an eminent British statesman, Henry Dundas. It was given the name by city founders, Edward and John Archibald, who came from Dundas, Ontario. They came to the area to build a flour mill that was known for having the best flour in the state.

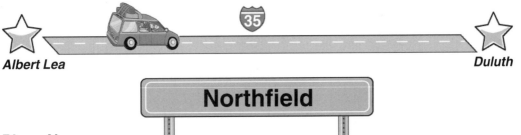

Northfield

Place Name
The town was co-founded by Ira Fields and his partner John Wesley North, whom the town is named after.

Historical Significance
In the 1870s and 1880s, important changes took place inside several small flour mills in southeastern Minnesota. Those changes laid the groundwork for a technological revolution that made Minnesota's milling industry the largest in the world.

The changes grew out of a desire by millers to improve the quality of their flour. Most Minnesota farmers raised hard spring wheat, which had a reputation for producing speckled flour. Drawing on European technology, Minnesota millers developed a method of refining their flour by sending it through a purifier that removes the specks, or middling, and by grinding the flour several times. Called the New Process, this method produced whiter, purer flour that was soon in demand by consumers.

One of the first to experiment with this new technique was Northfield miller Jesse Ames, who used a purifier as early as 1865. Within a few years, purifiers were found at the Archibald mill in Dundas, the Mowbray mill in Stockton, the Gardner mill in Hastings and the Faribault mill.

As the changes swept the milling industry in the 1870s, millers concluded that the traditional millstone, which required frequent redressing, was no longer efficient. They turned instead to rollers, already used in some parts of Europe. One of the earliest American attempts at roller milling occurred in 1872-73 at the Mowbray mill, where four-foot marble rollers were installed. Soon most Minnesota millers had replaced their old millstones, opting for more efficient porcelain-covered or iron rollers.

(Historical marker located on I-35 at the southbound rest area)

Local Landmark
A prep school started by Horace Goodhue, Jr. Opens in Northfield in 1867 with twenty-three students. Known as Northfield College the name would be changed to Carleton College following the generous donation from William Carleton of Charlestown, Massachusetts.

* * * *

Eight years later in 1875 classes begin at St. Olaf College, which grew out of the Reverend Julies Muus's preparatory school.

Prominent People
Actress Alexandra Holden was born in Northfield. She appeared in numerous episodes of the TV series Ally McBeal, playing "Jane Wilco".

> Nancy Ringham, a graduate of St. Olaf's starred in the Broadway revival of My Fair Lady opposite Rex Harrison in 1981 when the lead developed laryngitis.

103

Albert Lea

Duluth

General Trivia

Jesse James and his gang were chased out of Northfield trying to rob their first bank. Under the cover of night, they escaped on stolen horses, with only $290, on their way to Missouri.

Place Name

Ferris Webster, the town's namesake, came to the area from Franklin, New York, first settling in the area as a farmer before opening up a store here.

Place Name

A massive sandstone bluff that lies within the city limits gave Castle Rock its name. Both traders and Native Americans used the bluff as a landmark for traveling.

Place Name

As its name implies, Farmington is a excellent center for the farming community, hence it received this appropriate name.

Place Name

Named Prairie Lake when it was originally established, then changed to Lake Marion, the name was changed to its present name when it merged with another township.

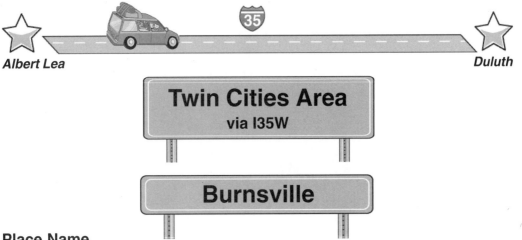

Albert Lea ⭐   ⭐ Duluth

Twin Cities Area
via I35W

Burnsville

Place Name

The land of Burnsville has had five owners: first, the Mdewakanton Sioux, then, in 1493 Spain laid claim to it, next, France obtained possession in 1682, Britain claimed it in 1763, Jefferson bought it from Napoleon in 1803. The Sioux, led by Little Crow, signed away the land to Governor Ramsey in 1851.

The pioneers who arrived in 1850 were primarily Irish and farmers by trade. William Byrne arrived in 1855. He donated land for a church, school and a cemetery and it has been assumed by many that "Byrnesville" township was named after him.

Historical Significance

Before the coming of the white man, the Mdewakanton band of Dakota Sioux lived in the Burnsville area.

Chief Black Dog's village was located on the isthmus of land between Black Dog Lake and the Minnesota River, the present site of the Black Dog Power Plant. There were perhaps as many as 250 Sioux living there when the first white man came.

Black Dog's band was often referred to as "the people who did not eat geese", because they found such a good market for geese at Fort Snelling. They also found a ready market for fish caught in Black Dog Lake among the Irish Roman Catholic settlers who were the first Europeans to settle in the area.

> Crystal Lake was another gathering site of the Dakota and they named the lake "Minne Elk". The Sioux watched deer at the lake from the top of what is now the Buck Hill Ski Area.

General Trivia

In 1950, Burnsville was still a quiet township with a population of 583 people. School was taught in a one-room schoolhouse containing eight grades. The "boom" started in 1962 and the population exploded

Industry

The manufacturing industry is the second largest industry in Burnsville with key companies such as, B. F. Goodrich, Aircraft Sensors Division, Pepsi Cola and Northern Tool & Equipment.

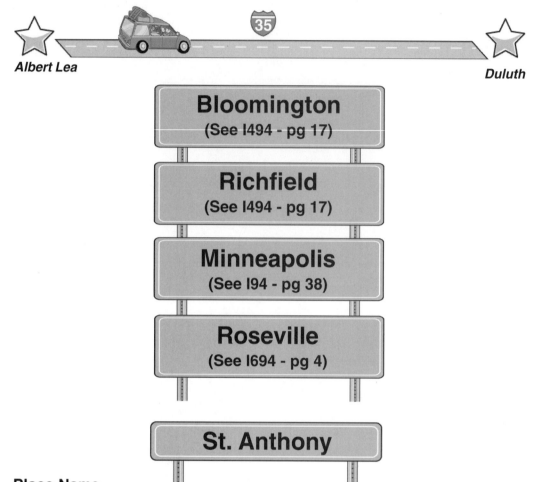

35

Albert Lea

Duluth

Bloomington
(See I494 - pg 17)

Richfield
(See I494 - pg 17)

Minneapolis
(See I94 - pg 38)

Roseville
(See I694 - pg 4)

St. Anthony

Place Name

Missionary Louis Hennepin named the falls on the Mississippi River after the Franciscan friar from Padau, Italy for all the favors provided by the Almighty through intercession by this great saint that became the patron and protector of all Hennepin enterprises.

New Brighton
(See I694 - pg 6)

Arden Hills
(See I694 - pg 6)

Mounds View
(See I694 - pg 7)

106

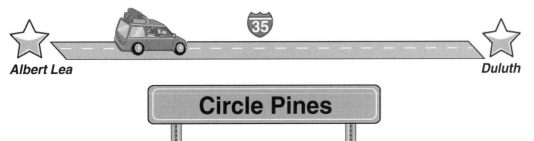

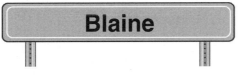

Circle Pines

Place Name

The original goal of this community was to be heavily comprised of cooperatives. The symbol for cooperatives is a Pine Tree with a circle around it. The city's name comes from this symbol.

Historical Significance

The idea for developing cooperatives in the city was prompted by V.S. Pedersen, who helped found the town. The notion of cooperatives somewhat died when Pedersen died. Yet, his legend still lives on in the city name.

Blaine

Place Name

Blaine was considered part of Anoka, Minnesota. In 1877, Blaine separated from Anoka and organized as a Township of its own.

In 1877 the first election was held and Moses Ripley was elected as the first Chairman of the Board of Supervisors. Ripley came to Minnesota from Maine. He persuaded his fellow Board Members to name the new Township in honor of James G. Blaine, a senator and three-time presidential candidate from Maine.

Historical Significance

Phillip Laddy was one the first settler in Blaine. He settled near the lake that bears his name, Laddie Lake.

In 1865 Blaine's first permanent resident was Green Chambers, a former slave of Kentucky.

I35 continues
on pg 109

107

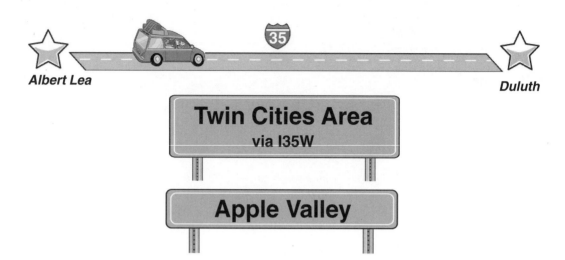

Twin Cities Area
via I35W

Apple Valley

Stephen Hesla, an Apple Valley resident, wrote the adventure / spy novel The Hawthorne Conspiracy.

Place Name
This town was named by developer Orrin Thompson after Apple Valley, California and for the apple trees planted at each home in the development.

Local Landmark
This is home to the Minnesota Zoological Garden.

Prominent People
Christopher Orr graduated from Apple Valley High School in Apple Valley, Minnesota in 1992. He starred in Law and Order, Sex in the City, The Mighty Ducks, and Beverly Hills 90210.

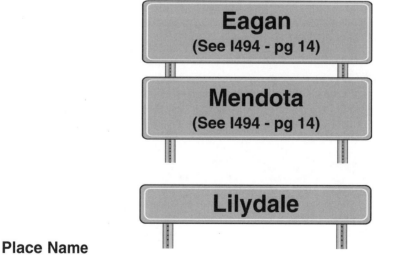

Eagan
(See I494 - pg 14)

Mendota
(See I494 - pg 14)

Lilydale

Place Name
The town was named for the many lilies that flourished in Pickerel Lake

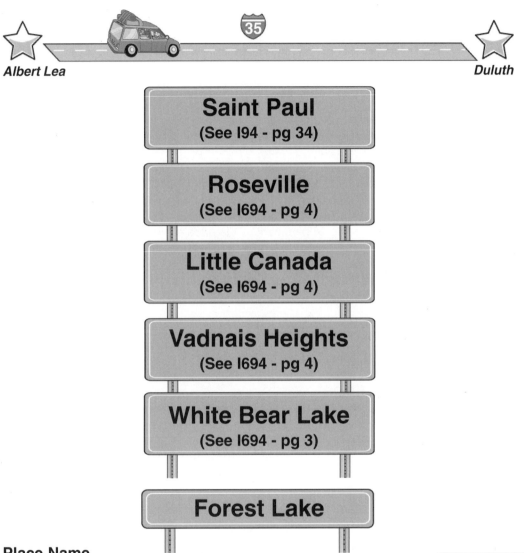

Saint Paul
(See I94 - pg 34)

Roseville
(See I694 - pg 4)

Little Canada
(See I694 - pg 4)

Vadnais Heights
(See I694 - pg 4)

White Bear Lake
(See I694 - pg 3)

Forest Lake

Place Name

Forest Lake got its name from the adjacent lake of the same name.

Historical Significance

Railroads were chartered in Minnesota as early as 1853, but it was not until 1862 that Minnesota's first railroad began to operate on ten miles of track connecting St. Paul with St. Anthony (now a part of Minneapolis). In 1870, the Northern Pacific Railroad began at Carlton, Minnesota and reached Portland, Oregon by 1884. By 1871, railroad lines had reached Minnesota's southern and western borders and by 1893 the Great Northern Railway extended from St. Paul to Seattle. Over 150 railroad companies received their charters and built rail lines into nearly every part of the state by World War I consolidating into about a half dozen major railroads. This immense transportation system was made possible by grants of public land to the railroads estimated in 1873 at over thirteen million acres worth

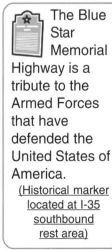

The Blue Star Memorial Highway is a tribute to the Armed Forces that have defended the United States of America.

(Historical marker located at I-35 southbound rest area)

Albert Lea   **Duluth**

over fifty million dollars.

Railroads were critical to the development of Minnesota; they connected its citizens, agricultural products, natural resources, and manufactured goods with the rest of the country. They promoted towns and cities along their routes, and opened new markets as goods and products were swiftly transported across the country.

The peak year of railroad trackage in Minnesota was 1929 with 9,500 miles. By the mid 1990s there were less than 5,000 miles of track remaining. Passenger service, except for the modest Amtrak effort, was discontinued by the mid 1970s. Decline and further consolidation has been the fate of Minnesota's railroads during the last several decades, and many small towns and rural areas are without rail service of any kind. Numerous miles of right-of-ways, once bearing ribbons of steel, now serve recreational uses; many former railroad depots have been adapted for new uses and are tangible reminders of the past.

<u>(Historical marker located at I-35 southbound rest area)</u>

Wyoming was the city where William Hamm, the owner of Hamm's Brewery was released after being kidnapped by mobsters from St. Paul in 1933.

Place Name
The town is named by the earlier settlers for the similarity between the area and that of the Wyoming Valley in Luzerne County, Pennsylvania which is traversed by the North Branch of the Susquehanna River. Another explanation states that name comes from the Delaware of Lenape Indians, which meant large plains or extensive meadows.

Prominent People
This was the residence of two women named T.A. Jenkins ad C.G. Carleton. They were the first women to attend a national political party convention as delegates.

Place Name
The name of the city comes from the Chippewa word, which means large and lovely; referring the name given to the beautiful lake in the area.

Place Name
This town was named after Jesse Taylor, the man who claimed the area.

110

Historical Significance

In the 1800s, this community was a large lumber center. It was incorporated in 1858, the same year that Minnesota became the 32nd state in the union.

It is a town that was settled mostly by New Englanders looking for new opportunity in the west. As a result, the architecture in this community reflects the heritage of those that founded it. In fact, the town has preserved more than one-third of its 19th century buildings.

Local Landmark

William Henry Carman Folsom, St. Croix River Valley lumberman and land speculator, chose this imposing site for his home in 1854. He, his wife Mary Jane, and their two small sons lived in an open barn on this property to prove up the claim while the five-bedroom home, reflecting both Federal and Greek Revival styles, was constructed. In 1855, after the family moved in, Mary Jane wrote to relatives in Maine, "We shall have plenty of room for as many as will come".

W.H.C. Folsom arrived in Taylor Falls in 1850 and actively involved himself in both the business and community development of his new home. Although he ran a store for 24 years, Folsom also helped operate a gristmill, a copper mining company, a bridge company, and a cemetery association. A member of the 1857 state constitutional convention, Folsom served five terms as state senator and one as representative. In his spare time, he wrote "Fifty Years in the Northwest," which is still a respected source of information on the early years of settlement in the area.

(Historical marker located at 272 W. Government Street)

> A member of the 1857 state constitutional convention, William Folsom served five terms as state senator and one as representative.

Geological

The Dalles of the St. Croix in Taylors Falls is a great place to visit if one is interested in geology, or can just appreciate the wonder of Mother Nature. Lava cliffs and strange rock formations can be seen 200 feet above the coastline.

* * * *

About 1.1 billion years ago, a great rift valley formed across the North American continent from the Lake Superior region southwest to Kansas. As this rift valley opened, basaltic lavas erupted into it, accumulating to a thickness of up to 20 kilometers in the Lake Superior region. The dark-grey basalt rock that form the St. Croix River gorge are made from these rift lava flows. Continental rifting with volcanism is common in the geological record and often leads to the breakup of continents and the formation of intervening ocean basins. For reasons not completely understood, the Midcontinent Rift here in North America failed to evolve to the stage of complete continental separation.

About 520 million years ago in the Lake Cambrian period, the North American continent was positioned with Minnesota near the equator. Shallow seas covered the region, into which great thicknesses of mainly quartz sand were deposited. These deposits are now the sandstone bluffs along this river valley and the rock faces exposed on the highway road cuts

111

south of this marker. Although most of the region then lay flat, the basalts in the Taylor Falls area stood high as rocky, cliff-ringed islands in a tropical sea.

The most recent geological event recorded here occurred about 12,000 years ago during the end of the Ice Age of the last two million years. As the last of the glaciers melted and receded to the north, tremendous quantities of sediment-laden glacial meltwaters were channeled into the St. Croix River valley. Here at Taylor Falls, a colossal torrent of abrasive currents carved down through the Cambrian sandstones and deep into the rift basalts now seen on the valley floor. The spectacular potholes in the lava rock, found in Interstate Park about 0.4 kilometers north of this site, attest to the high velocity of the raging glacial waters that carved the St. Croix River gorge.

(Historical marker on Hwy 8 and 95)

Place Name

Lindstrom was named for a pioneer farmer by the name of Daniel Lindstrom. He came to this area from Helsingland, Sweden where he was born.

Place Name

The town was named for one of its first settlers, Dr. Stacy Collins.

Place Name

The town gets it name because it crosses the North Branch of the Sunrise River.

Place Name

The name comes from the lake and river translated from the Ojibwe word, Memokage as "Sun-keep-rising".

Prominent People

Frank Lowden is born near Sunrise before moving to Illinois where he practiced law. His wife, Florence, is the daughter of George Pullman, the inventor of the railway sleeping car.

Frank could later manage some of Car King's enterprises following the death of his father-in-law, served in Congress, become governor of Illinois and lost a nomination for president.

Richard Widmark's daughter, Anne Heath Widmark, married baseball legend Sandy Koufax on January 1, 1969.

* * * *

Born in Sunrise, Richard Widmark grew up in Princeton, IL and attended Lake Forest (IL) College, where he first began acting.

Unforgettable in his screen debut (in 1947s 'Kiss of Death') as Tommy Udo, a psychopathic mob hit-man, who giggles gleefully even as he sends a wheelchair-bound old woman, portrayed by Mildred Dunnock, tumbling down a long stairway to her demise.

In 1979 he was the Friday night host for CBS Radio's "Sears Mystery Theater".

Stark

Place Name

Lars Johan Stark was born in Sweden in the town of Westergotland. He came to the United States, settling in Chicago City where he ran a mercantile business and farmed. He became a State Legislator.

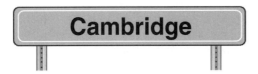

Cambridge

Place Name

The town was named by the Maine settlers who came to the area and named their new home after the town of Cambridge, located in central Maine.

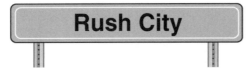

Rush City

Place Name

The village grew up along the Rush River where the St. Paul and Duluth Railroad cross the river. The naming of the river is from the various bulrushes that grew in the shallow river and lakes, and used to make mats.

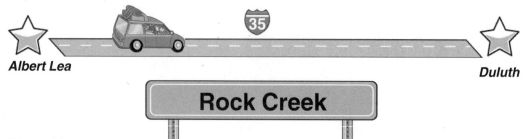

Duluth

Rock Creek

Place Name

The town is named after a tributary creek that flows south into the St. Croix River.

Pine City

Place Name

The area of land at the outlet of the Snake River from Cross Lake has played an important part in the history of the region. Its name comes from an Ojibwe word, pronounced "Sheng-wha-tah-nah," which has been translated both as "Pine City" and as "the steep end of a spur hills".

Historical Significance

Archeological evidence suggests that various peoples frequented the area from at least 6,000 B.C. Artifacts fashioned from native copper have been found in the valley, and early fur traders, geologist, and speculators heard rumors of copper deposits in the mid-1800s. But it was the construction of a logging dam at the Cross Lake outlet in 1950 that led to the first Euro-American settlement there.

In 1854 the Government Road under construction from Point Douglas (near Hastings) to Superior, Wisconsin, crossed the Snake River about one-half mile below the dam. The road attracted settlers, even though one traveler commented that there were enough mosquitoes to protect the country from extensive development. The town site of Chengwatana, established in 1856, was named the county seat when Pine Country was organized in 1857.

But the young community was born just in time for the national financial "panic" of 1857, which slowed its development. In the next few years several destructive fires and the railroad's bypass of the town spelled the end for Chengwatana. By the early 1870s most of the residents and businesses had moved to Pine City, which was now designated the county seat. Despite a brief copper mining "boom" in 1899, the town disappeared early in the 20th century. A W.P.A. dam built in 1936 on the site of the original logging dam is all that remains today to mark Chengwatana's place in history.

(Historical marker located on Hwy 61)

Beroun

Place Name

Czechoslovakia native Joseph Chalupsky came to the area with his family of four sons and five daughters to operate a general store and local sawmill. He suggested the name which translated in his native language means "an official or other important person".

114

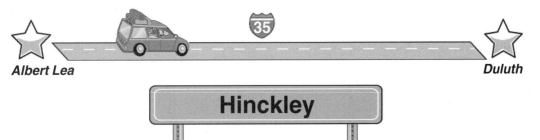

Hinckley

Place Name

This town is named for Isaac Hinckley. He was president of the Philadelphia, Wilmington and Baltimore Railroad Company for 16 years between 1865 to 1881. He was also a stockholder for the St. Paul and Duluth Railroad which later became part of the Northern Pacific Company.

Historical Significance

Between three and five o'clock on the afternoon of September 1, 1894, a ranging forest fire driven by strong southwest winds swept over the town of Hinckley, killing 248 residents. The conflagration burned over 480 square miles in parts of five counties, also consuming the surrounding towns of Brook Park, Mission Creek, Miller, Partridge, and Sandstone. At least 418 people died in the disaster.

Trains of the St. Paul and Duluth Railroad and the Eastern Minnesota Railroad carried nearly 500 people to safety through the burning countryside. More than 1,500 individuals lost their homes and possessions, with fire relief receiving donations from as far away as London and even Turkey as news of the tragedy spread. The mass graves of the Hinckley townspeople who died in the fire are marked by a state monument in Lutheran Memorial Cemetery.

> On Sept.1, 1894, a ranging forest fire driven by strong southwest winds swept over the town of Hinckley.

The Hinckley fire was among the worst of many that followed the end of large scale pine logging operations in northern Minnesota. As the virgin red and white pine was removed, a tinder-dry refuse of stumps, slashings, and brush provided ready fuel for several other disastrous fires including those at Baudette in 1910 and at Cloquet in 1918.

(Historical marker located on County Road 61)

Friesland

Place Name

Friesland is named for a province in The Netherlands.

Sandstone

Place Name

Named for the quarries of sandstone found on the bluffs of the Kettle River, the village of Sandstone was founded in 1887.

> Sandstone is a town that was modeled after its name. The Great Northern Railroad Roundhouse, the former Sandstone State Bank, as well as the 1901 red sandstone school building were all crafted from sandstone.

Groningen

Place Name

Groningen is named for the northeastern most province in The Netherlands.

Askov

Place Name

Founded in 1906 by the Danish Peoples Society. The town's name means "ash wood" and is also the name of Denmark's largest folk high school.

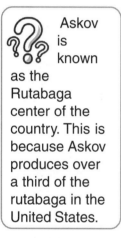

Askov is known as the Rutabaga center of the country. This is because Askov produces over a third of the rutabaga in the United States.

Geological

The light-brown sandstone that forms the cliffs along this part of the Kettle River valley is called the Hinckley Sandstone. This sandstone formed as a result of a major geological event. About 1.1 billion years ago, this continent Rift, which extended from the Lake Superior region southwest to Kansas. As this great rift valley opened, volcanic eruptions filled it with thousands of dense, basaltic lava flows. Then the rifting and volcanic activity stopped. Over time, the weight of the dense basalt caused the rift area to subside, or sag, forming a long basin. Streams and wind brought in sand, which accumulated in the basin. Eventually, deep underground, minerals carried by groundwater cemented the buried sand grains, forming sandstone. The Hinckley Sandstone, one of several sandstone units deposited, is cemented with iron oxide and silica. The iron oxide gives it its light-brown color, and the silica helps to make it one of the strongest sandstones in Minnesota.

During the Ice Age of the last two million years, glaciers repeatedly covered this area. About 10,000 years ago, as the last glacier here receded into the Lake Superior basin, meltwater collected at its southwestern edge, forming a great lake, called Glacial Lake Duluth. Water from this lake found an outlet and increasingly poured southward through the present-day Kettle River valley. That ancient river would make today's turbulent Kettle River look tame by comparison.

Torrents of water were channeled into fractures in the sandstone, which readily eroded down, leaving the blocky cliffs one sees along this stretch of the river.

Along the Hell's Gate Trail one can see kettles, or potholes, in the rock that in some places are 15 meters above the present river. These potholes are evidence that water once raged through this valley at levels much higher than today. Potholes commonly occur behind the base of a large boulder or other flow obstruction. They are made when turbulent water forms an eddy, or whirlpool, strong enough to swirl pebbles and cobbles around in one spot. There the swirling stones grind a cylindrical hole down into the bedrock.

(Historical marker located on Hwy 18, 2 miles east of I-35 in Banning State Park)

Finlayson

Place Name

The town is named for the original owner of the sawmill here, David Finlayson.

Historical Significance

Lumbermen first arrived in this area in the 1830s, logging the white and red pine stands along the St. Croix River. Sawmills were few and much of the pine lumber was floated down the St. Croix to the Mississippi River and on to other states. Logging camps, which supplied the timber, operated in the winter months with about 15 men and a few teams of oxen.

By the 1880s, the industry boomed with an influx of new wealth from lumbermen who had made fortunes in Michigan and Wisconsin and the new markets in the West. Sawmills powered by steam engines ripped through millions of logs annually as lumberjacks spilled into the forest of the north. Logging camps swelled to an average of 70 men, and horses replaced oxen. It wasn't long, however, before horses were replaced by steam powered equipment. In 1900, the peak year of the pine log harvest, the state produced over one billion board feet of logs, enough timber to build a nine-foot wide boardwalk around the earth at the equator.

Production began to decline after 1905, as pine timber was depleted and timber companies shifted their interest towards new pine stands in the Pacific Northwest and the South. By 1930, the pine sawmill industry died with the closing of the last sawmill near Virginia, Minnesota. After 100 years of logging most of the pine was gone.

Minnesota's timber industry was rekindled in the 1970s; over a dozen new forest product plants were built or expanded, producing paper, composite board, laminates and other items. Harvest of all forest products in the state in the 1990s matched harvest levels of 1900. Today the products of Minnesota's forests are marketed throughout the world and are found in your home, your car, and even in the ice cream you eat.

The timber industry grew quickly, however, and in 1840, lumbermen supplied the growing nation with 5 million board feet of lumber. Ten years later, 90 million board feet was harvested from the new Minnesota territory.

(Historical marker located on I-35 at the north bound Kettle River rest area)

Rutledge

Place Name

This small community started out as a lumbering town. The Rutledge Lumber Company was one of the largest employers to ever set up shop in the area. However, by 1910, Rutledge's lumbering days had ended. Even though the lumbering days are over, this small community is still keeping a part of its history alive in its name.

Willow River

Prominent People

The Town of Willow River was the birthplace to Ernie Nevers. Nevers was once considered the best college athlete of all time. In 1926, he played professional football and basketball in Chicago and professional baseball in St. Louis. Nevers was also appropriately elected to the pro football Hall of Fame in 1963.

Sturgeon Lake

Historical Significance

This town is named after the lake that it lays next to, which is in reference to the large rock sturgeons that weigh upwards to 100 pounds.

In the 1880s, when General Christopher C. Andrews began urging the state to consider the future of its forested lands, most Minnesotans could not believe that there might ever be a shortage of timber. But by the time of his death in 1922 the vast virgin pine forests were gone, lumber was being imported from the Pacific Northwest, and a series of devastating fires had claimed hundreds of lives and millions of acres.

Andrews served as captain, and colonel of the Third Minnesota Regiment of Volunteers during the Civil War, and finally as Brevet Major General United States Volunteers, at the close of the war. He was appointed minister to the combined state of Sweden and Norway in 1869, and while living in Stockholm he became interested in reforestation. When he returned to Minnesota he began his efforts to save parts of the state's remaining forests, to encourage replanting, and to start a school of forestry. he implemented the Swedish idea of only cutting the annual growth of trees for lumber each year and as a result is considered by professional foresters to be the father of "sustained yield" in the United States. He met with little success until 1895, the year following the Hinckley fire that killed more than 400 people. The legislature then passed a bill written by General Andrews and calling for the "preservation of forests and the prevention and suppression of forest fires." Andrews was named the state's first chief fire warden.

Forest preservation was difficult in regions where there were still hundreds of logging camps, miles of railroads with unclear rights of way, and acres of "slashing" - tree tops and branches left by the lumbermen. In spite of Andrew's efforts, carried out with almost no funding, terrible fires ripped through northern Minnesota in the early years of the 20th century.

In addition to his firefighting work, Andrews played a key role in the establishment of Superior and Chippewa national forests and the development of a forestry board to oversee the management of state forest reserves. He served the forest service for 26 years at an average salary of only $1,650, and his work, much admired today, was appreciated by only a farsighted few of his fellow citizens.

(Historical marker located on I-35 at the southbound rest area)

Moose Lake

Place Name

Moose Lake is probably the translation of a Ojibwe word for the nearby lake of the same name.

Historical Significance

When Moose Lake came to be in the 1860s, it embraced one hotel, many barns, and many Native American teepees. The 1870s brought more growth and prosperity to the town when the Lake Superior-Mississippi River Railroad was built.

The train engines were quite different in those days from what they are today. The engines were wood burning and thus, required additional fuel every five miles or so. Filling up so often made trips long and monotonous.

Moose Lake's early residents were involved in the logging industry much like many other towns along the St. Croix.

Geological

Toward the end of the great ice ages about 10,000 years ago, the glacier, which had pushed its way along the trough of Lake Superior, retreated toward the northeast and near Moose Lake crossed the divide between the Mississippi River and Lake Superior. When the lobe of ice was shrunken so that it lay wholly within the rim of the lake basin, Glacial Lake Nemadji was formed around the southwest margin of the ice.

The earliest outlet was at this, the western, end, when the lake stood 523 feet above the present level of Lake Superior and nearly reached the elevation of the State Hospital in the distance. During the centuries of drainage from here through the Moose River to the Mississippi, this channel was eroded downward to the present level. When lower outlets for the Lake Superior basin were opened, the Moose River Valley was abandoned as an outlet, and this part of the ancient watercourse became the basin of Moosehead Lake.

(Historical marker located on Hwy 61)

 In 1918 tragedy struck this small town. A forest fire wiped out 183 people in town. A 27-foot granite memorial at Riverside Cemetery was constructed in 1929 to honor the memory of the 453, men, women and children who perished

Barnum

Place Name

The town is named in honor of Duluth resident, George Barnum, who was the paymaster of the Lake Superior and Mississippi Railroad when it was being built.

Industry

In what used to be a proud lumber town, Barnum has made the transition to farming. They

are famous for raising Guernsey cattle and chickens. In fact, Barnum is actually one of the largest egg producers in the state.

Place Name

Combine the Dakota word mahto and the last syllable of the Ojibwe makwa, together to form the word Mah-to-wa, meaning "a bear".

Place Name

Carlton was originally named Northern Pacific Junction because of its location at the junction of that transcontinental line with the older Lake Superior and Mississippi line. The name was soon changed to Carlton after pioneer, Reuben Carlton.

Place Name

Scanlon is another one of those old lumbering towns that is located conveniently on the shores of the St. Louis River. It was named for the president of the Brooks-Scanlon Company, M. Joseph Scanlon. His company was engaged in the development of numerous logging enterprises in the area, as well as in other parts of the country such as in Oregon, Louisiana and Florida.

Historical Significance

The early Finns were very concerned about cleanliness. Each person had his or her own bathhouse. Non-Finnish residents used to think the Finns practiced magic. This is because the Finns used to drape themselves in white sheets everyday and retreat to small buildings. But these buildings were not used as places to practice magic, they were merely places used by the Finnish to wash up. Even though early residents jumped to conclusions about the Finnish ritual, after time the matter was "all cleaned up".

The Finns founded this small dairy community and gave it a Finnish personal name.

120

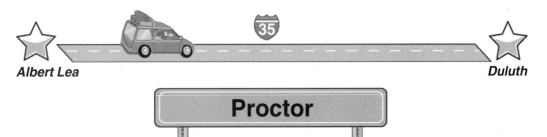
Proctor

Place Name

Proctor was originally named after Kentucky Governor, J. Proctor Knott. The citizens of Duluth chose the name for the town of Proctor in appreciation for the free publicity they obtained during Proctor's speech in Congress. His delivery of "The Glories of Duluth" mocked the city's effort to defeat a bill granting land to the St. Croix and Lake Superior Railroad.

Historical Significance

Railroading was the major industry of the town in its beginnings. Because of the railway, Proctor is one of the greatest iron ore transportation centers in the world.

Duluth

Place Name

The city is named for explorer Daniel Greyselon Sieur du Lhut. He claimed the region for the French in 1679 from the Sioux and Chippewa tribes.

Historical Significance

Older than the state of Minnesota itself, the city of Duluth was originally settled by Sioux (Dakota) and Chippewa (Ojibwa) tribes, who enjoyed the rich natural surroundings Lake Superior had to provide. They called Lake Superior "Gitchi-Gummi".

Daniel Greyselon Sieur du Lhut claimed the region for the French in 1679 from the Sioux and Chippewa tribes. From that point until the late 1800s, Duluth served as a large fur trading post.

Built on a natural harbor where the St. Louis River meets the Great Lakes, Duluth is located at the westernmost tip of Lake Superior, halfway between the Twin Cities and the Canadian border. This unique locale was a natural spot for a thriving city, especially since it's directly connected to the Atlantic Ocean via the Great Lakes/St. Lawrence Seaway.

At 2,342 freshwater miles from the East Coast, Duluth is host to the largest, farthest-inland seaport in the world. The location helped Duluth become a world center for lumbering, mining, shipping and other industries. This meant jobs, people and money. So much money, in fact, that Duluth was at one time home to more millionaires per capita than any other city in the world.

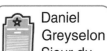 Daniel Greyselon Sieur du Lhut claimed the region for the French in 1679 from the Sioux and Chippewa tribes.

Geological

Duluth is built on a pre-historic volcanic mountain range and its altitude rises quickly from a scenic 600 ft. above sea level at the shoreline, to a dramatic 1,485 ft. along Skyline Drive.

* * * *

For about 20 million years as the rift valley opened, basaltic lavas erupted into it, accumulating to a thickness of up to 20 kilometers in the Lake Superior region.

 Lake Superior is situated over the Midcontinent Rift, which is a rupture in the North American continent that formed a great rift valley from the Lake Superior region southwest to Kansas about 1.1 billion years ago.

After the rifting and volcanic activity ended, the great thickness of dense basalt here depressed the crust into a troughshaped basin. As the depression formed, it was filled in by sediment eroded and washed in from the surrounding heights. Ultimately, the sedimentary deposits reached a thickness of many kilometers.

Over the past two million years, glaciers more than a kilometer thick have repeatedly advanced along the buried trough and scoured out much of the soft sedimentary rock that once filled it. The harder, erosion-resistant volcanic rocks along the margins of the trough now form the rocky coastline of much of Lake Superior.

Ten thousand years ago, as the glacial ice in the basin melted west to east, water ponded in front of the ice to form Glacial Lake Duluth. Eventually, the ice melted out of the eastern lake basin and a drainage way opened to the lower Great Lakes. When the eastern outlet first formed, it was lower in elevation than today and drained the lake to 60 meters below its present level.

Relieved of the great weight of this glacial ice, the earth's crust has been slowly rising. The rate of rebound is fastest where the load of ice has been most recently removed. Thus, the northeastern lake basin and its eastern outlets are rising faster, thereby tilting the basin toward the southwest and flooding the mouth of the St. Louis River. Duluth harbor, which was formed by this submergence, has been enlarged by the formation of Minnesota Point, a baymouth bar sand deposit washed there by easterly waves and shore currents transporting beach sand from Wisconsin.

(Historical marker located on I-35)

* * * *

Lake Superior is the largest fresh water lake in the world. It boasts 31,280 square surface miles. If that surface were completely frozen (which has only happened twice) there would be enough space on the ice for everyone in the world to spread out a 12' x 12' picnic blanket.

Superior has an average depth of 483 feet, and its deepest point is a staggering 1,333 feet below the surface.

Lake Superior is also large enough to hold all the other Great Lakes.

Not only this, but it is also the final resting-place for over 350 shipwrecks, including the famous Edmund Fitzgerald, which went down with all 29 men on board.

Local Landmark

In 1871, the natural entrance to the harbor was located on Superior's end of Park Point, a seven-mile sandbar (the world's longest) that formed the natural breakwater for the harbor.

As the story goes, Duluthians wanted the port of entry and the economy that trade would bring for themselves, and so in the last days and nights before the U.S. Army Corps of

Albert Lea   **Duluth**

Engineers were to name the official port, they dug, by hand, a waterway between the lake and the harbor, and thus opened the now famous canal.

When the St. Lawrence Seaway opened in 1959, Duluth became the westernmost Atlantic seaport in America. Today, freighters and cruise ships from around the world come to Duluth.

* * * *

The Aerial Lift Bridge in Duluth is one of its primary landmarks. It was patterned after the suspended car transfer bridge at Rouen, France.

Huge ocean liners have no trouble entering the city's port as a result of the bridge rising upwards to 138 feet in about 55 seconds.

The two-lane span weighs roughly 1,000 tons and is operated with the help of two 500-ton counterweights, each of which hangs a hundred feet above traffic.

> The Aerial Lift Bridge has been raised and lowered over 400,000 times, welcoming ships from around the globe.

* * * *

The Minnesota Point Lighthouse ruins stand at the tip of Minnesota Point.

* * * *

More than three billion tons of iron ore, along with millions of tons of grain, timber, fish, and coal, have passed through the Duluth-Superior harbor since the beginning of Minnesota's Iron Age.

The first ore from the rich Mesabi Range left the harbor for smelters on the lower lakes in 1892 and by 1916 yearly shipments had reached nearly 38 million tons.

Huge loading docks, (stretch 2,300 feet into the Lake) built first of wood and later of steel and concrete, could load four or five ore-carrying lake freighters simultaneously from nearly 400 railroad cars.

In 1953 an all-time yearly record 64 million tons of ore was shipped. As the rich hematite ore became scarce in the late 1950s, methods were developed to process and ship taconite, a plentiful lower grade ore.

(Historical marker located on I-35)

* * * *

Glensheen, is the illustrious mansion owned by state legislator Chester Congdon. Constructed from steel beams, the mansion boasts glorious gardens and antique furniture original to the home. Congdon's property encompasses 22 acres and is set on the shores overlooking Lake Superior.

General Trivia

Minnesota's oldest concrete pavement was built of portland cement concrete in 1909 and 1910 and ushered in the era of modern roads and streets in the state.

A distinct feature of these pioneer concrete pavements is the scored surface pattern of rectangular grooves. This indented design was used, according to the records of the day, to provide a firm and substantial footing for horses.

(Historical marker located at the intersection of East 7th Street and 29th Avenue East)

* * * *

Deadly fires have struck Minnesota throughout history. One unfortunate fire broke out just north of Duluth in 1918. The fire consumed 2,000 square miles of forest, killed 1,000 people and left 12,000 homeless.

In 1857, Duluth had bad luck as well. In 1857, the national monetary panic caused three-quarters of the Duluth residents to flee the area. Those that stayed concerned themselves with the business of keeping alive.

Prominent People

> Bob Dylan, considered by many to be the greatest songwriter of our time is from Duluth.

One of the most famous and influential rock stars in history was born in Duluth. Robert Allen Zimmerman was born in 1941. You may know him better by his stage name, Bob Dylan.

At age three, he gave his first performance on his father's Dictaphone inside his office. When he was a teenager, his first band was called "The Golden Chords". His original stage name was "Bob Dillon", and he was paid $400 for his first record. The first musician to combine a guitar with a harmonica in a frame-holder, Dylan's music was motivated by social events during the 1960s. Dylan believed so much in the message of his music, that he refused to perform on the Ed Sullivan show when they wouldn't let him play "Talkin' John Birch Society Blues".

* * * *

Losing his legs to frostbite after an airplane crash on Mount McKinley in 1981, Duluth native Ed Hommer would return on June 3, 1999; being the first double amputee to reach the summit (20,320).

* * * *

Actor Hank Harris Grew up in Duluth, Minnesota. He appeared in episodes of 7th Heaven, Providence, and the X-Files.

* * * *

Former model on "The Price Is Right" Gena Lee Nolin was born in Duluth. She also appeared in a number of episodes on the TV series, Baywatch.

General Trivia

Duluth is home to the nation's 9th largest marathon, Grandma's Marathon, in which more than 8,000 hearty souls brave the 26.2-mile course along Lake Superior's breathtaking North Shore.

This course is so beautiful and challenging that it's also home to the world's largest inline skating marathon, the Northshore InLine Marathon.

The city also hosts one of the longest dogsled races in the lower 48 states. The John Beargrease Sled Dog Marathon covers 470 miles from Duluth to Grand Portage. The race is named for a mail carrier that traveled the same course in the late 1800s by dogsled.

Albert Lea   **Duluth**

* * * *

Duluth is home to the world's largest freshwater port, the International Elks Curling Bonspiel, and the oldest community theatre in the United States.

HIGHWAY 169

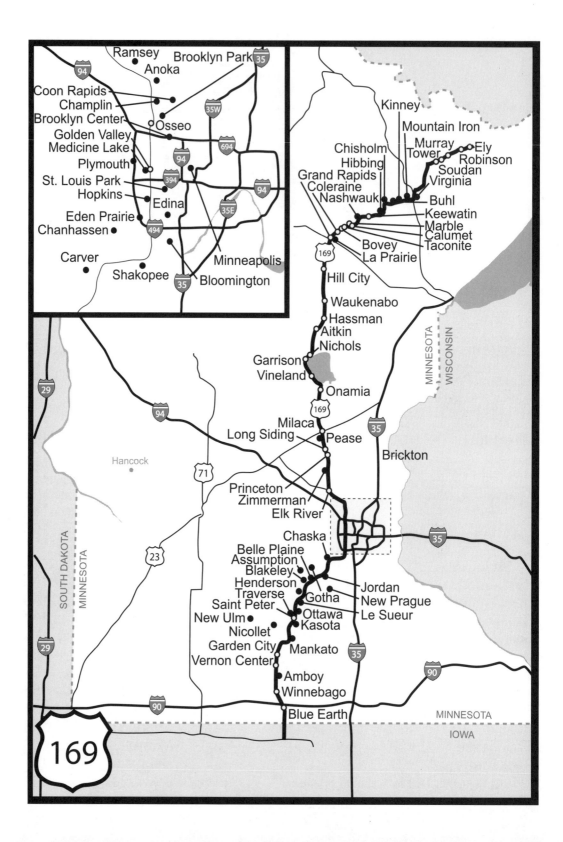

Ramsey
Brooklyn Park
Anoka
Coon Rapids
Champlin
Brooklyn Center
Osseo
Golden Valley
Medicine Lake
Plymouth
St. Louis Park
Hopkins
Edina
Eden Prairie
Chanhassen
Carver
Shakopee
Minneapolis
Bloomington

Kinney
Mountain Iron
Murray
Chisholm
Tower
Ely
Robinson
Hibbing
Soudan
Grand Rapids
Virginia
Coleraine
Nashwauk
Buhl
Keewatin
Marble
Calumet
Taconite
Bovey
La Prairie

Hill City
Waukenabo
Hassman
Aitkin
Nichols
Garrison
Vineland
Onamia
Milaca
Long Siding
Pease
Brickton
Hancock
Princeton
Zimmerman
Elk River
Chaska
Belle Plaine
Assumption
Blakeley
Henderson
Jordan
Traverse
Gotha
New Prague
Saint Peter
Le Sueur
New Ulm
Ottawa
Nicollet
Kasota
Garden City
Mankato
Vernon Center
Amboy
Winnebago
Blue Earth

MINNESOTA
WISCONSIN
SOUTH DAKOTA
MINNESOTA
MINNESOTA
IOWA

169

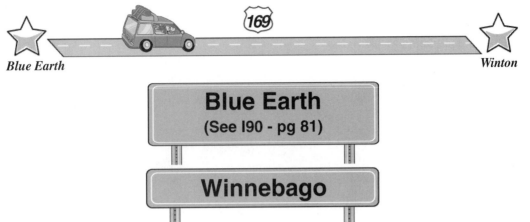
Blue Earth
(See I90 - pg 81)

Winnebago

Place Name

Named in recognition of the Winnebago Indians, whose reservations was in Black Earth County during the years 1855 to 1863.

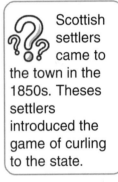

Scottish settlers came to the town in the 1850s. Theses settlers introduced the game of curling to the state.

Industry

In December of 1993, the town opened a revolutionary $30 million ethanol plant. The plant boosted industrial opportunities for residents throughout the town.

The plant initially provided 40 new jobs and 15 million gallons of ethanol a year. The plant also enables more than 500 farmers to sell five million bushels of corn a year to the plant. The crops are used to produce ethanol, which is an alternative to oil, used for the production of gasoline.

Amboy

Place Name

Amboy is situated near the Blue Earth River. It was given its name by the first postmaster, Robert Richardson for his former hometown in Illinois. Amboy is an Indian name meaning "hollow inside" or "bowl like".

General Trivia

There is supposedly a haunted old mill near here. Gottlieb Shastag, who was a settler from Holland, built the mill to grind corn. Shastag ran the mill for the entire city for 10 years.

Natives in the region made several attempts to destroy the mill because of the excessive noise that it produced. Although they were never successful in their attempt to destroy the mill, the construction of several mills in the area drove business away from Shastag's mill.

This led Shastag to believe that a devil in the form of a black rabbit, which was living there, was destroying his mill. In order to drive out this devil, Shastag stood guard, hoping the rabbit would show himself.

Meanwhile, Shastag boarded up the mill and placed signs all over and surrounded the property. He warned people to never enter the mill. His signs warned that anyone who entered the mill would die. Finally, in Shastag's attempt to destroy the rabbit, he was killed inside the mill by a revolving fan blade.

Ever since his death, no one has attempted to enter the mill for fear of losing his or her life as Shastag warned.

Place Names

Two early businessmen from the area, Col. Benjamin Smith and Benjamin McCracken came from Mount Vernon, Ohio and thus suggested the name.

Like many towns across the country, and President George Washington's home in Virginia are all named Vernon. Generally speaking it is in honor of the distinguished Edward Vernon, an admiral and hero of the expeditions capturing Porto Bello in 1739 and leading the attack on Cartagena four years later.

Place Name

This village was originally known as Watonwan for the local river. Then it was named Fremont for John Fremont, the Republican candidate for president in 1856. Two years later it was renamed Garden City in reference to the native floral charm of the area.

Garden City owes its growth to London millionaire, Sir Henry Wellcome.

Historical Significance

Sir Henry Wellcome provided hundreds of thousands of dollars for the growth and development of Garden City, which resulted in the construction of an athletic field, sidewalks, a water system, a sewage system, and an electric light plant. Wellcome was extremely dedicated to making Garden City the best it could be. He worked day in and day out in accomplishing this goal until the day of his death.

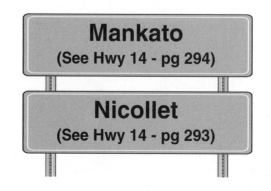

Mankato
(See Hwy 14 - pg 294)

Nicollet
(See Hwy 14 - pg 293)

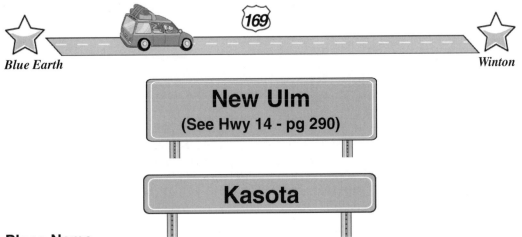

New Ulm
(See Hwy 14 - pg 290)

Kasota

Place Name

Kasota is the Dakota word describing the naked ridge or prairie plateau south of town. Approximately 3 miles long and averaging a half mile wide, the Kasota terrace valley is about 150 feet above the river and 75 feet lower than the general upland surrounding it.

Industry

The area is known for its pink colored limestone. Kasota Stone quarried from the area has been used in the construction of both the Minnesota and Wisconsin State Capitals and other important buildings across the country.

Saint Peter

Place Name

St. Peter was founded in 1853, by Captain W.B. Dodd, who named the city for the St. Peter River, which later became known as the Minnesota River.

Historical Significance

In 1857, there was an attempt to move Minnesota's capitol from St. Paul to St. Peter. The bill was passed by both houses and was waiting to be signed by the Governor. Unexpectedly, Representative Joseph Rolette took the bill and fled. He hid himself and the bill until the statute of limitations was expired. Meanwhile, the Governor signed a replica of the bill. However, since the bill wasn't the original, the Supreme Court didn't allow St. Peter to become the Capitol City.

Local Landmark

In 1871, Eugene St. Julien Cox, a man of eccentric tastes and "great vigor of mind" built a picturesque neo-Gothic Italianate house noted for its towered cupola, small balconies and carved eaves.

Cox began his law career in 1857 and built a thriving practice in the frontier village of St. Peter. After brief service as a Union officer in the Civil War, Cox enrolled fifty men into the "Frontier Avengers" and led this unit in the defense of New Ulm during the Dakota War of 1862.

After the wars, the "affable and genial and always daintily dressed" Cox was elected St.

Peter's first mayor. This was followed by his election to the Minnesota Legislature, first as a representative, later as a senator.

In 1877, he was elected judge of the ninth judicial district. Within four years, the Minnesota House impeached Judge Cox and the Senate organized a high court for trial purposes. He was mainly charged with intoxication "caused by the voluntary and immoderate use of intoxicating liquors, which disqualified him for discharge of his official duties".

In 1882, after a sensational five-month trail which included seventeen hundred pages of testimony and a petition for acquittal signed by four thousand people, Judge Cox was convicted and removed from his office as district judge by a bare two-thirds vote of the Minnesota Senate.

Nine years later, the legislature passed a resolution "vacating, annulling, and expunging all the proceedings of the impeachment and trial". Nevertheless, a few years later, E. St. Julien Cox left Minnesota and died in Los Angeles on November 2, 1898.

(Historical marker located at 500 North Washington Avenue)

St. Peter, the town is home to five Minnesota state governors, H.A. Swift, Horace Austin, A.R. McGill, A.O. Eberhart and John Johnson.

Prominent People

Despite the fact that politics couldn't flourish in St. Peter, the town is home to five Minnesota state governors, H.A. Swift, Horace Austin, A.R. McGill, A.O. Eberhart and John Johnson.

A statue of Johnson, who was the first executive to be born in Minnesota, rests on the grounds of the Nicollet County Courthouse. It is rumored that Johnson would have ran for President in the early 1900s, if it hadn't been for his sudden death.

Traverse

Place Name
The village name comes from the Traverse des Sioux, because this is where they would cross the Minnesota River.

Historical Significance
This ancient fording place, the "Crossing of the Sioux", was on the heavily traveled trail from St. Paul and Fort Snelling to the upper Minnesota and Red River valleys.

Here, on June 30, 1851, Governor Alexander Ramsey, Commissioner of Indian Affairs Luke Lea, Delegate to Congress Henry H. Sibley, and other government officials established a camp on a height overlooking the small trading post and mission on the riverbank. They had gathered to negotiate an important treaty with representatives of the Sisseton and Wahpeton Sioux for almost twenty-five million acres called the Suland.

This vast tract comprised most of Minnesota west of the Mississippi and south of the line between present-day St. Cloud and Moorhead, as well as portions of South Dakota and northern Iowa.

News of the signing of the Treaty of Traverse des Sioux on July 23, 1851, started a great land rush, which brought swarms of settlers to the fertile lands acquired by the United States from the Sioux.

(Historical marker located on Hwy 169)

Place Name

Founded by Frenchman named Antoine Young who built the areas first saw and grist mill, the town takes its name from a small tribe of Native Americans related to the Ojibwe known as the Ottawa.

Geological

Ottawa is home to the Ottawa Bluffs. This 63-acre span of bluffs towering over the Minnesota River is preserved by LeSueur County. The bluffs are home to perhaps the largest variety of plants and animals in the state.

Local Landmark

The accomplishments of the Mayo family in the field of medicine have brought fame both to its members and to Minnesota, for it was Dr. William Mayo and his two sons, William J. and Charles H., who founded the Mayo Clinic in Rochester, Minnesota, in 1903.

This town is named for Pierre Charles Le Sueur who explored the Minnesota River Valley in the 1600s.

Their little house was built by William W. Mayo in 1859. It is intimately associated with the Mayo family's early years in Minnesota, for here on June 29, 1861, the Mayo's first son, William J., was born.

His father had immigrated to the United States from England in 1845. By 1854 the doctor was living with his wife in Indiana. He left the family there when he departed suddenly in search of relief from the effects of malaria, saying to his startled wife, "Good-bye, Louise. I'm going to keep driving until I get well or die".

Dr. Mayo's travels took him to St. Paul, the rude capital of Minnesota Territory, where he settled with his family. In 1859 he moved to Le Sueur, where he built a house with the help of his brother James. In 1863 he again moved, this time to Rochester, where in 1889 he was asked to become the medical director of St. Mary's Hospital, the nucleus of the future Mayo Clinic.

(Historical marker located 118 N. Main Street)

Industry

In 1903, fourteen of Le Sueur's leading businessmen met in the back of the Cosgrove Harness Shop to start a canning factory. They called it the Minnesota Valley Canning Company. Sixty-seven shares of stock at one hundred dollars per share were sold that evening. The sale provided enough money to buy one kettle, seed, sugar, salt and cans. Corn was brought in from the fields with horse-drawn wagons. Women husked the corn by hand for three cents per bushel.

The gentle laughter of the Jolly Green Giant can still be heard echoing through this valley.

Eleven thousand seven hundred cans of white cream style corn were sold that first year. The profit from this was enough to buy two more kettles. The company continued to grow, and in 1907 it began canning peas under the Blue and Gold label. In 1925, the Green Giant brand of peas was added. Vacuum packed Niblet brand yellow whole kernel corn was introduced in 1929. Though the company continued to expand, packing a variety of vegetables and opening canning facilities throughout the United States, only corn and peas were ever canned in Le Sueur.

In the early 1940s, during World War II, many of the local men went into the military service. That left a shortage of help. Laborers from Mexico and Jamaica and German prisoners of war were assigned to help harvest the vital food crops needed.

In 1950, the Minnesota Valley Canning Company changed its name to the Green Giant Company. In 1978, one year before the company was acquired by Pillsbury, its national sales were over $485 million, and its net earnings were over $10 million.

Over the years, the canning company had a direct impact on the positive growth and development of the County of Le Sueur. The Le Sueur plant closed in 1995.

(Historical marker located on Hwy 112)

Geological

Geologically young when compared with ancient rivers such as the Nile or the Amazon, the Minnesota River is only about 12,000 years old. It occupies a channel that was cut by the Glacial River Warren, when it drained Glacial Lake Agassiz, the largest lake to have ever existed. This all occurred at the end of the last glacial age, when the glaciers covering Minnesota, in some cases to a depth of over a mile, melted away.

Starting at the South Dakota border, at Browns Valley, the Minnesota River is the state's second largest river. It joins the Mississippi at the foot of Historic Fort Snelling, after traveling a distance of some 355 miles. By geological definition the Minnesota is an "under fit river," the term applied when a river occupies the channel of an earlier river. While the ancient valley is up to two hundred and fifty feet deep and in places 5 miles wide, the Minnesota is just a shallow, meandering river. During flood stages it swells beyond its banks, due to runoff from its extensive drainage basin.

History is abundant along its banks. Exposed by the waters are rocks that are more than 3.8 billion years old, attesting to the age of the earth. Ruins stand today as reminders of former homes, villages, military posts and sanitariums that once served the residents of the area. Indian villages and crossing sites that predate the European settlement of the region

are also found along its course. Hundreds of steamboats once slowly traveled the river. Their use ceased with the coming of the railroads.

While the water flows by in an endless trip to the sea, and the life style changes with each passing year, the past will always be present here in the Minnesota Valley.

<u>(Historical marker located on Hwy 169)</u>

Place Name

The town is named in honor of Joseph Brown's fathers only sister, Margaret Brown Henderson and her son Andrew.

Joseph Brown later would be honored by the naming of Brown County, founded and edited the area's first newspaper, the Henderson Democrat.

Place Name

A group of Bohemian and Bavarian settlers came to the area in the mid 1800s at the urging of Bishop Cretin of St. Paul.

Named for the capital of Bohemia, the ancient city of Prague, from where many of the early settlers immigrated from.

Local Landmark

St. Wenceslaus Church is one of the largest churches in Minnesota.

Place Name

Elias Drake and I.N. Dean founded this community in 1867 and named this railway village in honor of Captain Russell Blakeley, who captained steamboats cruising from St. Paul, Minnesota to Galena, Illinois.

Place Name

Minnesota territorial judge, Andrew Chatfield founded the town in 1854. In French, Belle Plaine means "beautiful prairie".

Assumption

Place Name

The Catholic Church in the area referred the name in commemoration of the ascension of the Virgin into heaven.

Gotha

Place Name

Named for Gotha, the ancient city in central Germany.

Jordan

Place Name

After a very intense and somewhat heated discussion on trying to select a name for their town, William Holmes suggested the name for the River Jordon in Palestine.

Some people believe that the name was partly due to writings of author Carl Schurz. The German immigrant described the gently sloping banks on this part of the Minnesota River as being as beautiful as the Rhine.

Carver

Place Name

The river in the area that was known by the Dakota as the Odowan, their native word for song or hymn, was changed to the Carver River by Captain Jonathon Carver himself.

Chaska

Place Name

The German town of Chaska is the seat of Carver County. Chaska is a Native word meaning "first".

Historical Significance

By 1804 Jean B. Faribault was trading in furs for the Northwest Company near the "Little Rapids" of the Minnesota River, south of this point, and in

Chaska was also the name of the two Sioux Chiefs that camped near the town.

136

this vicinity.

His fur post of 1842 on the site of Chaska became the nucleus for the first Catholic Mission in Carver County under Father Ravoux.

(Historical marker located on U.S. highway 212)

Industry

In 1979, Pillsbury moved its headquarters to Chaska after it bought Green Giant.

Nordic Track exercise equipment was invented in Chaska.

* * * *

The M.A. Gedney Company has been making pickles in Chaska since 1881.

General Trivia

Chaska had the honor of hosting one of the U.S. Open golf tournaments.

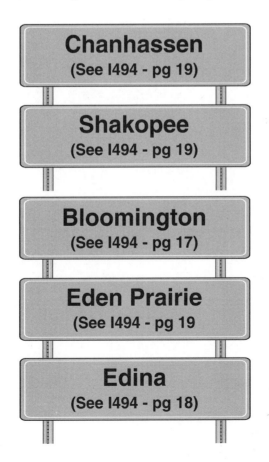

Chanhassen
(See I494 - pg 19)

Shakopee
(See I494 - pg 19)

Bloomington
(See I494 - pg 17)

Eden Prairie
(See I494 - pg 19)

Edina
(See I494 - pg 18)

Blue Earth

Winton

169

Hopkins
(See I494 - pg 21)

St. Louis Park
(See I494 - pg 21)

Minneapolis
(See I94 - pg 38)

Golden Valley
(See I494 - pg 23)

Medicine Lake
(See I494 - pg 23)

Plymouth
(See I494 - pg 24)

Brooklyn Center
(See I694 - pg 9)

Osseo

Place Name

This town's name comes from Longfellow's poem, The Song of Hiawatha, which tells the story of Osseo, the "son of the Evening Star," told at Hiawatha's and Minnehaha's wedding by Iagoo.

Brooklyn Park
(See I694 - pg 10)

Champlin

Place Name

Settled in the 1850s by Swiss and Yankees, Joseph Holt, Samuel Colburn and John Cook at the mouth of the Rum River. They named it after John Cook's wife, Elen Champlin, whose father was Commodore Stephen Champlin.

Stephen Champlin was a navy career officer, commander of the Scorpion, the gunboat responsible for firing the first shots in the battle of Lake Erie on September 10, 1813.

Coon Rapids

Historical Significance

In 1847 the Federal Government surveyed the land and found a well traveled road running through Anoka County which Coon Rapids is a part of. This road was laid out in 1835 for military to use and it is said that it may be the oldest road in this part of the country.

In 1843 trade was established from St Paul to Pembina in the Red River Valley by Norman W. Kittson and the road became the Red River Ox Cart Trail. Note: The trail closely follows the present East River Road/Coon Rapids Boulevard alignment.

* * * *

Agriculture was the first industry in the Coon Rapids area with local farmers owning from 90-600 acres.

In 1881, Dr. D.C. Dunham organized the first brick yard, known as the Anoka Pressed Brick and Terra Cotta Company. It represented the first non-agricultural industry in Coon Rapids. A legacy left by that brick industry is still visible today and is known as the "Clay Hole".

* * * *

In 1898, the Great Northern Development Company proposed to build a dam below the Coon Creek Rapids with a power generating plant on the east side of the river.

The actual construction by the Mississippi River Company did not start until 1912, and was operating by 1914. Northern States Power Company ran the dam until 1969. It was acquired by the Hennepin County Park Board and serves as Coon Rapids Dam Regional Park today.

Geological

About 20,000 years ago, a glacier from the Ontario region passed through the Lake Superior basin and reached the Twin Cities area. As the glacier ice melted, it deposited the St. Croix moraine at its margin. A moraine is a deposit of sediment (clay, silt, sand, gravel, and boulders) left by a melting glacier. The St. Croix moraine forms a belt of hills that crosses the Twin Cities and extends northwest to St. Cloud. As the moraine was deposited, it buried some blocks of stagnant glacial ice that were left stranded in an ancient valley.

This area lies within the southern part of the Anoka sand plain, a vast area of sand stretching from St. Cloud to the St. Croix River valley. Much of the sand was deposited about 12,000 years ago in Glacial Lake Anoka. Fed by meltwater from glacial ice in northwestern Minnesota, the lake formed on the northern side of the St. Croix moraine. The hidden ice blocks buried earlier in the moraine eventually melted to create a gap through which Glacial Lake Anoka drained, abandoning its former outlet to the east through the St. Croix River valley. With this gap, the general course of the Mississippi River was established between the sites of north Minneapolis and Hastings.

After Glacial Lake Anoka drained, the Mississippi River meandered across the flat surface of the former lake bottom. The shifting river formed two distinct terrace levels before becoming entrenched in its present narrow floodplain. As the Mississippi cut below the lower terrace, it encountered many boulders in the glacial sediment just upstream from the dam. The boulders formed a barrier to erosion on the river bottom, creating the Coon Creek rapids, now submerged behind the dam.

Downstream from the dam, the river has cut its channel into reddish, clay-rich sediment from a glacial lake that existed before Glacial Lake Anoka. The red clay was mined along Coon Creek by various companies from just before 1880 to about 1910.

<u>(Historical marker located off West River Road on the bank of the Mississippi River)</u>

Anoka

⭐ The name Anoka came from two Indian words, the Dakota word A-No-Ka-Tan-Han meaning on both sides of the river, and the Ojibwa word On-O-Kay meaning working waters.

Historical Significance

The area was surrounded by Dakota but later the Ojibwa pushed the Dakota westward across the Mississippi. The territory of Anoka then became a neutral ground between the two tribes.

* * * *

The two rivers, the Rum and Mississippi, run together in the city. These two rivers played an integral part in Anoka's settlement. Father Lewis Hennepin first visited the area in 1680 and settlers came to stay in 1844.

The first logging operation took place in the 1840s where the logs floated down the Rum River to the Mississippi River to the sawmills in St. Anthony.

General Trivia

It is believed that Anoka was the first city in the United States to host a Halloween celebration to divert old-time Halloween pranks.

This celebration has been held every year since 1920 with the exception of 1942 and 1943, when they canceled because of World War II.

Anoka, is known as the Halloween Capital of the World!

* * * *

Jonathan Emerson was an early settler that constructed a monument of himself in the city cemetery just one year before his death. The eerie monument has engraved in it an epitaph that reads, "Remember me as you pass by for as you are now, so once was I".

Prominent People

Anoka is home to World War II Congressional Medal of Honor winner Private Richard Sorenson.

* * * *

It is also home to Gretchen Elizabeth Carlson, who was Miss America in 1989.

* * * *

Prairie Home Companion humorist Garrison Keillor is born in Anoka. His show made its first live broadcast from Macalester College in Saint Paul in 1974, having national broadcasts four years later.

Ramsey

Historical Significance

This city started with the vision of being a thriving river port. Developers including Governor Alexander Ramsey even had grand illusions of moving the state capitol here. It was supposedly probable that the bill would pass, unfortunately according to the county historical records someone stole the bill until after the Legislature had adjourned.

Elk River

Alexander Ramsey, for whom the town was named, started governing Minnesota in 1849. After his years as Governor were over, he represented Minnesota in the United States Senate.

Place Name

Elk River is the county seat of Sherburne County. It is named after the neighboring river which was named by Zebulon Pike for the herds of elk found roaming in this area when he traveled up the Mississippi in the fall of 1805.

Geological

Just North of the Elk River is the Anoka Sand Plains. This is a 858 square mile triangular shaped plain where the wind has eroded all of the topsoil. The result is the creation of huge sand dunes, some upwards of 20 feet high, which look eerie and out of place here in the Midwest.

* * * *

Minnesota was largely covered by glaciers many times during the last million years. The ice flowed across the state from both the northeast and the northwest. As it advanced along separate points, it scraped up, crushed, and carried with it thousands of cubic kilometers of rock debris, called glacial drift. This was deposited in a thick layer over much of the state.

About 25,000 years ago, a tongue-shaped lobe of ice called the Superior lobe advanced across Minnesota from the northeast. This ice eroded the mostly igneous bedrock in Ontario and the Lake Superior region and deposited a reddish, sandy, and rocky drift. Soils that developed from this drift are not the most fertile.

More recently, about 16,000 years ago, another lobe of ice advanced across Minnesota from the northwest. This was named the Des Moines lobe because its point of furthest advance was Des Moines, Iowa. Drift deposited by this ice contains crushed pieces of sedimentary marine shale and limestone eroded from the Winnipeg Lowlands in southern Manitoba. Soils developed from this drift are typically gray to brown, full of clay, and rich in lime, magnesia, and potash. These soils are quite fertile and good for agriculture.

In the Elk River region, deposits from both the northeast and the northwest occur in close proximity. Most of the quite fertile material at the surface was deposited by an eastern offshoot of the Des Moines lobe called the Grantsburg sublobe. The older Superior lobe deposits are close to the surface, however, and may be mixed with those above. Thus, the fertility of the soils in the Elk River region will vary depending on the proportionate mix of the two parent drifts.

River terrace deposits of sand and gravel are also common near Elk River. The Mississippi River established its present course during the final decline of the glaciers. Water from the melting ice followed a number of different routes until finally cutting the valley in which the river now flows. Sandy terraces mark former river courses.

(Historical marker located on Hwy 10)

Local Landmark

The National Grange of the Order of Patrons of Husbandry was founded in Washington, D.C., on December 4, 1867. This date marks the birth of organized agriculture on American soil. Oliver Hudson Kelley first advanced the idea of a farm fraternity. As first secretary and one of the founders of the National Grange, he maintained official headquarters here until 1870.

(Historical marker located on Hwy 10)

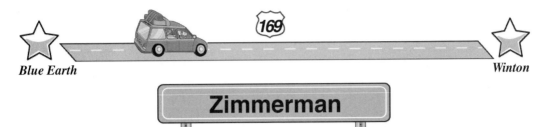

Zimmerman

Place Name

This town was first known as Lake Fremont, after the nearby lake. It was renamed after local farmer, Henry Zimmerman, when the Great Northern Railroad was completed in the area.

Princeton

Place Name

Founded in 1856, this town was named in honor of John S. Prince, a local fur-agent who helped establish the village.

Brickton

Place Name

Just north of Princeton used to be the small thriving village of Brickton. Back in the late 1880s to early 1900s, the main business here was a brickyard which turned out 20 million bricks a year.

The factory closed in 1929 because the clay resources gave out and the transportation costs were too high to continue. The area was converted into farmland.

Long Siding

Place Name

This Great Northern Railway station was named for Edgar Long, a landowner and lumberman from the area.

Pease

Place Name

This town started as a result of Benjamin Soule from Maine, building a local sawmill on the east branch of the Rum River. When the railroad was completed from Princeton to Milaca, Soule built another mill closer to the tracks. The station became known as Soule Siding.

After the Hinckley fire destroyed the sawmills in 1894, the Dutch migrated here to settle. Establishing a post office, the name was changed from Soule Siding to Pease.

Either the railroad officials named it in honor of James Hill's friend from Anoka, Granville Pease; or possibly it was a misspelling for the word Peace, the name suggested by the settlers for their home.

Milaca

Following the general traditions of French Explorers and traders, explorer Nicolet referred to this region as having "all sorts of lakes," or simply as Mille Lacs, meaning thousand lakes.

Historical Significance

Milaca was started by a lumber company, which was owned by James J. Hill. He built houses on the site known as Oak City and rented them to his workers.

Geological

Almost all the lakes in Minnesota were formed by glacial action. Many small lakes formed after the glacier receded and blocks of ice buried in the sediment melted, leaving holes, called kettles, that filled with water. Other lakes occupy basins that were scraped out of solid rock by glacial ice. Lake Superior is a prominent example of a lake bottom scoured by glacial ice. Lake Mille Lac, by contrast, is not really in a basin. It is surrounded on the north, west and south sides by a moraine, a ridge of sediment (silt, sand, gravel, and boulders) left along the edge of a glacier. With the land on the eastern shore also being of higher elevation, the moraine effectively dams the drainage to the south to form one of the largest lakes in the state.

The Mille Lacs moraine was formed about 15,000 years ago near the end of the last, or Wisconsin, glaciation, by a tongue-shaped lobe of ice called the Superior lobe, which flowed into the areas from the northeast. This ice carried sediment derived from rock along the Superior basin and the North Shore, which was later deposited beneath the ice and at its margin. At its maximum, the Superior lobe extended beyond Minneapolis to the south and St. Cloud to the west. Its decline was punctuated by several minor readvances, such as the one that deposited the Mille Lacs moraine.

About 12,000 years ago, another lobe of ice advances from the northwest and overrode the northern part of the Mille Lacs moraine, sending its meltwater into Lake Mille Lacs. Once this influx of meltwater ended, precipitation and small streams maintained the water level in Lake Mille Lacs, much as they do today.

(Historical marker located on Hwy 47)

General Trivia

Mille Lacs consistently produces a harvest of between 200,000 and 500,000 walleyes each year. The average walleye weighs nearly two pounds.

Each year 11 billion eggs are deposited through natural spawning, a miracle of nature that results in a hatch of 2.2 billion fry.

Mille Lacs Lake harbors more than one million catch able size walleye. Often called the "Walleye Capital of the World",

Onamia

Place Name

Onamia is located on Onamia Lake; which receives their name from the Ojibwe meaning dancing ground. Because the dance symbolizes either petition or thanksgiving, it is, in a manner of speaking, the Ojibwe word for these dances. The site of the city of Onamia was the place the early American Indians used for these dances.

Historical Significance

The site where the first day's fighting (of the Battle of Kathio) occurred in a decisive three-day battle between Chippewa and Sioux Indians about 1750. A large war party of Chippewa, armed with guns, marched from Lake Superior and made an early morning raid on the Sioux village near the base of Cormorant Point. Fighting with bows and arrows that were no match for the invaders' firearms, the surprised Sioux made a brave defense but were overwhelmed. A few escaped southward to the main Kathio village along the outlet (Rum River) of Mille Lacs. There on the second day, the Chippewa again wiped out most of the Sioux, who tried to take refuge in their semi-permanent lodges. Gunpowder, dropped by the Chippewa through smoke holes at the top, exploded in lodge fires and killed most of the Sioux occupants. A remnant of the Sioux escaped after dark to a third village on Aquipaquetin Island at the north end of Lake Onamia. They made a last stand there on the third day, then fled by canoe down the Rum River. The Battle of Kathio drove the Sioux forever from their ancient Mille Lacs villages southwestward to the prairies and ensured the Chippewa a permanent home in northern Minnesota's forest and lake country.

(Historical marker located on Hwy 169)

Local Landmark

Crosier College is located in town. Started by the Crosier Fathers, who came to Onamia in 1913. The order was started in Belgium in 1211, and the mother-house is at Agatha, Holland. Onamia and Hastings, Nebraska are the only English-speaking branches of this order in existence.

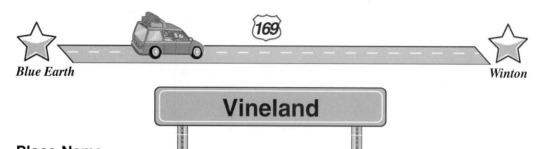
Vineland

Place Name

Leif Steenerson, the first settler, suggested the name to commemorate Leif Ericsson's, voyage from Greenland, around the year 1,000, when he explored the country, probably the coast of Maine or Massachusetts, he named Vinland or Vineland in reference to the grape vines.

Place Name

Oscar Garrison came to Minnesota in 1850 first settling in the Lake Minnetonka area. A land surveyor and civil engineer he platted the town of Wayzata before moving north to the St. Cloud area. Working for the U.S. Forestry he continued to examine the Upper Mississippi region, eventually making a homestead claim in the area which later incorporated a town named after him.

Historical Significance

Named from the fur trader's phrase "the thousand lake region", this lake is 1250 feet above sea level and covers 200 square miles. It formerly included much low ground and several adjacent lakes. When visited by Du Luth in 1679, Sioux villages, now indicated by numerous burial mounds, lined the lake shore.

(Historical marker located on Hwy 169)

Geological

This part of Minnesota was covered by glacial ice a kilometer or more thick at least four times during the last million years. As the glaciers moved in from Canada, they brought with them enormous quantities of glacial drift (silt, sand, gravel and boulders) that was deposited under the ice and at its margin, in sheets or in irregular hills and depressions.

About 15,000 years ago, near the end of the last, or Wisconsin glaciation, a tongue-shaped lobe of ice, called the Superior lobe, advanced into this area from the Lake Superior region. During the final decline of this ice lobe, it temporarily advanced again; and at its point of furthest progress, it deposited a pile of drift, called an end moraine, along its margin. This end moraine encircles Lake Mille Lacs on the north, west and south. With the land on the eastern shore already of higher elevation, the moraine blocked the drainage to the south. As a result, the bounded area was flooded, and one of the largest lakes in the state was formed.

Mille Lacs is 29 kilometers long and 22 kilometers wide. Its surface is 381 meters above sea level, and its depth of 8 to 11 meters is rather uniform throughout. Overflow from the lake is discharged to the south through the Rum River, which flows from Vineland about 112 kilometers to Anoka, where it empties into the Mississippi River.

(Historical marker on Hwy 169)

Place Name

The town is named after ore prospector James Nichol. He was a foreman for the Merritt brothers who discovered the first large iron ore bed on the Mesabi Range near Mountain Iron.

Place Name

The city of Aitkin was named after William Aitkin. He was a fur trader who established a permanent settlement on the Mississippi River in 1831.

Historical Significance

This community resulted because of the logging companies who sent logs down the Mississippi River to this spot during the late 1800s to early 1900s.

Place Name

Although the town name is altered slightly, it comes from the Ojibwe who called the nearby lake, Wakonabo sagaiigun, the lake of the broth of wakwug; or broth of moss growing on rocks or trees. It is believed that the Native Americans ate the moss to prevent starvation during the winter months when game was scarce.

Place Name

The town takes it name from the glacial debris left behind to form the hilly region referred to as Piquadinaw by the Ojibwe, meaning it is hilly.

Historical Significance

When the early settlers came to the area they called the larger hill southeast of town, Poquodenaw Mountain, which was shortened later to Quadna Mountain.

147

The town established around 1900 was the site of the National Wooden Ware Company, which produced wooden tubs and barrel staves.

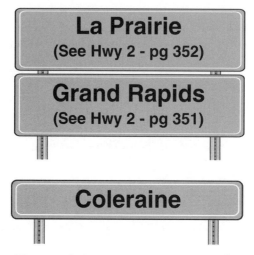

La Prairie
(See Hwy 2 - pg 352)

Grand Rapids
(See Hwy 2 - pg 351)

Coleraine

Place Name

The town's name honors Thomas Cole, president of the Oliver Mining Company, who was influential in the early development of the Mesabi Range iron mines.

Historical Significance

In the past, the quiet town of Coleraine has been referred to as a "model village". This is a tongue-in-cheek nickname since the town was purchased by the Oliver Mining Company for its employees in the 1800s

. The city is located on scenic Trout Lake among rolling green hills. The Oliver Mining Company is responsible for designing and building almost all of the modern business buildings and architecturally diverse residences. The city also houses a junior college which provides a fine education to the hundreds of students that choose to attend it.

Ole R. Mangseth was inducted into the National Ski Hall of Fame.

Prominent People

Coleraine is also the home of Ole R. Mangseth. Mangseth was born in Norway, but he lived his childhood years in Coleraine. He is honored at the Ski Museum in Ishpeming, Michigan and was given the privilege of being inducted into the National Ski Hall of Fame. He is an excellent ski jumper that owes much of his fine talent to the challenging hills just west of his home in Coleraine.

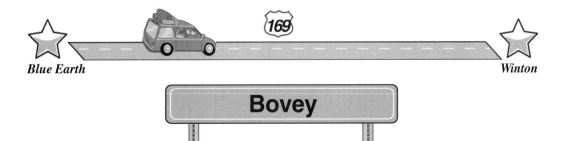

Bovey

Historical Significance

The town of Bovey was incorporated as a city in 1904. They barely had enough people to meet the legal requirements in order to have a village government. However, the popular mining industry began to attract more and more people until the homes in the village were occupied by people wanting to mine the great lands of Bovey.

Taconite

Place Name

The town was planned by the Oliver Mining Company which opened the Holman Cliffs Mine and takes the name of the mineral mined.

Industry

Taconite was home to the earliest mining on the Mesabi Range. The first experimental ore-washing plant was constructed in Taconite as well. Besides iron ore, diamonds were mined in the city.

Marble

Place Name

This town was named for the light yellowish magnesium limestone rock that resembles marble which is used for building or ornamental purposes because of the hardness, durability and ability for polishing it.

Calumet

Geological

The lowest layer visible on the mine face is a thick exposure of reddish-brown sedimentary rock called the Biwabik Iron Formation. About 1.9 billion years ago, this rock layer formed underwater, near the shoreline of a shallow sea. In that marine environment, blue-green algae grew. Now classified as a type of bacteria, these ancient microbes were photosynthetic: they made their own food from water, carbon dioxide, and sunlight, and gave off oxygen

Calumet bears the French name which describes the ceremonial pipe smoked by the Ojibwe during special occasions such as signing treaties like when they ceded the entire Arrowhead region.

as a by-product. At that time, the seas contained much dissolved iron, and when oxygen was introduced, it combined with the iron. The resulting iron oxide precipitated from the seawater, mixed with silica sediments on the seafloor, and eventually solidified into sedimentary rock. Much later, groundwater infiltrated the rock and circulated, especially along the faults and fractures. The water concentrated the iron by leaching out silica and caused further oxidation, producing an enriched ore containing 55 percent or more iron by weight.

About 95 million years ago, during the Cretaceous period, another shallow sea advanced over this area. The erosive action of rivers, waves, and weather broke down the surface of the Biwabik Iron Formation and produced a layer of boulders, cobbles, pebbles, and sand-sized particles on top of the iron formation. As the sea level rose, finer sediments were deposited on the seafloor. Fossilized clams, oysters, snails, fish teeth, turtle bones, crocodile bones, and plant debris are all found within these sediments, now called the Coleraine Formation. Most of this formation has been eroded or mined. Only a thin, patchy layer remains, and it is mostly hidden by vegetation. However, excellent exposures exist at the east end of the mine.

At the top of the mine is a light-colored layer of glacial sediment (clay, silt, sand, gravel, and boulders), which was mixed and deposited by glaciers that repeatedly covered this area during the Ice Age of the last two million years. Meltwater streaming from the edge of a glacier has in some places sorted the glacial sediments by size. The glaciers last receded from this area about 11,000 years ago.

(Historical marker located on Hwy 169)

During its 67 year history, the Hill-Annex Mine produced over 75 million tons of ore. This mine was the first mine to use electricity in its operation.

Nashwauk

Place Name

The town takes its Algonquin name from the Nashwaark River near Fredericton, New Brunswick, Canada.

Historical Significance

This town got its start as a lumbering site, logging the thickly dense pine forest. However, it wasn't necessarily easy because they didn't have any rivers or streams to float the logs to the mill. Therefore the Wright-Davis Lumber Company built a railroad south to the town of Jacobson where the logs could be shipped down the Mississippi River. Eventually James Hill would buy the companies interest, adding the railroad to his vast transportation empire.

Ore was discovered in 1900 and resulted with the development of the Hawkins Mines. Followed by the opening of the LaRue and Headley Mines, once the railroad was expanded into the area.

Blue Earth   **169**   *Winton*

Keewatin

Place Name

Taken from the Ojibwe word Giwedin, meaning north. The town's name also is translated as the northwind.

Mesabi Range

Henry Longfellow's Song of Hiawatha called it "the Northwest Wind", or home wind which they spelled Keewaydin, the way it was pronounced.

Geological

The dramatic history of the Mesabi Range dates back over 2.5 billion years when a mountainous terrain, perhaps similar to the California Coast Ranges today, extended from Minnesota to the Hudson Bay. The mountains slowly eroded down to their granite cores, and about two billion years ago the region was flooded by a sea that encroached from the south. Along the shallow margins of that sea, chemical sediments made of iron oxides and silica, which were precipitated out of the seawater, accumulated on the ocean floor to form the Biwabik Iron Formation. Evidence of primitive life forms (mostly algae) is preserved in the Biwabik and iron-formations of similar age around the world. It is believed that oxygen produced by the photosynthesizing algae modified the chemistry of the seawater and enabled iron and silica to precipitate from the ancient oceans.

Farther out to sea, fine sediments (mud, silt, and fine sand) accumulated to form the shale and siltstone of the Virginia Formation. As the sea level rose and submerged the eroded mountains, deeper water covered previously shallow environments where the iron-formation had been deposited. In the deeper water, fine sediments were also deposited over the iron-formation. As the iron-formation was buried under the younger sediments, the increasing pressure and temperature converted it to solid rock.

At some point after rock was formed, groundwater infiltrated and circulated through the Biwabik Formation, especially along its faults and fractures. The water effectively concentrated the iron by leaching out silica and caused further oxidation to produce the soft ores first mined on the Mesabi Range. With the gradual depletion of those enriched ores, most mining since the 1950s has instead extracted the magnetic mineral magnetite from unoxidated ore (taconite).

<u>(Historical marker located on Hwy 169 on 13th Street in Hibbing)</u>

Hibbing

Place Name

The town was named after Capt. Frank Hibbing, who purchased light and water systems for the town. This resulted in miners and lumberjacks flooding into the town.

Historical Significance

Valuable ore was found under Hibbing's streets. When it was, an iron company bought the land, and in 1919 moved the village to its present location, a mile farther south. Many buildings were pulled by log-haulers. Others were cut and pulled in halves.

Industry

> ❓❓❓ The Hull-Rust-Mahoning pit has been called the "Grand Canyon of the North," a fitting title for the world's largest open pit iron mine.

The Hull-Rust-Mahoning pit actually began as separate mines, named for their owners, first dug in 1895, that gradually merged into one. Today this enormous pit measures 1.5 x 3.5 miles with a depth of 600 feet. Because of its size and the important developments that took place here, the Hull-Rusk-Mahoning Mine played a key role in making Minnesota the leading iron-ore producer in the country.

Sitting in the midst of the Mesabi Range, the largest of Minnesota's three iron ranges, this mine owed its dominance to its particular iron formations. Here, vast stretches of high-grade, soft ore lay in shallow deposits that could be scooped up with giant steam shovels, machinery perfected at this site. Using the open pit method, mining companies removed huge quantities of iron ore quickly and economically, dumping it into rail cars that were moved out of the mine on tracks circling the slopes of the pit.

Large mining operations required extensive financial resources. Small local developers were soon driven out, and the wealthy ones with names like Rockefeller and Carnegie took over. In 1901 J.P. Morgan consolidated their mining and manufacturing operations as United States Steel, creating what was then the biggest corporation in the world.

The Hull-Rusk-Mahoning Mine developed rapidly in the early 1900s, when demand was high for iron and steel to build railroads, bridges, and skyscrapers. In its peak production years during World War I and II, this pit supplied as much as one-fourth of all the iron ore mined in the United States.

(Historical marker located off Third Avenue East in Hibbing)

> 🏆 Bob Dylan and Kevin McHale attended Hibbing High School.

Local Landmark

The Hibbing High School building is an interesting site. Built in 1921, this $4,000,000 structure is E-shaped.

* * * *

The Park School is known as the "Glass School" because of its large wall areas of structural glass. It was designed by J. C. Taylor.

* * * *

The Village Hall is made of red finishing brick, is modeled after Faneuil Hall in Boston and houses all the departments of municipal administration. There are four murals of the history of Minnesota and of the mining industry; two others symbolize Law and Justice.

Prominent People

Roger Maris, who would hit sixty-one home runs in the 1961 season to break Babe Ruth's single season record, which stood for thirty-four years. His record would be broken by Mark McGwuire and Sammy Sosa thirty-seven years later.

New York Yankee Roger Maris was born in Hibbing.

* * * *

Starting with one old Hupmobile, Andrew Anderson and Carl Eric Wickham established the first bus line between the towns of Hibbing and Alice in 1914 which would eventually be the start of the Greyhound bus system.

* * * *

Legendary prosecutor and author Vincent Bugliosi was born in Hibbing on August 18, 1934, is one year younger, to the day, than Roman Polanski (August 18, 1933), the husband of Sharon Tate, one of the Charles Manson Clan's murder victims.

Vincent Bugliosi prosecuted the Manson Clan, and authored a book about the case, Helter Skelter, and co-authored the screenplay for the memorable 1976 TV movie.

* * * *

Local choreographer and dancer Greg Rosatti appeared in the hit film Grease.

Chisholm

Place Name

Named in honor of the principal explorer of the Mesabi Range, Archibald Mark Chisholm. He started as the paymaster of the Chandler and Ely mines on the Vermilion Range before moving to Hibbing to become a bank cashier. Later dealing in mining and real estate he discovered several productive Mesabi mines as well as copper mines in Arizona and New Mexico.

Local Landmark

The 85-foot high bronze and steel Iron Ore Miner Statue pays tribute to all the men who worked in the early ore mines of the Mesabi Range.

They toiled with purpose, those miners of ours... moving tons of iron for massive steel towers. This devotion to a nation, they adopted as one, makes the heritage of the iron range foremost 'neath the sun. The legend lives. They were the "iron men" who dug the mines and contributed to the building and expansion of this country, during an industrial age. They helped to provide the iron needed when freedom was threatened.

Today, as the industrial age ebbs, and the technical age advances, the iron men are honored with a shrine that tells us they will never be forgotten.

This area is well known for its mining. Since the Mesabi Range was first opened, 45 mines have shipped ore from the Chisholm district.

The magnificent sculpture evokes strength and embodies past history and ensures continued remembrance of the "iron men".

Look at the contentment in the chiseled face, and you will see the souls of all the iron men who ever were. This statue, the third largest free-standing memorial in the United States, is a lasting tribute to the Mesabi, Vermilion, Cuyuna and Gogoebic ranges' men of steel, who carved out of a sylvan wilderness the iron ore that made America the industrial giant of the world.

They shall live forever! Yes, the iron man lives. By Veda Ponikvar.

(Historical marker located on Hwy 169)

Prominent People

The movie Field of Dreams is based on W. P. Kinsella's novel Shoeless Joe, which celebrated Chisholm's own Archibald "Moonlight" Graham. His only game as a major league player was with the New York Giants.

Place Name

Lumbering was still prevalent when miners from the Sharon Ore Company from Sharon, Pennsylvania came to the area establishing their mine claim. Deciding that a new town was needed, they built theirs, naming it after Frank Buhl the president of the company.

Place Name

Shortly after the Sharon Mining Company established their mine in nearby Buhl, O.D. Kinney discovered ore in this area. The Republic Iron and Steel Company leased the land to establish their mining operation.

A 2 1/2 ton, 10-foot high statue of Merritt stands in the heart of the city.

Place Name

As its name suggests, the City of Mountain Iron was literally built on a mountain of iron. It was here in 1890, that Leonidas Merritt first discovered iron ore, launching the mining era that uncovered the fabulous wealth beneath the Mesabi Range.

Historical Significance

The first development work was done by Captain A.P. Woods in 1891-1892. A shaft was sunk in 1892 and the first ore was taken from the mine for shipment. The first car of ore was shipped from Mountain Iron October 17, 1892 and was sent to Duluth where it was on exhibition. This shipment of 20 tons assaying 65 per cent metallic iron, was sent in standard wooden ore car No. 342. 4,245 tons of ore were shipped during the year 1892 from the Mountain Iron Mine.

(Historical marker located on Hwy 169)

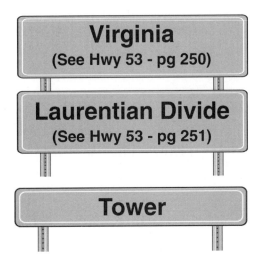

Virginia
(See Hwy 53 - pg 250)

Laurentian Divide
(See Hwy 53 - pg 251)

Tower

Place Name

The town is named in honor of Harvard graduate, Charlemagne Tower. Tower came to live in Duluth where he was president of the Duluth and Iron Range Railroad Company and also managed the Minnesota Iron Company. He later served as the U.S. ambassador to Austria-Hungary, Russia and Germany.

Historical Significance

The history of this region includes repeated battles between Sioux and Chippewa who both desired the excellent hunting and fishing area.

Later, when the white settlers came, this became a fur-trading town.

It also was the scene of Minnesota's gold rush. Tower is also the oldest mining town in Minnesota, having been founded in 1882.

> Lake Vermilion was called Sah-Ga-Ee-Gum-Wah-Mah-Mah-Nee by the Chippewa. This means "Lake of the Sunset Glow".

* * * *

On October 28, 1865, geologist Henry E. Eames returned to St. Paul after initiating a survey of the mineral wealth present in the Lake Vermilion area only to find an abundance of rumors concerning a valuable gold strike on the shores of that lake. A number of gold mining companies were quickly organized, and a St. Paul newspaper dispatched a special correspondent to the Vermilion gold field. Hundreds of men, including recently discharged Civil War veterans, made their way to Duluth, where

they purchased food and supplies for the trek north to the supposed gold fields.

During the winter of 1865-66, many of these men were employed by the mining companies to break open a road from Duluth to Pike Bay of Vermilion. This road followed inpart an old Indian trail from the Head of the Lakes. The improved trail stretched 85 miles to the north, and, in time, became known as the Old Vermilion Trail. At first only a winter road, it was improved in 1868-69 by George Stuntz, who directed a resurvey and construction project financed in part by government funds.

The gold prospectors created a log cabin and shack community named Winston City. In 1866 it boasted several stores, a hotel, four saloons, and a post office. But gold was not found in quantities sufficient to cover the cost of mining. In 1867 the disappointed miners deserted their gold-diggings, and Winston City shortly became the first ghost town of the Vermilion Range.

(Historical marker located on Hwy 169)

Soudan

Place Name

D.H. Bacon the general manager of the Soudan Mine named the town and mine because of the extreme winter weather, the severe cold was in strong contrast to the tropical heat of the Africa region of Soudan (or Sudan).

Historical Significance

The first shipment of iron ore from Minnesota came from the Soudan Mine in 1884; by 1900 Minnesota was the leading iron ore producer in the United States.

The Soudan Mine headframe sits atop the largest iron deposit in the Vermilion Range, one of the three vast iron ranges in northern Minnesota. On the nearby Mesabi Range, where the ore was soft and close to the surface, it could be scooped up with steam shovels, giving rise to open pit mining. But on the Vermillion range, ore deposits were embedded deep in hard rock that required drilling and blasting. These mining methods made the Soudan an underground operation, with a shaft that descended nearly 2,400 feet and tunnels that ran almost a mile from end to end.

Pennsylvania investor Charlemagne Tower and his son Charlemagne Junior were the first to develop the riches of the Vermilion Range. After buying more than 20,000 acres, they brought in experienced miners to work the new mine at Soudan and founded the town of Tower to serve the fast growing population. To ship the ore, they built the Duluth and Iron Range Railroad, linking their mine to the town of Two Harbors on Lake Superior, where they constructed an ore dock.

At its peak in the 1890s, the Soudan Mine employed 1,800 men and shipped more than half a million tons of ore a year. In 1901, years after Tower had sold it, the mine came under the control of the newly formed United States Steel Corporation.

The Soudan Mine remained in almost continuous operation until it closed in 1962, not because its resources were depleted but because changing economics and technology made

underground mining too expensive. In 1963 U.S. Steel gave Minnesota's oldest and deepest mine to the state, which established it as a state park in 1965. Its name was changed in 1985 to the Soudan Underground Mine State Park.

(Historical marker located on Hwy 169 near the Visitor Center)

Place Name

The village was named after a Tower Lumber Company foreman.

Place Name

This former Duluth, Missabe and Iron Range Railroad station was named for a lumberman who was camped beside the lake in the vicinity.

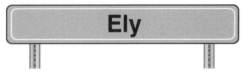

Place Name

Named to honor one of the financial promoters of the construction of the Duluth and Iron Range Railroad, Mr. Arthur Ely of Cleveland, Ohio. Ely was also instrumental in the development of the Tower iron mines.

It is also said that the town's name may be in honor of Rev. Edmund Franklin Ely, a missionary to the Ojibwe, who established a mission school in the area.

Local Landmarks

The International Wolf Center open here in June 1993, is a nonprofit educational organization focused on the worldwide environmental education about the preservation of wolves.

* * * *

The Boundary Water Canoe Area Wilderness, known simply as BWCA, comprises of one million acres of rivers and lakes extending 150 miles from Canada's Quetico Provincial Park along the border from Lake Superior to International Falls.

Prominent People

Not satisfied with his expedition to the North Pole accomplishment, Steger was determined to reach the South Pole. However, he didn't just want to reach it, instead he decided to travel across the entire continent of Antarctica

Local science teacher Will Steger and outfitter Paul Schurke joined up together in 1986, along with a team of 7 men, 1 woman, and 49 dogs to retrace Robert Peary's original 1909 expedition to the North Pole.

from the Pacific Ocean to the Atlanta. Joined by a team of 6 men and 36 dogs, they spent 220 days on their journey before completing their expedition on March 3, 1990.

* * * *

Anne Bancroft, the only women in Steger's expedition to the North Pole, learned to handle the dog team. Traveling an average of 20 miles a day, Bancroft completed the 500 mile journey to become the first woman ever to reach the North Pole.

Place Name

The town is named for a member of the Knox Lumber Company of Duluth which did a lot of the logging around the Ely and Winton area. His name is William Winton.

HIGHWAY 75

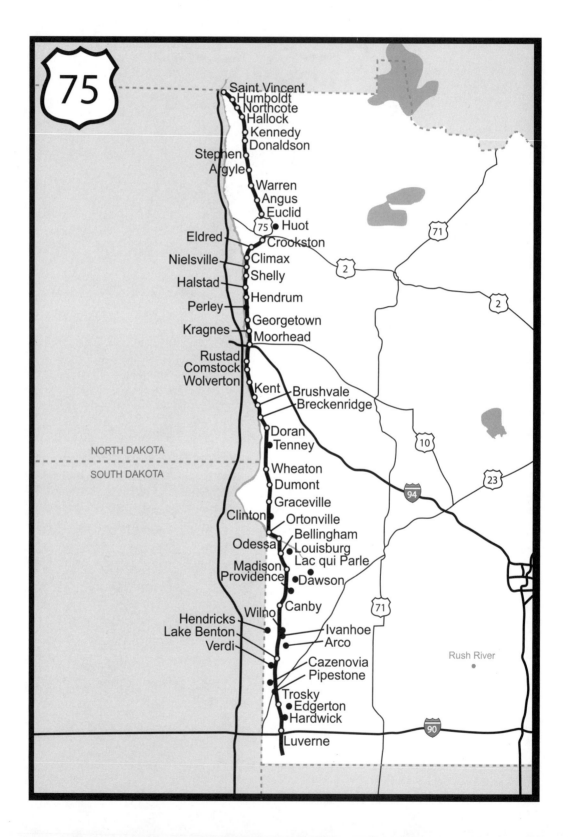

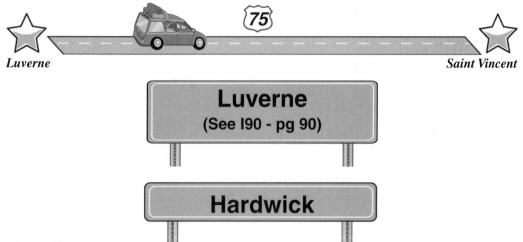

Luverne
(See I90 - pg 90)

Hardwick

Place Name

The town is named for the master builder of the Burlington, Cedar Rapids and Northern Railway, J.L. Hardwick.

Edgerton

Place Name

Wesleyan University graduate, Alonzo Edgerton moved to Mantorville where he practiced law prior to serving as captain of the Tenth Minnesota Regiment. Returning to the state as a brigadier general he settled in Kasson, and became a state senator. Eventually Colonel Alonzo Edgerton would become a U.S. Senator and for whom this town is named.

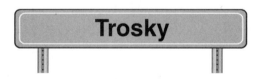

Trosky

Place Name

By all accounts, this is the only town in the United States called Trosky, which might explain why the significance of the name is unknown.

Pipestone

Place Name

When settlers came to Pipestone, they originally called it "Tall grass Prairie" after the eight-foot tall grass that blanketed the region. The name was later changed in reference to the red pipestone quarry.

Historical Significance

The pipestone quarries have an importance that goes beyond their size. There is evidence pipestone was quarried at least since the time of European exploration. Many explorers of the Minnesota region refer to the existence of a quarry of the red stone.

161

A French explorer in 1684 wrote that while Indians used many pipes, those made from red stone (as at Pipestone) were the most esteemed and their use "had the same effect as a flag of friendship among the Whites".

The relatively soft stone is found as a layer in the very hard Sioux quartzite stone. Sands in a shallow sea were cemented together to form the Sioux quartzite. The softer pipestone is formed of a different material.

It is thought to have been laid down at a different period of different materials and ended up soft enough to be carved into things such as pipes.

Today, only Native Americans are allowed to quarry pipestone. It is a laborious task, involving uncovering the vein of pipestone with the Sioux quartzite.

Local Landmark

Pipestone National Monument was created by an act of Congress in 1937 to preserve the pipestone quarries and elements of Native American culture. Special attractions include Winnewissa Falls, Leaping rock, and a marker from the Nicollet Expedition.

Large granite boulders have long been known as the Three Maidens. With smaller fragments, they once formed one large single boulder some 50 feet in diameter. The boulder was deposited by glaciers.

> Pipestone National Monument was created by an act of Congress in 1937 to preserve the pipestone quarries and elements of Native American culture.

* * * *

The Calumet Inn's history has been compared to the legendary phoenix, rising to re-open after disaster. The first grand hotel was located one block north of the present structure, where the First National Bank now stands at the corner of 2nd St. NW and Hiawatha Avenue. The 60-room facility was built by the Close Brothers, English land agents, at a cost of $25,000 and was destroyed in two hours December 15, 1886 by fire.

Townspeople desperately wanted a grand hotel to serve the trains which were the lifeblood of the early community. Two bankers announced plans to build a new bank at the corner of Hiawatha Avenue and Main Street, the present Calumet location. It was decided to include the hotel with the bank. The corner door would be for the bank and east and north doors would be for the hotel.

The new Calumet Hotel would include 50 rooms in three stories and cost $30,000. The Sioux Quartzite, the primary building stone, was taken from quarries at Pipestone. Darker stone for trim came from quarries at nearby Jasper. Construction began in the spring of 1888. The grand opening was Thanksgiving Day that year.

General Trivia

Gargoyles placed in the Sioux Quartzite building stone at 102 E Main are a popular sight. The stone faces are the work of early builder Leo H. Moore. Moore operated a stone quarry just north of Pipestone. The gargoyles are typical of his work, and a link to the community's European heritage where gargoyles adorn churches and public buildings.

The larger work entitled "Moses," near the center of the building, is his masterpiece. To Moses' left is a vacant niche where the legend is a full length "Eve" reposed. She was a bit

too much for the tender sensibilities of early residents, however, and was removed. To where is a local mystery.

Prominent People

Guitarist Roger Steen from the rock band, "The Tubes" was born in Pipestone.

* * * *

Beside episodes of Seinfield, Philip Bruns appeared in St. Elsewhere, Mr. Belvedere, Amazing Stories; plus the movie Flashdance, Dead Men Don't Die and others.

* * * *

Native actress Anne Lange appeared in a couple TV episodes of Sex and the City, Law and Order, as well as numerous made for TV movies including For Love or Money and Cry Baby Lane.

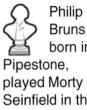 Philip Bruns, born in Pipestone, played Morty Seinfield in the first episode of Seinfield in 1990.

Place Name

Many of the farmers that came to this area, came from Madison County, New York, giving their new home the name of their former village.

Place Name

Actually the name of this town commemorates Giuseppe Verdi, the renown Italian operatic composer. However, it is quite appropriate considering "verdant" is a descriptive for greenness and certainly the color of the green landscapes that extend throughout the area every spring.

Arco

Place Name

Officials for the Chicago and North Western Railroad named this city after the ancient Italian city of Arcola. To avoid any confusion with another railroad station by the same name in Washington County, they adjusted the name slightly.

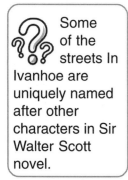

Some of the streets In Ivanhoe are uniquely named after other characters in Sir Walter Scott novel.

Ivanhoe

Place Name

The town was named for the hero in the Sir Walter Scott novel.

Wilno

Place Name

This town was settled by Polish immigrants who named their town after Wilnius, of old Poland, which is now the capital of Lithuania. They also named their streets for Polish heroes or other homeland cities.

Local Landmark

The Church of St. John Cantius has become known as the "Cathedral in the Cornfield" because of being the center of Polish-American farming.

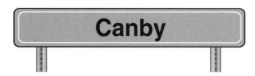

Hendricks

Place Name

Norwegians settled this community, located on Lake Hendricks, at the mouth of the Lac Qui Parie River, and were both named for the Commissioner of the General Land Office, Thomas Andrews Hendricks.

Canby

Place Name

Canby, located on the Lac qui Parie River, was named for Edward Richard Sprigg Canby.

A graduate of the U.S. Military Academy, Canby served both during the Mexican War and Civil War. He was the Louisiana commander in charge of the U.S. Army departments west of the Mississippi River and later captured the city of Mobile, Alabama.

It is the seat of Yellow Medicine County. Yellow Medicine County got its name from the roots of the yellow moon seed. This seed was used by Natives for medicinal purposes.

Place Name
Founder Roger Williams named the township for the capital city of Rhode Island.

Place Name
Dawson rests on the West Fork Lac qui River and is named for St. Paul banker, William Dawson.

Prominent People
Ex-Secretary of Labor James Day Dodgson was born in the town in 1915.

Theodore Christianson, a three-time Minnesota Governor and a Senator, was from Dawson.

Place Name
The town was named from Claus Moe's suggestion of his hometown in Madison, Wisconsin.

Historical Significance
Jacob Jacobson led Iowa settlers to the town and found it in the late 1800s. He later ran for Governor of Minnesota but ended up losing.

Madison is the seat of Lac qui Parle County, which has an interesting translation. It is a Native phrase meaning "lake that speaks".

Bellingham

Place Name

This town name was given by Phebe (Morese) Bellingham after her father-in-law, Charles, who was the patriarch of the large family (of seven sons and one daughter) that settled here.

Louisburg

Place Name

Ole Thompson owned the land this town was developed on and given the name for his father, Louis Thompson.

Odessa

Place Name

One explanation of the city's name is that wheat seeds were brought here from Odessa, a city in southern Russia.

Another explanation is that the town was named after A.D. Beardsley's daughter, Dessa, who died of diphtheria at the age of three.

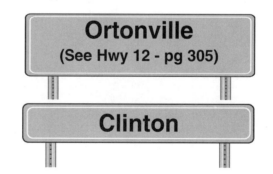

Ortonville
(See Hwy 12 - pg 305)

Clinton

Place Name

The people voted to name their town after the village of Clinton in Oneida County, New York.

Graceville

Place Name
Since this community was founded by a Catholic colonist, it is believed to be named in honor of Thomas Langdon Grace, a St. Paul bishop for 25 years.

Local Landmark
About 1866 a trading post on the Fort Wadsworth Trail was established on Tokua (Togua) Lake a mile west of Graceville. Early in 1878 Archbishop (John) Ireland, after erecting a church on the present town site, located several hundred families in the vicinity through the Catholic Colonization Bureau.

Dumont

Place Name
The town's name was suggested by officials of the Chicago, Milwaukee and St. Paul Railroad for a French trader in the area who provided food for their men.

Wheaton

Place Name
The surveyor for the Fargo and Southern Railroad, Daniel Thompson Wheaton, from Morris suggested the town be called Swedenburg in honor of the Swedish landowners Swan C. and Ole Odenborg. However they chose his name instead.

Tenney

Place Name
Lumberman, John Tenney was the original owner of the land the town site was built on.

Doran

Place Name
Railroad magnate James Hill named this village after his Irish friend Michael Doran who came to this country engaging in farming and banking before becoming a state senator.

167

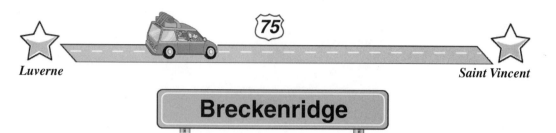

Breckenridge

Place Name

In 1857, settlers came to the area located at the confluence of the Otter Trail and Bois de Sioux Rivers, founded it, and named it after Vice President John C. Breckenridge. Breckenridge is also the seat of Wilkin County.

Historical Significance

When the Civil War started, many of the town's residents left the town to enlist.

On August 23, 1862, its remaining citizens were warned, and most of them fled to Fort Abercrombie. Scoffing at the warning, three men, Edward Russell, Charles Battle, and Martin Fehrenbach, stayed behind and were killed by the Indians. After the Sioux Uprising, Breckenridge remained a virtual ghost town until 1871 when the St. Paul and Pacific Railroad reached here and ushered in a period of booming growth.

<u>(Historical marker located on U.S. highway 75)</u>

Brushvale

Place Name

Brushvale was named for the farmer, Joseph Brush, whose land the town was located on.

Kent

Fort Abercrombie, begun by U.S. troops in August 1857 to protect the northwest frontier against the Indians.

Place Name

Kent was named by railroad officials for a county in England.

Local Landmark

On the west banks of the Red River, at the head of navigation, about one mile west of here, stood Fort Abercrombie, begun by U.S. troops in August 1857 to protect the northwest frontier against the Indians.

The post withstood several Sioux attacks during the outbreak of 1862, and was garrisoned until its abandonment in 1877.

<u>(Historical marker located on Hwy 75)</u>

Wolverton

Place Name
Established as Nora Township the name was changed shortly thereafter in honor of Dr. William Dilts Wolverton, the Fort Abercrombie physician who owned the majority of the land in the area.

Comstock

Place Name
Solomon Gilman Comstock for whom the town is named, came to Minnesota from Argyle, Maine. He was admitted to the bar and then elected as a state legislature representative, State Senator and Congressman.

Rustad

Place Name
The village was named for Norwegian immigrant Samuel Rustad, a local merchant.

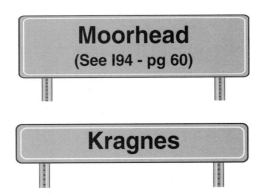

Moorhead
(See I94 - pg 60)

Kragnes

Place Name
Norwegian immigrant, Aanund Ole Kraaknes, one of the areas first settlers, changed his name to Andrew Kragnes when he came to the area. He was influential in the establishing the community, building a elevator, lumberyard, store and machinery agency.

Georgetown

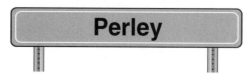

⭐ When the village was established as a trading post for the Hudson's Bay Company, they called it Selkirk after Lord Selkirk. Later it was renamed in honor of Sir. George Simpson, the governor of the Hudson's Bay Company.

Historical Significance

Hudson Bay Company was chartered by King Charles II of England on May 2, 1670, on its agreement to pay "two Elkes and two Black Beaver" in rent for rights of trade, commerce and governmental powers over the territories lying within the entrance of Hudson Strait. The region encompassed the drainage basin of the Red River of the North, an area equal to 1/3 North America. Rents were to be paid whenever the reigning sovereign of England set foot on "Rupert's Land". First immigrants to Minnesota were Scotchmen from Red River Settlement established near present-day Winnipeg in 1812.

Fur trading and barter was the way of life of the territories. Fur trading posts were built on Red River, the one on this site being erected in 1859. Reconstructed around this marker is the warehouse in which furs were stored for transportation by dog team, oxcart, and pirogue to York Factory in Hudson Bay and shipped by sailing vessels to London.

Georgetown was named after Sir George Simpson, Governor-in-Chief of Rupert's Land. It marks the confluence of the Red and Buffalo rivers and a crossing of the first overland highways in Minnesota, the Red River Oxcart Trails.

(Historical marker located on Hwy 75)

Perley

Place Name

George Edmund Perley graduated at Dartmouth College before coming to Morehead to settle and practice law. He later served as a state representative.

Hendrum

Place Name

When the township was founded in 1881, it was named by the Norwegian settlers after a group of farms from their native homeland.

Others believe the town may have been named for Johanas Hagen's wife, who helped organize the town, Olava Hindrum Hagen.

75

Luverne　　　　　　　　　　　　　　　　　　　　　　　　　　*Saint Vincent*

Halstad

Place Name

This community was named for Norwegian immigrant Ole Halstad, a pioneer farmer.

Prominent People

Skitch Henderson, who was born in England, later moved to and grew up in Halstad. It was here that his aunt taught him how to play the piano. His talent grew to the point that Skitch became the musical director for Frank Sinatra and Bing Crosby.

In 1954, Skitch Henderson became the first "name" band to play for Steve Allen on the Tonight Show.

Shelly

Place Name

Vermont native John Shely came to Minnesota and was the first homesteader in the area. He later became a wheat buyer in Ada before moving to Duluth where he was the state's assistant grain buyer.

Nielsville

Place Name

Nils Olson came to the United States from his native Norway. Once established in the area he changed his name to Nels Paulsrud. The local mail was delivered to his home referred to as Old Nielsville. When the new post office was opened they no longer called it old, just plain Nielsville.

Climax

Place Name

The name comes from the ancient Greek word meaning a ladder or stairway. Here, it refers to the highest point of achievement obtained by Climax Tobacco advertisements.

Eldred

Place Name

John Elg donated land to the Great Northern Railway for a right-of-way here and was named after him, with a slight change in the form.

Crookston
(See Hwy 2 - pg 342)

(See Hwy 2 - pg 342)

Huot

Place Name

Huot is a small village that lies on the border of the Red Lake River that was named for an early French Canadian homesteader, Louis Huot.

Local Landmark

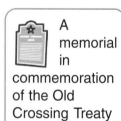

A memorial in commemoration of the Old Crossing Treaty is located here.

The Old Crossing Treaty was signed by the chiefs of the Red Lake and Pembina tribes, and by United States Representative, Alexander Ramsey. The treaty gave the United States a great portion of the Red River Valley- nearly 10 million acres.

* * * *

A nearby trail winds through the surrounding lands to the Ox Cart Trail. This monument contains a giant cottonwood tree. This tree pays tribute to the early settlers. Ox cart trains followed this trail often to pick-up and drop-off.

Euclid

Place Name

When Springer Harbaugh moved here to manage the Lockhart farm, he suggested the name after Euclid Avenue in Cleveland.

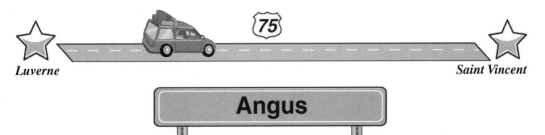

Place Name

Angus is named after the Montreal banker, Richard Bladworth Angus, who financed the construction of the Great Northern Railway line in the area.

Place Name

Warren Wilson, a prominent settler in the area was honored with the naming of the town.

Historical Significance

Warren is the seat of Marshall County. It had to put up a fight to have this honor. In 1881, the Marshall County commissioners voted to move the county seat from Warren to nearby Argyle. Thus, the safe containing all the legal documents and money pertinent to the county seat was moved to Argyle. For about 10 years, residents of both towns attempted to steal the safe back. This happened so often that in the end, a vote decided that Warren would serve as the county seat.

Argyle

Historical Significance

In 1879, James J. Hill bought the Great Northern Railway and accepted the task of completing the line from Crookston to the Canadian border.

What he didn't know was that there was already a settler located in the area of the middle River where Argyle is today. The man was a French Canadian named Gervais. This comes as no surprise since the French Canadians had been coming to the Red River Valley since the beginning of the 1800s.

Gervais was cunning, and he had staked a claim right in the path of the railway line, calling his community Louisa in honor of the French king. However, the James J. Hill group outsmarted Gervais and located their railroad town just south of the Gervais property and subsequently south of the river.

> The name of the town was suggested by Hon. Solomon Comstock for Argyle, Maine where he was born.

Stephen

Place Name

Stephen was adopted from the name of a farm established here by Lord Ramsey. Ramsey called it the "Stephen Farm" in honor of Lord Mount Stephen who was a Canadian railway official.

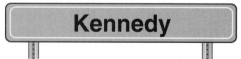

Donaldson

Place Name

Donaldson is named after Captain Hugh Donaldson who was a former Civil War officer and manager of the Kennedy Land Company who owned several thousand acres of adjoining farmland.

Local Landmark

The extravagant Donaldson-Ryan property in the town demonstrates Donaldson's elitism. Back in these times, when anyone in the community wanted a job or wished to buy property, they had to talk to Donaldson in order to do so. Thus, the town's name tells quite a bit about its history and development.

Kennedy

 It is even believed by some that the Old Pembina Trail route was used by a Norse-Gothic group as early as 1362.

Place Name

Scottish immigrant John Stewart Kennedy came to the United States in the mid 1800s. Settling in New York he worked as an iron merchant, banker and railway director.

Operating a bonanza farming project here, he convinced officials of the St. Paul, Minneapolis and Manitoba Railroad to build a station here. This would enable his company, The Kennedy Land and Town Company, to expand trading opportunities.

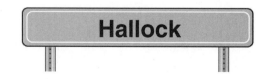

Hallock

Place Name

Hallock is the seat of Kittson County. The seat is named Hallock in honor of Charles Hallock who was a famous journalist, editor, and founder of Forest and Stream magazine.

Mr. Hallock financially supported the community in its early days. Being an avid sportsman, he constructed the Hallock Community Rink so that citizens could play hockey at their leisure.

The Old Pembina Trail lies in the Hallock vicinity. The trail is unmarked but was used for decades by pioneers and Natives in early times. The trail was also used by ox carts to haul fur and wood.

Norman Kittson, for whom the county is named, also used the trail extensively. Kittson made his ox cart usage extremely profitable. He made a profit by hauling loads in large trains by ox cart. This way he could haul more goods in one trip as opposed to many. For example, Kittson's first train carried $2,000 worth of furs. As he gradually increased the cart size, he gradually increased his profit to well over $15,000.

Place Name

Northcote is named after Sir Henry Stafford Northcote. He was a wealthy English statesman and financier who helped to settle the town.

Place Name

The town was named in honor of many of the former Great Northern Railway German stockholders; or to commemorate an eminent German scientist and author, Baron Alexander von Humboldt, who traveled throughout South America and Mexico in the later 1700s, early 1800s.

Place Name

The town was named after St. Vincent de Paul, who was known for his outstanding work with the poor.

HIGHWAY 71

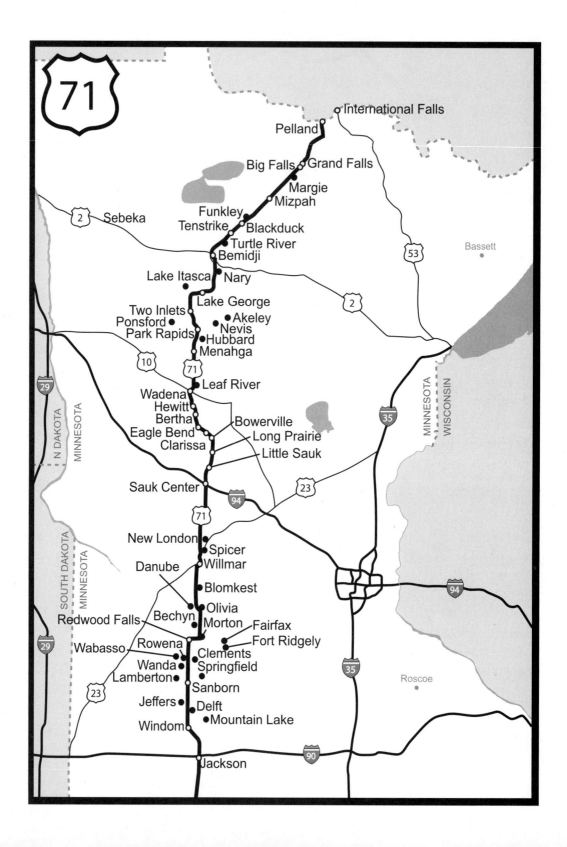

71

International Falls
Pelland
Big Falls   Grand Falls
Margie
Mizpah
Funkley
Tenstrike   Blackduck
Turtle River
Bemidji
Lake Itasca   Nary
Lake George
Two Inlets   Akeley
Ponsford   Nevis
Park Rapids   Hubbard
Menahga
71
Leaf River
Wadena
Hewitt
Bertha   Bowerville
Eagle Bend   Long Prairie
Clarissa   Little Sauk
Sauk Center
71
New London
Spicer
Danube   Willmar
Blomkest
Olivia
Bechyn   Morton   Fairfax
Redwood Falls   Fort Ridgely
Rowena   Clements
Wabasso   Springfield
Wanda
Lamberton   Sanborn
Jeffers   Delft
Windom   Mountain Lake
Jackson

Sebeka

Bassett

Roscoe

2

53

2

23

10

29

35

94

94

35

23

29

90

N DAKOTA
MINNESOTA

SOUTH DAKOTA
MINNESOTA

MINNESOTA
WISCONSIN

178

Jackson
(See I90 - pg 86

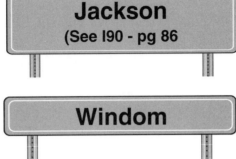

Windom

Place Name

Windom is the seat of Cottonwood County named for William Windom. Mr. Windom had a distinguished background as a statesman and as a member of President Garfield's and President Harrison's Cabinet.

The TV announcer, Johnny Olsen, for such shows as Family Feud, Password Plus and Tattletales was born in Windom.

Mountain Lake

Place Name

The village was originally named "Midway" when it was founded in the mid 1800s, because it was located midway between the railroad line that travels from St. Paul to Sioux City, Iowa.

The name was later changed to Mountain Lake after settlers saw a tree-covered island that jets out from a lake lying southwest of the city.

General Trivia

Mountain Lake has the oldest known human dwelling in the state. Evidence of this dates back to 100 B.C.

Delft

Place Name

Originally known as Wilhelmine, a common female name in Holland, John Bartsch and Henry Wieb named the town after a city in Holland.

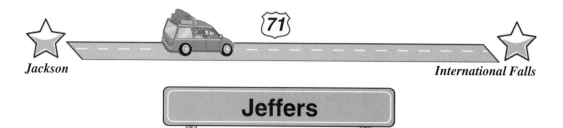
Jeffers

Place Name

The town was named for one of its more wealthy landowners, George Jeffers, whose land was purchased for part of the village.

 The Jeffers Petroglyphs were created by Native Americans thousands of years ago.

General Trivia

Part of the town was platted by Frank Peavey, the president of the Interstate Land Company, and as a result many of the streets are named for previous employees of the Peavey Elevator.

Local Landmark

The Jeffers Petroglyphs contain more than 2,000 pictures carved by these Native Americans on red quartzite rock. These pictures are an accurate reflection of what the early life and culture of the Native Americans was like.

Sanborn

Place Name

The town is named for an railway company officer, Mr. Sherburn Sanborn.

Local Landmark

Sanborn is the home of the McCone Sod House. This unique house was constructed from virgin prairie sod. It is a fine replica of the 1870s "Soddie Home"

Springfield
(See Hwy 14 - pg 286)

Lamberton
(See Hwy 14 - pg 285)

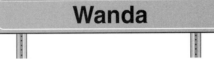

Place Name
The name of the town comes from wanenda, the Ojibwe word meaning to forget.

Place Name
Named for a Swedish immigrant farmer, Peter Clements.

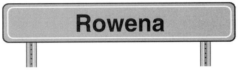

Place Name
The town's name bears the name of the Cedric ward in Sir Walter Scott's Ivanhoe; who is the rival of Rebecca and marries Ivanhoe.

Place Name
The site was developed by the Chicago and North Western Railroad and given the Ojibwe word (Wabos) for rabbit.

Wabos, pronounced Wahbose, is used in Longfellow's Song of Hiawatha.

Place Name
This city has a very scenic location on a high bank of the Redwood River. The river drops almost 150 feet in a three-mile span. This causes cascading waterfalls and white rapids, which gives the city its name.

Historical Significance
Redwood Falls became a city in 1891. It has an extensive history as a port town and was heavily influenced by Army Colonel Sam McPhail. McPhail financed Redwood County for two years so that the county could get on its feet.

* * * *

Near here are buried the repatriated remains of Mdewakantan Dakota. Many Dakota cooperatively worked for years with the State of Minnesota, the Bureau of Indian Affairs, and the Minnesota Indian Affairs Council to repatriate these remains. Used in an American Indian contest, to repatriate means to return to the place of one's ancestry. The Lower Sioux Mdewakanton Community has returned the remains of more than 80 of their ancestors to their homeland through multiple repatriations.

Chief Marpiya Oki Najin was one of thirty-eight Dakota men hanged at Mankato on December 26, 1862, for alleged crimes they committed during the U.S.-Dakota War of 1862.

The U.S.-Dakota War of 1862, a six week struggle, resulted from many years of uneasy interaction between Dakota, Euro-americans and the U.S. government. A devastating result of the War was that the majority of Dakota either left their traditional homelands or were forcibly exiled to areas farther west. When these Dakota died, they were buried in the area of their most recent residence rather than in their ancestral homelands in Minnesota.

Most of the Dakota whose remains are buried here resided in South Dakota or Nebraska at the time of their death. The remains of Chief Marpiya Oki Najin (Cut Nose) are of special concern to the Dakota. Chief Marpiya Oki Najin was one of thirty-eight Dakota men hanged at Mankato on December 26, 1862, for alleged crimes they committed during the War. After the hanging, doctors from Mankato and nearby towns stole the bodies of the dead Dakota men. For many years, the bodies were used for medical research and anatomical studies. Chief Marpiya Oki Najin's and those of two others are the only known remains of the thirty-eight Dakota hanged in Mankato to be recovered and properly buried.

While the remains of many Dakota have been repatriated to their ancestral homelands, the remains of many more are still awaiting repatriation and burial in a respectful manner with proper Dakota ceremonies.

(Historical marker located off Co. Rd 2, 1 mile south of Hwy 71)

Prominent People

Near this spot (in Redwood Falls Cemetery) lie the remains of Wowinape (Place of Refuge), a survivor of the Dakota War of 1862. Wowinape was the son of Taoyateduta (His Red Nation), known to whites as Little Crow, spokesman and leader of the Dakota in that tragic war. In July, 1863 Wowinape was with his father when he was killed. He fled to the Dakota Territory but was captured, tried and sentenced to hang. Reprieved and in a prison camp, he became literate in the Dakota language, a Christian convert, and took the name Thomas Wakeman.

Pardoned in 1866, he went to the Santee Reservation and later homesteaded with other Dakota at the bend of the Big Sioux River in Dakota Territory. Thomas Wakeman married Judith Minnetonka in January, 1874. He farmed and carried the U.S. mail. Impressed by the Y.M.C.A.,he worked with friends to found the first Indian chapter at Flandreau, Dakota Territory, on April 27, 1879.

Ill with tuberculosis, he returned to boyhood scenes and died at Redwood Falls, Minnesota on January 13, 1886. In his lifetime, he made a path between Dakota Indian and Euroamerican worlds.

(Historical marker located on N. Redwood Road)

General Trivia

Redwood Falls holds The Minnesota Inventors Congress, the oldest and the most successful inventors fair in the nation.

Place Name

Henry Morgan, an explorer/author traveled through Minnesota in route to Manitoba and across the Missouri River to the Rocky Mountains writing numerous books including the history of the American beaver.

> Morton was named for Henry Morgan, often called "the Father of American anthropology".

Historical Significance

On a summer day in 1862 the Redwood Ferry landing on the Minnesota River (2 miles east of Morton) was the scene of the first attack against military troops in one of America's most tragic Indian wars.

Early in the morning of August 18, 1862, a large party of Dakota (Sioux) warriors, enraged by delayed annuity payments and near-starvation conditions on their reservation, attacked the nearby Lower Sioux Agency. Surviving agency employees crossed the river on the Redwood Ferry and fled to Fort Ridgely some 13 miles downstream.

Discounting warnings of the Indian's strength and determination, the fort's commandant, John S. Marsh, set out toward the agency with interpreter Peter Quinn and 46 soldiers of the Fifth Minnesota Infantry. They found the Dakota waiting in ambush at the ferry. In the ensuing fight, Quinn and 23 soldiers were killed swimming across the river. The remaining men eventually made their way back to Fort Ridgely, which was itself attacked on August 20 and 22.

The war in the Minnesota River Valley claimed the lives of at least 450 whites and an unknown number of Dakota before it came to an end at Camp Release on September 26, 1862.

<u>(Historical marker located on Hwy 19)</u>

Geological

Near the end of the last glacial period, this site overlooked a colossal river called Glacial River Warren. Between 11,700 and 9,500 years ago, there were two separate spans of time during which this immense river flowed for a total of about 1,000 years. With its headwaters near the site of Browns Valley, it was the main outlet for Glacial Lake Agassiz, an enormous glacial meltwater lake. At its maximum, this lake covered the combined areas of the Red River valley, northwestern Minnesota, and much of Canada southwest of Hudson Bay. The tremendous power of Glacial River Warren cut through layers of sediment (clay, silt, sand and gravel and boulders deposited by glaciers) and clay-rich deposits of weathered bedrock all the way down to scour some of the oldest bedrock in North America.

Morton contains the largest quarry in Renville County. Rainbow granite is quarried here. This type of stone is well known for its tremendous quality. It is one of the oldest and hardest stones available.

Some of the bedrock exposed on the valley floor is as old as 3.6 billion years. It is called Morton Gneiss (pronounced "nice"), and it formed deep in the earth's crust, where extreme heat and pressure changed, or metamorphosed, an earlier kind of rock. The extreme conditions may have resulted from small continental masses colliding and combining, the process that built the early North American continent. The beautiful and distinctive banding of colorful minerals within the Morton Gneiss make it an attractive building stone, which is used around the world.

Above the Morton Gneiss and visible in places along the valley walls is a layer up to 45 meters thick of gneiss decomposed by weathering. This deep and intense weathering occurred about 100 million years ago when Minnesota's climate was subtropical. Prolonged exposure to a warm atmosphere and acidic rainwater caused clay minerals of the kaolin group. These white kaolin clays are mined throughout the river valley and are used for cement, bricks and ceramics.

In most places, the kaolin deposits are buried by tens of meters of glacial sediment, deposited during the Ice Age of the last two million years. Glacial sediment can be seen along the valley walls, and the modern Minnesota River exposes more in the valley bottom.

(Historical marker located on Hwy 19)

Fairfax

Place Name

This town was given its name by the president of the Minneapolis and St. Louis Railroad company, Eben Ryder, for his native county in Virginia.

Fort Ridgely
(See Hwy 14 - pg 287)

Bechyn

Local Landmark

Bechyn is situated near the Birch Coulee State Park. This 80-acre park was established in 1895 to commemorate the Native American battles in 1862. The Lower Agency building in the park is the site where the first attack occurred in the 1862 uprising.

Olivia

Place Name

The town is named after the friend of a prominent railroad official. Chief Engineer Albert Bowman Rogers may have suggested the name after the woman who was the first station agent in Ortonville. Her name was Olive. Or perhaps it was for the official of the Chicago, Milwaukee and St. Paul Railroad, Russell Sage's wife, Margaret Olivia.

General Trivia

Olivia is Minnesota's "corn capital". In fact, Corn Capital Days is an annual celebration of the town's booming agricultural industry. In 1978, the head of the town's festival parade was singer, Olivia Newton John.

Prominent People

Native Kathleen Winsor is the author of the novel Forever Amber.

> A giant 25 feet tall ear of corn made of fiberglass towers above some of the trees in the town's Memorial Park.

Danube

Place Name

The town was named after the European river, the Danube.

Blomkest

Place Name

The town originally named in honor of the mayor of Hutchinson and called Kester, after C.E. Kester. However, the name was often confused with a similar sounding town's name (Kiester) in the southern part of the state, that they changed the name to Blomkest. The new name is a combination of the original and that of an early native Swedish settler, Blom Olof Anderson.

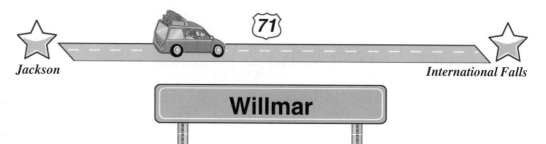

Willmar

Place Name

Willmar was founded in 1869 by the St. Paul and Pacific Railroad and named after Leon Willmar. Willmar, a Belgium native, was living in London working as the agent for the European bondholders of the St. Paul and Pacific Railroad Company.

Geological

The agricultural land of the Willmar region has a history that dates back 60 million years, when an inland sea covered the Great Plains from the Gulf of Mexico to the Arctic Ocean. As the adjacent land eroded and life in the sea flourished, sediments for sandstone, shale, and limestone were deposited on the sea floor and eventually became rock. Later, when the sea level dropped, these sedimentary rocks were exposed on dry land.

About 14,000 years ago, during the end of the Ice Age of the last two million years, glaciers advancing southward from Canada scraped up and carried great quantities of those sedimentary marine rocks from Manitoba and northwestern Minnesota. When the ice melted, rock fragments, crushed by the moving ice, were left as a layer of glacial drift across the state. This drift was rich in lime, magnesia and potash, so became a great natural resource as the parent material for fertile soils over much of the state.

Earlier glaciers also advanced across Minnesota from the north-northeast about 25,000 years ago. This ice eroded the igneous bedrock in Ontario and the Lake Superior region and deposited a reddish, more sandy and rocky drift. Soils that developed from this parent material are not as fertile.

Most of the surface material in the Willmar region is the rich, fertile sediment deposited by the more recent glaciers from the northwest. The belt of hilly topography and abundant lakes northwest of Willmar, however, once marked the edge of a glacial lobe from the north-northeast. The margin of that ice left piles of sediment there at its farthest advance, forming a glacial deposit called a terminal moraine. While this moraine is buried under the more recent drift from the northwest, its effect on the topography is still very evident.

(Historical marker located on Hwy 71)

Guri Endresen-Rossland whose heroic deeds have resulted in her being acclaimed one of the most outstanding heroines of the nation.

Prominent People

A monument has been placed to honor Guri Endresen-Rooseland and other early settlers of the Solomon Lake community. The settlers were predominately immigrants from Hardanger, Norway. Among the special characteristics of these pioneers were their courage and faith in Almighty God.

No one of them exemplified these characteristics more than Guri Endresen-Rossland whose heroic deeds have resulted in her being acclaimed one of the most outstanding heroines of the nation.

During the Sioux Indian Uprising of 1862, a band of

Indians attacked the Endresen cabin, killing the husband, Lars, and a son, Endre. Guri Endresen escaped with her infant daughter, Anna, by hiding in the cellar. After the Indians left, she hitched the family oxen to a cart and set out with her child for refuge at Forest City, some thirty miles away. En route she stopped at the homes of other settlers, attending to the needs of those wounded in the massacre. Some she took with her. All travel was by darkness.

Following the submission of Chief Little Crow and his warriors, Guri returned to the family homestead to rebuild her home.

<u>(Historical marker located on Hwy 5)</u>

Local Landmark

The Vikor Lutheran Church Congregation was organized at the Endresen cabin in 1871. It was named after the Vikor Church in Norway which was built by Lars Endresen.

> Willmar is famous for Kaffe Fest, a festival celebrating the Scandinavian tradition of having a cup of coffee. Needless to say, the caffeine intake is at its highest level during this sociable festival.

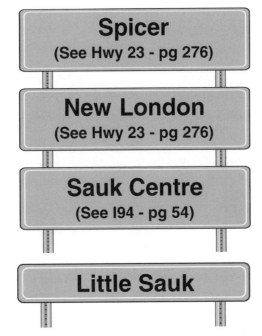

Spicer
(See Hwy 23 - pg 276)

New London
(See Hwy 23 - pg 276)

Sauk Centre
(See I94 - pg 54)

Little Sauk

Place Name

Named in reference to the band of five Sauk Indians living in the Lake Osakis area.

Long Praire

Place Name

Named for the river that winds its way through a long and relatively narrow prairie.

Historical Significance

In 1848, an Indian agency was established in the region. Some Winnebago from Iowa were moved here to serve as a buffer between the Chippewa and the Sioux.

In 1851, Francis Vivaldi established a mission school for the Winnebago tribe. Vivaldi ended up leading a fairly significant life. He was appointed as consul to Rio de Janeiro and Argentina by President Lincoln.

Browerville

Place Name

As an artist, Kieselewski was the youngest person ever to be awarded the prestigious Prix de Rome Prize.

Browerville was named for Abraham D. Brower. He was a pioneer in the region and became the chairman of the first board of county commissioners in 1867.

Local Landmark

St. Joseph's Catholic church is one of the most notable sites in the town. Located in the heart of the city, its Romanesque style architecture complements its surroundings.

The church contains some of the most beautiful sculptures in the northwest. Joseph Kieselewski is the Browerville sculptor responsible for these outstanding works of art.

Clarissa

Place Name

Land speculator, George Bischoffsheim owned the name in the area, despite the fact he never visited the area. The town was given its name by his agent, George Howe, who slightly altered the name of Clarisse Bischoffeheim.

Eagle Bend

Place Name

This town receives its name for its location on a notable bend on Eagle Creek

Bertha

Place Name

The town is named after the first white settler in the area, Bertha Ristau, the wife of the local postmaster.

Hewitt

Place Name

The town was started on land donated by Henry Hewitt who was an area farmer.

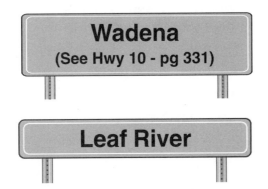

Wadena

(See Hwy 10 - pg 331)

Leaf River

Place Name

The name comes from the name given to the mountains and river by the Ojibwe, referred to as Leaf Hills.

Sebeka

Place Name

The name of this town is a modification of the Chippewa word, "Se-be-kaun". In English, this word translates to "by the made ditch or channel". Because of its location on the Red Eye River, the early settlers were probably trying to come up with a word meaning "by the river". Apparently, "by the channel" was the closest they could come.

Place Name

Menahga is a Chippewa word meaning "blueberries".

Local Landmark

Menahga has a statue of Saint Uhro standing in the heart of town. Uhro is holding a pitchfork with a grasshopper impaled on the tines.

Uhro was a hero in Finland for driving the grasshopper plague out of his county with a mysterious chant.

Place Name

Originally known as Mantor, after the county. It took its name from former Minnesota Governor Lucius Frederick Hubbard, who began flour milling in the area around 1870.

Place Name

It was the park like setting beside the banks that inspired Frank Rice to suggest the name.

Prominent People

Congressional Medal of Honor Recipient, Lloyd C. Hawks is from Park Rapids.

Many fishing dreams have been inspired by the world's largest tiger muskie statue here.

Place Name

The town was named for either Ben Nevis in western Scotland, the highest mountain in Great Britain, or for Nevis, an island of the West Indies.

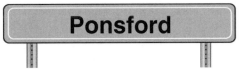

Akeley

Place Name

Healy Cady Akeley built a large sawmill here and established the Akeley Lumber Company. With the depletion of the available pine timber, his sawmills would eventually close. Nevertheless the city would be developed on large tracts of timber land previously owned by Akeley.

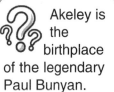

Akeley is the birthplace of the legendary Paul Bunyan.

Local Landmark

There is the world's largest statue of the legendary Paul Bunyan, the greatest lumberjack ever, kneeling down on one knee, gently offering his big hand.

Ponsford

Place Name

Ponsford was named for Orville Ponsford, an early settler.

Historical Significance

For some time after the first settlement, roads were mere trails and kept open with great difficulty. Snow shoes were used by almost everyone and "many a sack of flour was carried weary miles on the shoulders of a man trudging through the trackless snow".

Two Inlets

Place Name

Name refers to the two inflowing streams that come together at the north end of Two Inlet Lake.

Lake Itasca

Historical Significance

The name Itasca was coined specifically from the Latin words "Veritas Caput", literally meaning "true head", by Henry Rowe Schoolcraft in 1832.

Led by Ozawindib, an Ojibwe guide who knew the upper reaches of the Mississippi River and its headwater lakes, Schoolcraft was able to document the true source of America's

greatest river, a feat that had eluded many previous explorers, including Zebulon Pike, Lewis Case, and Giacomo Beltrami.

(Historical marker located in Itasca State Park)

The name Itasca was coined specifically from the Latin words "Veritas Caput", literally meaning "true head", by Henry Rowe Schoolcraft in 1832.

Local Landmark

Lake Itasca rests by the Itasca State Park on the Mississippi River. This is one of the most famous state parks in the nation because within it lies the headwater of the Mississippi River. From this spot, the mighty river flows 2,500 miles into the Gulf of Mexico.

The park is also home to some very rare wildlife. Trumpeter Sans and Bald Eagles can be seen gracefully perched in the park's trees.

Geological

The diversified scenery of Minnesota, of which the Itasca Park area is one phase, is due to the location of the state in the approximate center of the continent. Situated midway between the Atlantic and Pacific oceans, Hudson Bay and the Gulf of Mexico, the state has within its boundaries three principal divides in the watersheds of North America. Minnesota lacks the rugged topography and high elevations found in most continental divides. Its highest elevation 2,300 feet on the Mesabi Range, is in close proximity to its lowest, the surface of Lake Superior, 602 feet above see level.

The general surface of the state slopes from the north-central portion near Itasca Park, in four directions toward its distant and opposite corners.

The 10,000 lakes of Minnesota cover 5,600 square miles, an average of 1 square mile of water for every 15 of land. This unprecedented supply of water, which has a surface exceeding the water area of any other state, finds its way to the ocean through the Hudson Bay, the Great Lakes and the Gulf of Mexico.

(Historical marker located at Peace Pipe Springs in Itasca State Park)

Place Name

The lake and town were named for an early pioneer by the name of George Kraemer.

Place Name

This railway station was named for the cruiser, Thomas Nary of Park Rapids. As a cruiser he was responsible for selecting timber lands that lumbering manufacturers in Minneapolis could purchase.

Bemidji
(See Hwy 2 - pg 347)

Turtle River

Place Name

Turtle River name is actually a translation from an Ojibwe word. David Thompson suggested the name because he said the shapes of many of the small bays in the area gave the appearance of a turtle.

Tenstrike

Place Name

Almon White suggested the name alluding to getting down all ten pins with the first ball, known as a strike, while bowling.

Blackduck

Place Name

Named after the river which derived its name from the Cormorant, a ring necked duck the Ojibwe translated to mean black.

Funkley

Place Name

Matt Fisher requested the name in honor of a county lawyer, Henry Funkley.

Mizpah

Place Name

The name meaning watchtower in Hebrew, was given to a parting salutation in reference to the bible verse; (Genesis 31:49) "The Lord watch between me and thee, when we are absent from one another."

Place Name

Name for the daughter of Westley Horton, the area postmaster.

Place Name

First known simply as Ripple the name was changed when the Minnesota and International Falls railroad arrived, to describe the swift and beautiful rapids of the Big Fork River.

Place Name

The Big Fork River descends 29 feet over gneiss and mica schist ledges giving a grand description of the falls.

Place Name

Two brothers, Joe and Frank Pelland, from Quebec, Canada settled near the junction of the Rainy and Little Fork Rivers.

Local Landmark

Just slightly south of Pelland is the Grand Mound. The largest Mound stands 40 feet high and measures 325 feet around. Four other smaller mounds are located at the Mouth of the Big Fork River. The mounds date back more than 2,000 years ago and were created by the Laurel Tribe.

> The Grand Mound is the largest Indian burial mound in the Upper Midwest.

International Falls

Historical Significance

The Rainy River serves as the boundary between the United States and Canada between Rainy Lake and Lake of the Woods.

From the late 1600s to the 1820s the chain of waterways of Minnesota's border lakes formed a segment that was the thoroughfare of a vast fur trading empire. At its longest, this water route stretched from Montreal to Lake Athabasca, and over it a treasure in furs from the North American wilderness reached the markets of Europe and Asia. A mainstay of this commerce were the rollicking, indomitable men who paddled the trader's canoes and packed his goods on their back over portages. Mainly French-Canadians, they were called "voyageurs", the French term meaning travelers.

Over these waters early each summer they paddled fur-laden canoes eastward to inland depots like Rainy Lake, Grand Portage, or Michilimackinac; each July they returned, carrying trade goods and supplies to the isolated wintering posts. They were a fiercely proud breed, who could paddle eighteen hours a day or carry a load of 450 pounds and yet retain a lusty joy in their work. Decked out in gay sashes and ostrich plumes, they strutted, quarreled, consorted with the Indians, and lightened their toil with French folk songs, gay and rhythmic or hauntingly sad. Today their route, scarcely touched by the modern world, remains open to all who seek adventure.

> The town was originally named Koochiching, but was later changed to International Falls to reflect its location on the Canadian border near the waterfalls of the Rainy River.

(Historical marker located off Hwy 71 and 11)

* * * *

As part of the fabled "Voyageurs Highway" of rivers and lakes, Rainy Lake and the Rainy River saw a traffice of fur trade canoes for nearly two centuries before the first steamer, the Louise Thompson, was put into service in 1875. Her mission was to help build a canal and locks at Koochiching Falls, connecting the lake and the river and encouraging the movement of Canadian homesteaders into the area around Fort Francis, Ontario. Work on the canal was soon abandoned, however, when the development of the Canadian Pacific Railroad bypassed Fort Francis and opened more desirable frontier areas further west.

Steamer traffic on the 90 miles of river "highway" from Fort Francis to Rat Portage (later Kenora) on Lake of the Woods boomed with the area's settlement in the 1890s. During 1894 a total of 27 steamers and 29 barges carried a total of 2,100 tons of freight and 20,086 passengers on the lake and river system.

The big boat news of 1897 was the maiden voyage of a new steel steamer, the Kenora, hailed as a "floating palace" with electric lights and accommodations for 200 passengers. The editor of the local newspaper confidently expected that such a "first class steamer would

result in summer resorts" on both sides of the Rainy River.

Steamer traffic declined in the 1900s with the arrival of railroad service. By the time the expected summer resorts were a reality, the steamers that had carried excited passengers on delightful summer excursions were gone.

<u>(Historical marker located on Hwy 53)</u>

Industry

The Boise-Cascade paper milling process is really quite interesting. First the pulpwood is sent through slashers, which cut the wood into shorter lengths. Then these smaller pieces are sent through barking drums, where all the bark is removed. The chip machines then slice the sticks that remain into even smaller pieces. The wood is then cooked and steamed in an acid that disintegrates the wood. After the process is complete, the wood is transformed into a fine fiber. This pulp mix is combined with sulphite pulp, treated, and finally drained. Lastly, this liquidy mix goes through a series of hot drying rollers and emerges as dry paper in less than one minute.

General Trivia

The name and climate of International Falls eventually became the inspiration for Rocky and Bullwinkle creator Jay Ward to call the characters imaginary hometown "Frostbite Falls".

International Falls is the headquarters of the Border Patrol and continues to thrive as an industrial center.

There are three branches of the Border Patrol. These employees can be identified by the color of their uniforms. Immigration Border Patrol Agents wear forest green. Customs Border Patrol agents wear dark gray. Lastly, Customs Inspectors wear dark blue.

These agents work their hardest to make crossing the border as safe and easy as possible. To prevent the prevalent problem of "border-jumping", drivers are encouraged to avoid picking up hitchhikers.

* * * *

Minnesota paid tribute to Smokey the Bear in International Falls by constructing a statue of the forest fire prevention hero.

Local Landmark

Opening in 1975, Voyageurs National Park is Minnesota's only National Park with 219,000 acres of water, forests, swamps and islands.

Prominent People

Jim Bakker, along with his wife, Tammy Faye LeValley (from International Falls) would co-found the Praise the Lord Ministry establishing the largest Christian television network in the world.

Tammy Faye divorced her husband when he was serving time in jail on fraud and conspiracy charges, a charge for which she escapes conviction, and marries Roe Messner.

HIGHWAY 61

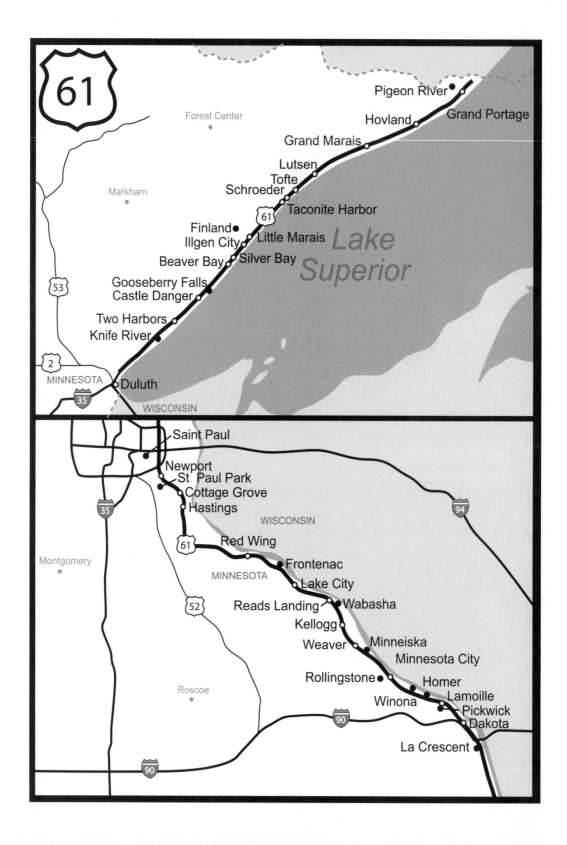

198

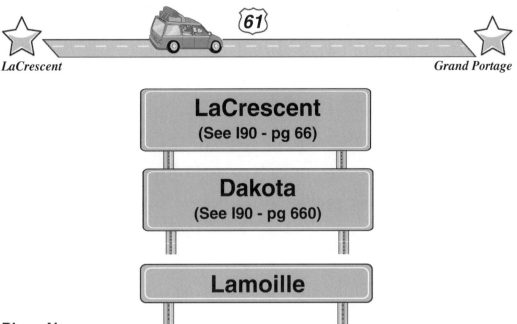

Place Name

This town was established at the point where the stage route crossed the Mississippi River. Both the town and the river have the same name as a river and county in northern Vermont.

Local Landmark

Near the little village of LaMoille rests the historic King Estate. Three separate properties make up this impressive estate: a main house, a studio house, and a caretaker's cottage. It is a mixture of Pueblo Revival, Prairie, and Viennese architectural elements.

Local Landmark

The Pickwick Mill is situated by the town dam, near the Mississippi River on Big Trout creek. This stone building was constructed in 1856. Originally, the building had six floors, but the top two were destroyed in a tornado in 1907.

This town gets its name from the Charles Dickens serial published from 1836-37 known as the Pickwick Papers.

Place Name

Although many communities across the country have similar names bearing the name of the early Greek epic poet, this town was given its name by Willard Bunnell for his brother's birthplace in Homer, New York.

Historical Significance

Francois du Chouquette, known as the first white man to settle in the area, built a small home in what is now Homer in 1830. As a blacksmith, he was hoping to trade with the nearby Wabasha tribe. When Sac and Fox raids on the Sioux became prevalent in the area, du Chouquette made the decision to relocate.

Local Landmark

The Gothic Revival Bunnell House is a cottage that was constructed in 1855. The house was built by the first settler after Francois du Chouquette, Willard Bunnell. He wanted to have a panoramic view of the Mississippi River. The two-story porch that faces the river allows for a fantastic view. The lower floor of the one-and-a-half story house is comprised of stone and ornate Gothic detail.

Place Name

Winona is a variation of the name given to every first-born Sioux girl in a family (Wenona).

Historical Significance

In 1851, Winona was a completely barren land. Occasionally, fur traders and Natives would make their way through the land, but seldom would anyone decide to settle here.

 Early river men called this region "Sand Prairie" or the more common name, "Wapasha's Prairie" after the powerful Chief Wapasha of the Dakota Sioux tribe.

As the nation pushed its growth west, explorers Father Louis Hennepin, Zebulon Pike, George Catlin, and the French fur traders at one time or another came upon the area known today as Winona.

Captain Orren Smith believed Winona had the potential to be more than just a place to pass by. He wanted to settle a town in the Winona vicinity that could be used as a stopping point for ships to refuel. His vision caused him to drop off his carpenter and friend, Erwin Johnson, in Winona. Smith ordered Johnson to settle the town. This was hard to do in barren lands without trees. Consequently, Smith retrieved wood for buildings and homes from the adjacent Wisconsin River bank and Winona began its early development.

Within two years of its founding, Winona was a full-fledged river town with a population of 300. Settlers from the east and immigrants from Europe journeyed up the Mississippi to Winona. Winona was the last source of supplies before heading west to establish new homes and farms. Wheat became the money crop, and by the 1860s, the nation's wheat belt was in the Upper Midwest.

To improve access to the river for grain shipments, railroads were built. In 1862, the Winona and St. Peter Railroad was constructed west from Winona. This later became the Chicago and Northwestern Railroad. Winona's market access soon extended to the South

Dakota border.

Railroad expansion eliminated the more gentile passenger steamboat, but river traffic increased as towboats bulled giant rafts of lumber from northern Wisconsin forests to Winona and other cities down the length of the Mississippi.

Between 1870 and 1900, Winona became one of the major timber processing and marketing centers in the nation.

Wealth was created by entrepreneurs who were in the wheat business. Money made from western agriculture and transportation businesses built numerous mansions in the community.

Just when things were looking up, tragedy struck in 1878. A scorching hot and dry period with very little precipitation killed the entire wheat crop. This tragedy taught farmers the value of diversification in planting. With time, the farmers successfully bounced back.

Geological

From Winona to LaCrosse, the Mississippi River valley displays its greatest depth as it extends vertically through more than 240 meters of a sedimentary-rock plateau. Here, Highway 61 follows the narrow strip between the river and the steep bluffs that mark the valley's western wall. The valley walls are composed of sandstone and carbonate rock, which formed from sand and lime mud deposited about 500 million years ago in a warm, shallow sea that covered much of what is now North America. The lower, more sloping parts of the valley walls are composed mostly of weakly cemented sandstone, which erodes easily. On the upper parts of the walls, steep cliffs shape the bluffs. The cliffs are composed of dolostone, a chemically altered limestone that is resistant to erosion.

Bluffs are formed as the Mississippi or a tributary cuts into the soft sandstone, initiating sandstone rock falls that undercut the dolostone. The dolostone then breaks along vertical joints, leaving steep cliffs. Two of the most prominent bluffs in the area, King's Bluff and Queen's Bluff, are visible on the west side of the valley. Both are within Great River Bluffs State Park and are designated Scientific and Natural Areas by the Minnesota Department of Natural Resources for their unusual geology and rare biological communities.

These bluffs are within the "Driftless Area," an area of deeply eroded stream valleys primarily east of the Mississippi River and covering southwestern Wisconsin. During the Ice Age of the last two million years, glacial ice never passed over and leveled this area, and no drift, or glacially carried sediment (clay, silt, sand, gravel, and boulders) was deposited here. However, the landscape before you was blanketed with a layer of loess, a windblown, tan-colored rock dust. This dust was carried by winds from floodplains still bare of vegetation, which were repeatedly loaded with very fine sediment by streams that drained melting glaciers. Today, a distinctive and fertile soil has developed in the top of the loess, which helps to give rise to the diverse and sometimes unique plant communities found on these bluffs.

 The valley walls are composed of sandstone and carbonate rock, which formed from sand and lime mud deposited about 500 million years ago in a warm, shallow sea that covered much of what is now North America.

(Historical marker located on Hwy 61)

Local Landmark

"Sugar Loaf" towers 85 feet above the top of a 500-foot bluff.

On the southern edge of town lies the man-made bluff known as "Sugar Loaf". The Sioux used to hold ceremonies on top of it when it was just a large hill in the backdrop of Winona.

The quarrying operation that resulted in the unusual formation at the top of Sugar Loaf provided limestone to build Winona's sidewalks and trim for many brick buildings before work was discontinued before World War I.

Rising over Winona, the peak in its original configuration as a rounded dome with a fringe of evergreen on the crown was well known to early explorers, traders, tourists and river boat pilots.

An often repeated legend says that the mountain was Chief Wabasha's red cap, originally presented to him by a British officer.

(Historical marker located on Hwy 14 and 61)

* * * *

A migration from Poland in the late 1800s to the area resulted in the largest concentration of Kashubian Poles in the United States. As a result Winona established the Polish Cultural Institute.

* * * *

Winona is also home to a very strange type of prairie grass. At Goat Prairie in Great River Bluffs State Park, there is a prairie grass that grows on a slope so steep that only goats are able to graze it. It can withstand both the intense heat of summer and the below freezing winter evenings. Very few plants can survive throughout a whole year in such rapidly changing weather conditions.

* * * *

Winona's newspaper, "The Daily Republican", claims to be the first published daily paper after Minnesota's admission into the union.

* * * *

Winona also opened the first college west of the Mississippi, which is now part of Winona State University.

Prominent People

Winona Ryder's real named is Winona Horowitz. She was named after her hometown.

Winona Ryder made a name for herself in big screen productions such as Beetlejuice, Reality Bites, and Girl, Interrupted.

Ryder dedicated the film Little Women (1994) to Polly Klass, who was kidnapped and brutally murdered. She offered a $200,000 reward for anyone with information on the subject, and remains a strong supporter in the Polly Klass Foundation.

* * * *

Swimmer, Tracy Caulkings is from Winona. In 1978, a 15-year-old Caulkins took five gold medals in the world championship. In the 1984 Olympics, she took an additional three gold

medals. Throughout her successful career, Tracy has collected a total of 48 national titles. She also set 61 American records and five world records.

* * * *

Settling in Winona, William Windom, originally from Belmont City, Ohio would represent Minnesota in the United States Congress as a congressman and a senator. He later became secretary of the treasury under President James Garfield and Benjamin Harrison.

> William Windom's likeness appeared on the 1891 two-dollar bill.

* * * *

Former POW Gordon Larson, played himself in the movie *We Can Keep You Forever*.

* * * *

Producer Helene Lynn-Nash was originally from Winona. She was the associate producer of the TV movies, *Jewel*, *Fatal Judgment*, and *Mafia Princess*.

Place Name

Robert Pike named this area for the territory a colony of New York settlers were coming to establish on behalf of the Western Farm and Village Association.

Historical Significance

Minnesota City sits serenely on the freely flowing Mississippi waters. A group of New York mechanics called the "Western Farm and Village Association" had hopes of coming to the mystic land with a dream of change. Unfortunately, the dream of happily inhabiting this colony transformed into tragedy.

In 1852, steamboat captains came up the Mississippi and ran into several of these men who were bound for the city. The captains who knew the land well assured the men that the utopia they were searching for didn't really exist. The Minnesota City area was heavily overgrown. The travelers were in obvious disbelief and continued to press on for the perfect place they were seeking out. At the time, they referred to the city as Rollingstone.

Once the settlers got to their utopian land, they realized it was far from perfect. It was difficult and dangerous to get to because there were steep fords that had to be crossed. Many of them ended up suffering because of their lack of knowledge about farming and pioneer life. Many people died from disease or starvation, and the few who remained either moved back to New York or roughed it out and tried to develop farms.

Nameless graves of the dead now rest within the city. The discovery and settlement of Minnesota City is one of the most tragic stories about the settlement of Minnesota.

Rollingstone

Place Name

Although the name "Rolling Stone" didn't work for Minnesota City, it did work for another establishment just up the road. Rolling Stone is settled on the banks of the Rolling Stone River.

Historical Significance

The town was founded immediately after the Civil War by German colonists.

General Trivia

This town is unique in that it has close to 60 Native American burial mounds. Some of the mounds stretch more than 100 feet in length. Some of the mounds have been excavated discovering many beautiful Native American relics.

Place Name

This town get its name from the Whitewater River in the area. The Dakota translation Minne or Mini means water, and ska means white.

 The Weaver Dunes Scientific and Natural Area conservation center displays America's largest population of extremely rare Blanding's Turtle.

Place Name

This town started out as a railroad village named for William Weaver, the areas first settler from New York State.

Place Name

This town was named by the officers of the Chicago, Milwaukee, and St. Paul Railroad Company, in honor of a Milwaukee gentleman, L.H. Kellogg, who furnished the depot signs.

Historical Significance

Kellogg was the thriving transportation hub of the area in the 1800s. Tons of cabbage was

produced in the vicinity and hauled to the train depot for shipment.

Today the sandy soil and hot weather produces the sweet watermelon that is harvested in late August.

Rumor has it that the farmers use a spend breed of dogs to help determine when the melons are ripe. A breed of "lassie" sniffs the melons on the vines and paws at the fruit if it is ripe enough for picking. Amazing, they call this breed of dogs, "melon collies".

> Lark Toys is one of the largest children's specialty toy stores in North America and features the amazing hand carved Lark Carousel.

Wabasha

Place Name

The town was originally named Cratte's Landing in honor of Oliver Cratte. He was an Englishman who built a blacksmith shop in the picturesque town as early as 1838. This shop created the expansion of the city into a successful trading post. Its early trading post days contributed to the growth of the city.

Wabasha is renamed in honor of the Sioux Chief Wa-pa-shaw. Translated from Sioux, this means "Red Leaf".

As a general in the British Army, Chief Wabasha, leading 200 Dakotas, attacked Spanish positions at St. Louis in 1780. This is Minnesotans only known involvement in the Revolutionary War.

Local Landmark

Wabasha boasts the oldest hotel in Minnesota. The Anderson House on Main Street was constructed in 1856. The famous Anderson House Hotel is not only famous for its age, but it is also famous for a special feature that it offers guests. In the 1970s, the hotel started rent-a-cat service. Interested guests can rent a cat to keep them company at night.

* * * *

Wabasha also contains an Eagle Watch Observatory. This observatory is recognized by both the state and the nation for having the best area to view the Bald eagle in its natural habitat.

Between November and March, anywhere from 50 to 100 bald eagles call Wabasha their home. The eagle prefer this place because the waters of the Mississippi remain unfrozen here, making hunting for these graceful birds much easier.

> Wabasha is home to the films, "Grumpy Old Men" and "Grumpier Old Men".

General Trivia

The films "Grumpy Old Men" and "Grumpier Old Men" were based on local lore and followed the story of two-ice fisherman on the upper Mississippi River. A Hastings native, Mark Johnson, wrote the screenplay with the film action taking place in this town, the home of Johnson's grandfather.

Prominent People

Larry Bradenburg, born in Wabasha, almost turned down his role in Mo' Money in 1992 which led to other roles including guest appearances in Ally McBeal, Touched by an Angel, The Practice, West Wing and Boston Public; as well as the movies, Fargo, Mighty Joe Young and others.

Place Name

Charles Read came to America from England when he was tens years old. He served in the American army in the Canadian rebellion, was captured by the British and expected to be hanged, was pardoned and returned to the United States to take charge of a trading post along the Mississippi River that would eventually bare his name.

Historical Significance

When it was originally founded, Reads Landing was one of the busiest ports on the Mississippi.

In lumbering and steamboat days, Reads Landing was the industrious gathering place for all the workers and inhabitants of the surrounding area. The taverns in town did excellent business because of the town's reputation as a gathering place. By the 1850s almost 20 hotels and boarding houses were constructed for the travelers coming in and out of Reads Landing.

Reads Landing eventually became one of the largest wheat shipping ports in the country.

Today, however, all of the signs of the eventful river days are long gone. Only a fraction of the many buildings that once stood in the town now remain.

Geological

Lake Pepin, a widening of the Mississippi River, occupies the river valley north of Reads Landing for a distance of 35 kilometers. The lake was created by the delta of Wisconsin's Chippewa River, which enters the Mississippi directly east of this site. The Chippewa, a relatively small river, has a much steeper gradient, or slope, than the Mississippi. This steeper slope causes a faster flow, which transports more sand and coarser gravel than the Mississippi can remove. Consequently, the sediments brought in by the Chippewa dam the Mississippi back in this gorge, thus forming Lake Pepin.

But this scene was not always so tranquil. About 10,000 years ago, near the end of the last glacial period, this site was submerged by a colossal river that spanned the gorge. The immense volume of water came from the combined discharge of Glacial River Warren draining Glacial Lake Agassis, Glacial River St. Croix draining Glacial Lake Duluth, and many smaller tributaries. That tremendous current eroded this gorge to its present width and flushed it clean of sediment, right down to the bedrock.

After the glacial melt waters were gone and the Mississippi dwindled, sediment from the Chippewa dammed the main channel. At that time Lake Pepin extended for 100 kilometers,

all the way back to where St. Paul is today. Where the Mississippi first entered the lake, its sediments deposited to form a delta. The delta has since advanced downstream by progressively filling in the head of the lake and thus reducing its length.

The top of the bluffs that line the shores of Lake Pepin are about 140 meters above the surface of the lake. The walls of the gorge are composed of sandstone, shale and dolostone.

These rocks were deposited as sediment in a warm, shallow sea that covered the area of southeastern Minnesota and much of North America about 500 million years ago. The rock-walled gorge extends 46 meters below the lake surface. It has been filled to the present lake bottom mostly with clays that have settled out of the still waters of the lake.

<u>(Historical marker on Hwy 61)</u>

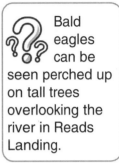

Bald eagles can be seen perched up on tall trees overlooking the river in Reads Landing.

Place Name

Lake City is nestled on the scenic shores of Lake Pepin and thus its location gives it its name.

General Trivia

This lake is simply a widening of the Mississippi River and is the widest point on the Mississippi.

This stretch of Lake Pepin is well known for its sudden, strong winds that often times catch boaters off guard. In 1890, the Seawing shipwrecked just North of Lake City, claiming 98 lives. Thus, boaters in this region must always be ready for the unexpected.

Invention

In 1922, Ralph Samuelson bought two Pine boards, heated the boards, and finally placed them in a vise for two days so that they curved upward. He attached these funny-shaped boards to his feet, and then he attached a rope to his brother's boat. By 1925, Samuelson was "water-skiing" atop the waters of Lake Pepin at 80 mph.

A statue honoring Samuelson and his challenging outdoor invention was built in Lake City in 1976.

Ralph Samuelson is hailed by the American Water Ski Association as the "Father of Water Skiing".

Frontenac

Place Name

Frontenac Station was established as the post office and railroad station for the early settlement of Frontenac. The town was named after Louis de Baude Comte de Frontenac.

Historical Significance

In September 1727, a party of French soldiers and traders, under the leadership of Rene Boucher, Sieur de la Perriere, built a fortified post on Lake Pepin from which they traded for two years with the Dakota (Sioux) Indians. They were there to secure an alliance with the Dakota in order to gain access to the fur and possible mineral wealth of the area and to eventually press westward in search of the "Great Western Sea".

Accompanying the group were two Jesuit missionaries, Michel Guignas and Nicholas de Gonner. A letter from Father Guignas to the Governor General of New France, Marquis de Beauharnois, reported that "the day after landing axes were applied to trees, and four days later the forest was entirely finished". Variously referred to as the "Post Among the Sioux" or "Fort Beauharnois," it included several trading houses, a guardhouse, quarters for the members of the party, and a chapel named in honor of St. Michael the Archangel.

Several trading posts were built on Lake Pepin by the French from 1686 until they abandoned the area in the 1750s during the French and Indian War. Most are believed to have been located on the east side of the lake, but the remains of only one, near Stockholm, Wisconsin, have been found. The locations of all the others, including Fort Beauharnois, are unknown.

(Historical marker located on Hwy 61 in Frontenac State Park)

The breathtaking scenery is so inspirational, that several famous authors and artists come to the area to write and paint. This includes "House of Vanished Splendor", written by William McNally.

Local Landmark

The first Episcopal bishop of Minnesota, Henry Whipple, built the Little Gray Episcopal Church in 1867 that is found along the shores of Lake Pepin in Frontenac.

Geological

Frontenac State Park offers a magnificent view of the Mississippi River valley. The valley is carved into rock that was deposited as sediment in a warm, shallow sea that covered the area of southeastern Minnesota and much of North America about 500 million years ago. The upper parts of the bluffs are composed mostly of dolostone, a chemically altered limestone that is resistant to erosion. The lower parts are mostly weakly cemented sandstone. This layering of resistant rock over erosive rock helps keep the bluffs steep.

During the Ice Age of the last two million years, tremendous torrents of glacial melt water repeatedly discharged from huge glacial lakes in the region of northern Minnesota and Canada. The forceful currents eroded

this river valley to its present width and flushed it clean of sediment, right down to the bedrock. This colossal river was much higher than the Mississippi is today, and locally it flowed through both the main channel before you and a secondary channel, which passes just south of the bluffs along Highway 61/63.

Today, the Mississippi River is but a trickle compared to its volume when it drained melt water from the glaciers. Its much slower current is unable to wash away all the sediment that tributary streams carry into the valley, so the valley is slowly filling. Here, the valley contains Lake Pepin, a river lake formed behind the delta of Wisconsin's Chippewa River. The Chippewa enters the Mississippi near Wabasha, about 27 kilometers downstream. Its delta is large enough to dam the Mississippi back into this valley. Two other rivers have built deltas into the lake near here; the Rush River to the north on the Wisconsin side, and Wells Creek to the south on the Minnesota side. Visible just downstream on the right-hand shore are Willow Point and Sand Point (more distant), both parts of the Wells Creek delta.

(Historical marker located on Hwy 61 in Frontenac State Park)

Place Name

Zebulon Pike came to the Red Wing region in 1805. Upon arrival, Pike realized the Dakota were already peacefully settled in the region. The Chief of the Dakota was named "Whoo-pa-doo-to" which means "Wing of Scarlet". The name Red Wing resulted from the chief's name.

Historical Significance

By 1836, Swiss Protestants set up a trading post in Red Wing, and thus the city was on its way to quick development.

The 1900s marked the beginning of the potter and clay pipe manufacturing industries. A host of other industries developed as well. These include plate glass, linseed oil, dairying, leather, shoes and wood products.

Industry

Red Wing Pottery was one of Red Wing's most unique industries that produced crocks, water coolers, and cemetery monuments, as well as top quality sewer pipe from 1877 to 1967.

William Sweasy established the world-renown Red Wing Shoe Company in 1905.

Local Landmark

The St. James Hotel is another fine Minnesota site that is hailed on the National Register of Historic Places. In 1977, the Red Wing Shoe Company purchased the hotel and fully restored it to its original romantic Victorian style.

* * * *

209

> "The most beautiful prospect that imagination can form," wrote 18th century explorer, Jonathan Carver about the view from Barn Bluff. "Verdant plains, fruitful meadows, and numerous islands abound with the most varied trees... But above all, reaching as far as the eye can extend, is the majestic, softly flowing river".

Composed of various Paleozoic rocks, including sandstone, siltstone, and dolomite, and capped by some 35 feet of sand, gravel and loess deposited by glaciations, Barn Bluff has also been known as "LaGrange," or "Twin Mountain". Rising some 343 feet above the modern city of Red Wing, it is one of the best known natural features along the Mississippi and was climbed by many of Minnesota's early tourists, including Henry David Thoreau. Topographical engineer Stephen H. Long, who climbed it during his 1819 mapping expedition, found "the sublime and beautiful here blended in a most enchanting manner," and artist Henry Lewis called the view "incredibly beautiful" while remarking unfavorably on a "mass of rattlesnakes" to be found there.

Lewis also reported on an "Indian Legend" about the bluff. Many hundreds of years ago, according to the story, a mountain twice as big stood in this place. The inhabitants of two Dakota villages quarreled over possession of the mountain, and to settle the dispute without bloodshed, the Great Spirit divided it into two parts. He left one part here, and moved the other half downstream to the second village. The portion that was moved, according to Lewis's interpretation, rises above today's city of Winona and is called Sugar Loaf.

(Historical marker located on Hwy 61)

Geological

During the great ice ages the landscape of Minnesota was profoundly altered by continental glaciers in four major epochs of glaciation. In this area, as elsewhere, the closing stage of each epoch was characterized by the release of floods of melt water which eroded the broad valley of the Mississippi River 200 feet deeper than the present channel. Because the tributary streams carried less water than the main river they were unable to cut down so rapidly and consequently their valley floors had steeper slopes.

As the volume of melt water diminished with the depletion of the ice, the velocity of the main stream was reduced and it was no longer able to remove all of the sediment contributed by its high-gradient tributaries. Thus the valley was filled to its present level and exhibits a remarkable series of meanders, oxbow lakes, side channels, sloughs, swamps and tillable land.

(Historical marker located on Hwy 61 and 63)

Prominent People

Eugenie Anderson settled at a large farm in Red Wing. She was heavily involved in political movements in Minnesota. Her hard work and dedication paid off in 1949 when Harry Truman became President. Truman rewarded Anderson with the position of Ambassador to Denmark. She became the first woman in the United States to become an Ambassador to a foreign country. In 1951, Anderson also became the first female American to sign a treaty when she signed for the U.S. in a treaty of friendship with Denmark. In 1962, President Kennedy named her to be Ambassador for Bulgaria.

* * * *

For those of you who enjoy puffed rice, you can be thankful for Alexander Anderson of Red Wing. He discovered the food in 1901 while working for the New York Botanical Gardens. He tried cooking rice by putting some in a sealed test tube. When he opened the airtight tube the grain exploded. The puffy, eight time bigger than normal, rice was much easier to digest than other starches. Hearing of his invention, Minnesota grain companies brought him to the area to refine his process. His patent was purchased by Quaker Oaks who introduced the food at the St. Louis World's Fair in 1904.

Puffed Rice was invented by Red Wing native Alexander Anderson.

* * * *

William Colvill was born in New York state on April 5, 1830. As a young lawyer he moved to Red Wing in 1854, becoming the town's first city attorney.

On April 19, 1861, one week after the Confederate fired on Fort Sumter, a citizens' meeting was held at the courthouse in Red Wing in response to a call for Union soldiers. Colvill and 49 others eagerly enlisted as members of the "Goodhue Volunteers". Colvill is said to have leaped over the backs of others attending the meeting to be the first to sign the rolls. When the men were mustered into the army as Company F, First Minnesota Volunteers, they numbered 114, and they had elected Colvill captain.

He was a full colonel when, on the afternoon of July 2, 1863, he led the First Minnesota in a bloody charge against a far larger Confederate force at Gettysburg. There, the First bought for the Union Army a few minutes of precious time and thus turned the tide of battle. But 215 of the regiment's 262 officers and men, including Colonel Colvill, lay dead or wounded on the battlefield. General Winfield Scott Hancock, who ordered the charge, observed that "No soldier, on any field, in this, or any other country, ever displayed grander heroism".

As a disabled veteran, Colonel Colvill returned to Red Wing. He served as a member of the state legislature in 1865 and 1878, and was attorney general of Minnesota from 1866 to 1868. He died in Minneapolis on June 12, 1905.

(Historical marker located on Hwy 61)

Hastings

Place Name

The town's name was the result of drawing lots between several of its proprietors which Henry Hastings Sibley was the winner's preference.

Historical Significance

Hastings is the seat of Dakota County. It was originally known as Oliver's Grove, because in 1819 Lt. William G. Oliver and his troops camped here. Among the group was Joseph R. Brown, who became Hasting's first settler. He was the drummer boy, about fourteen years old, when he established a trading post here in 1833.

Local Landmark

Hastings has some very impressive Victorian architecture. One example is the limestone mansion of General William Gates Le Duc. The house was the first to be built in the Victorian Gothic style, and was copied exactly from Robert Downing's book of architectural designs. Until this time, the New England and Greek revival styles had prevailed.

* * * *

Just northwest of Hastings stood the home of Ignatius Donnelly, author, orator, politician, reformer, and prophet who was easily the best known Minnesotan of his time, both in the state and throughout the world

Donnelly, a lawyer from Philadelphia, moved west to Minnesota and launched a national campaign to attract settlers to Nininger City, a promising village of more than 500 residents when it was laid out around 1856. After the town melted away during the panic and depression of 1857, Donnelly turned his astonishing energy to politics, serving one term as lieutenant governor and three terms in Congress. For nearly 40 years his restless search for fair and effective social and economic institutions led him to play a role in virtually every agrarian reform movement of the late nineteenth century.

In addition to his fiery campaigns on behalf of farmers and workers, Donnelly wrote several unconventional and widely read books of popular science, including Atlantis, The Great Crypogram, Ragnarok and Caesar's Column in which he predicted the collapse of American society in the year 1988.

Donnelly lived at his Nininger City home until his death on January 1, 1901. Despite efforts to save it, the house was dismantled in 1949.

<u>(Historical marker located on County Road 42 & 87)</u>

Geological

Hastings lies just south and east of the limits of the last glaciation. About 20,000 years ago a lobe of ice, called the Superior lobe, advanced from the Lake Superior basin and crossed the ancient bedrock valley of the Mississippi River between St. Paul and Hastings. There it filled the valley with ice and sediment (silt, sand, gravel, and boulders). Glacial ice trapped in the valley was then covered by more sediment as the ice lobe slowly receded. The melting lobe deposited a large amount of sediment along its edge, creating a swath of hills of which a portion curves around the Twin Cities on the south and west. This deposit of glacial sediment is called the St. Croix moraine. Melt water streams flowed out from the Superior lobe, breached the moraine, and built a broad outwash plain of sand and gravel. This outwash deposit buried the Mississippi River valley south of the moraine as far as Hastings.

About 16,000 years ago another lobe of ice, the Des Moines lobe, advanced from the northwest through central Minnesota and eventually extended as far south as Des Moines, Iowa. Locally, melt water from its eastern margin drained eastward and carved a river valley to the Mississippi River at the present site of Hastings. The modern Vermillion River is but a shrunken remnant of that stream.

Ice blocks buried within the St. Croix moraine and filling the ancient bedrock valley of the Mississippi were insulated by sediment and melted very slowly. Eventually, their

melting continued to recede, large volumes of melt water flowed through the Mississippi again, forming numerous terraces and re-exposing the bedrock valley. When the influx of glacial melt water ended, the volume of water in the Mississippi decreased to what we see today.

<u>(Historical marker located near the junction of Hwy 61 and 55)</u>

Prominent People

William Le Duc moves to Hastings where he establishes a mill that is the first to offer spring wheat flour. This early entrepreneur originally from Ohio, started a law office in Minneapolis, authored three books on the territory, was a Civil War general, and was instrumental in the development of the Remington typewriter.

* * * *

Native Mark Steven Johnson was the writer of Grumpy Old Men starring Jack Lemmon and Walter Matthau.

 The battleship Minnesota is launched at Newport News, Virginia after being christened by Rose Marie Schaller of Hastings.

Place Name

The town refers to the settlers cottages mingled within the tracts of groves and prairies.

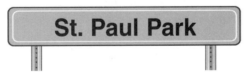

Place Name

One of the founders, Charles Parker built one of the largest hotels in the area, called the Parker House. When the city was name it added Park to the city name.

Place Name

Mrs. James Hugunin suggested the name similar to other towns of the same name in Rhode Island, Kentucky and in 30 other states.

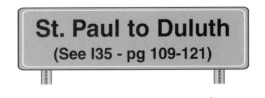

St. Paul to Duluth
(See I35 - pg 109-121)

Knife River

> ⭐ The name of the town comes from the Ojibwe word "Makomani". This word means "sharp rocks". These types of rocks characterize the land and nearby river waters.

Prominent People

The Arthur V Rohweder Memorial Highway was designed in recognition of the eminent leadership and outstanding contributions of Arthur V. Rohweder to the achievement by Minnesota of notable success and national prominence in all areas of accident prevention.

Serving as Superintendent of Safety and Welfare for the Duluth, Missabi and Iron Range Railway Company for forty-two years; as one of the founders, and President of the Minnesota Safety Council for twenty-five years; as First National President of the Veterans of Safety in 1941; as Vice-President and member of the Board of Directors of the National Safety Council for twenty-five years; and as Safety Consultant to eight Governors of Minnesota, Arthur V. Rohweder was dedicated to the cause of saving lives and eliminating sorrow and suffering attendant upon all types of accidents, and he worked unselfishly and tireless toward that end.

(Historical marker located on Hwy 61)

Two Harbors

Place Name

Two Harbors has gone through many different name changes. When it was platted in 1856, it was referred to as the village of Burlington. As time went on, residents decided that they liked the name Agate Bay better. Finally, in 1907, the town got the name that it has today, Two Harbors. The name results from the city's two harbors, Agate Bay and Burlington Bay.

Historical Significance

Originally, the town was a logging center. But when Two Harbors was connected to the town of Tower by railroad in 1884, the city became the state's first iron ore port. The iron ore industry caused the city to grow. Unfortunately, by the time the 1950s rolled around, most of the "grade A" iron ore was already unearthed. Today Two Harbors relies on fishing and tourism.

Geological

The story of the Lake Superior agate begins 1.1 billion years ago, when basaltic lava repeatedly erupted here and flowed out over the landscape.

When basaltic lava flows over the earth's surface, the gases it contains form bubbles,

which slowly rise in the viscous liquid. Rapid heat loss at the top surface of a flow causes the lava just below the surface to solidify quickly. This quick-hardening lava captures the bubbles within it, creating a zone of porous rock along the flow top.

Sometime after the lava flows in the Lake Superior region solidified, warm groundwater containing varying dissolved chemicals percolated through the basalt, especially through the porous zones, and lined the gas cavities with layers of different minerals until the cavities were filled. A common cavity-filling mineral is called chalcedony, which is a type of quartz with microscopic crystals shaped like fibers. When chalcedony is color-banded, it is known as an agate. The colored bands are due to small amounts of impurities (such as iron, copper, and aluminum) that are precipitated cyclically in every other layer of the fibrous quartz. In the layers receiving impurities, the quartz fibers formed are thinner and twisted. The center of an agate is often filled with coarsely crystallized quartz.

Since the time that agates and their basalt host formed, this continent has drifted very slowly several times across tropical climate zones, by a global process called plate tectonics. Under tropical conditions, intense chemical weathering caused the basalt to break down, but not the more resistant agate.

By the time the Ice Age began, about two million years ago, basalt flows near the surface of the land were very weathered, weakened and rich in hard agate nodules. As enormous glaciers advanced from the north and scoured the Lake Superior basin, they ground away the basalt and picked up the agates, transporting some as far away as Kansas. Many agates in Flood Bay may actually have been carried from areas in Ontario, where similar rocks are found.

<u>(Historical marker located on Hwy 61)</u>

Local Landmark

The Silver Creek Cliff and Lafayette Tunnels are located southwest of Two Harbors. The tunnel was completed in 1994 for almost 24 million dollars. Another tunnel was completed earlier in 1989 for a lot less at only 14 million.

* * * *

The Edna G., the Great Lakes first steam powered tugboat, operated through both World War I and World War II. It survived some of our nation's greatest history until it finally retired in 1981.

* * * *

Splithouse Rock Lighthouse opened in 1910 due to some tragic accidents along the North Shore. The house closed in 1969 but has since been restored by the Minnesota Historical Society. The lighthouse is one of the most visited lighthouses in the United States.

* * * *

The Peter Toth Indian Sculpture was donated to the state in honor of the state's Native American Heritage.

> The city houses the original office of the Minnesota Mining and Manufacturing Company, or more popularly referred to today as 3M. This establishment was used by 3M in 1902.

Castle Danger

Place Name

There are several theories behind its intimidating name. Some believe the town got its name from its castle-like formations and because Lake Superior is so dangerous in this particular area. Still, others believe the town is named after a ship called "Castle", which surrendered to the stormy lake waters. Evidence behind this theory has never been proved.

Historically, more than 300 ships have foundered into the nearby waters.

Local Landmark

It is true that Lake Superior is dangerous. Historically, more than 300 ships have foundered into the waters. The reason for so many ship-wrecks is that weather is so unpredictable on the lake. Storms can come on so suddenly that boaters don't have ample time to escape from the eye of the storm. Storms can be so severe that they can actually create waves up to 30 feet high.

There is a bluff that lies just South of the town of Castle Danger that is named for one Lake Superior shipwreck in particular. Lafayette Bluff is named after the Lafayette Iron Ore ship that sank in 1905. The storm that caused its wreck in that year is one of the worst ever recorded. The storm lasted in excess of three days with winds averaging 43 miles per hour. Gusts were clocked near 70 miles per hour. This storm led to the construction of a much-needed lighthouse in the region.

Gooseberrry River received its name from the Ojibwe for "gooseberry" in reference to the gooseberry bushes growing along the riverbank.

Gooseberry Falls are five falls in total, two of which have a total drop of 75 feet.

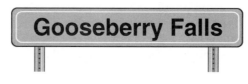

Gooseberry Falls

Geological

About 1.1 billion years ago, this continent began splitting apart along a rupture called the Midcontinent Rift, which extended from the Lake Superior region southwest to Kansas. During a period of about 20 million years, thousands of lava eruptions flowed out over a flat landscape. Layer upon layer of flows accumulated until the growing stacks reached a thickness of up to 20 kilometers in the Lake Superior area. Most of these flows solidified into the dark volcanic rock called basalt.

The waterfalls of the Gooseberry River reveal the layering of these lava flows. When basaltic lava erupts at the earth's surface, the gases it contains form bubbles, which slowly rise in the viscous liquid. Rapid heat loss at the top surface of a flow causes the lava just below the surface to solidify quickly. This quick-hardening lava captures the bubbles within it, creating a zone of porous rock along the flow top. Because the interior of a lava flow stays liquid longer, its gases have time to escape, leaving a solid

section. After the flows here accumulated, warm groundwater percolated through the layers for a long time, altering minerals and softening the porous flow tops more readily than the solid interiors. This process left each flow supported by the weakened porous top of the flow underneath it.

If you walk on the flows, you will see some polygonal patterns of cracks in the basalt. The geometric shapes are actually the tops of rock columns that extend down into each flow. The columns formed parallel to the direction the heat was lost when each lava flow cooled. Slow, uniform contraction of the rock during its cooling created the pattern of cracks, called columnar joints.

> Slow, uniform contraction of the rock during its cooling created the pattern of cracks, called columnar joints.

The columnar joints of a flow and the erosion of the weakened flow top underneath it work together to partition a flow into poorly secured columns. These columns are broken apart by weathering and frost, and the rushing water of the river removes the chunks from the downstream edge of the flow. Thus, the way in which these ancient lava flows erode produces waterfalls in the shape of giant stair steps.

(Historical marker located on Hwy 61)

Local Landmark

The classic steel arch bridge that spans this gorge is impressive for its simple beauty and elegance. Equally remarkable, but not as obvious to the onlooker, is the massive underground foundation that keeps this bridge sound and secure. To construct a foundation on rock is normally routine, but at this site, with its unusual geology and rugged terrain, nature created a considerable challenge for the builders.

Many years before construction began, a team of geologists and engineers began studying this site. They were searching for a subsurface material that would support the enormous forces exerted by the bridge and its traffic. Initially, it seemed as if the basalt rock exposed in the gorge would be sufficiently strong for this task. Lurking beneath the hard, resistant surface, however, lie weaken layers, each lava flow contains a solid, strong middle section, with much weaker, porous zones above and below. These porous zones are the result of gases that were trapped in the rapidly cooling outer portions of each flow. Groundwater later percolated through these zones for a long time, and they weathered to a near-soil condition. Complicating matters further, sagging of the Lake Superior basin has caused the rock layers in this area to dip about ten degrees to the east. Together, these factors made the design of the 16 different footings that support the bridge an intriguing problem.

Subsurface core drilling and the detailed mapping of outcrop, or exposed rock, helped geologists predict the three-dimensional extent of the solid portions of the lava flows. This study was made more difficult by the inability to drill at some of the foundation locations, because of the adverse terrain and the team's desire to preserve the natural beauty of the area. After the solid and weak layers in the rock were carefully mapped, construction plans were drawn up and the bridge was built. Predictions of the subsurface layers proved reliable, and only minor adjustments were required during construction.

(Historical marker located on Hwy 61)

Beaver Bay

Place Name

The town takes its name from its location on the Beaver River as it flows into Lake Superior.

Historical Significance

Beaver Bay is the oldest settlement on the Lake Superior shoreline. The town was first settled by people of German descent in 1856. These people opened the region's first sawmill, which provided an industrial base for the area.

The German immigrants gave the native Ojibwe the opportunity to work as well in the sawmill. The town has since been known for its strong ties to Native Americans.

The Ojibwe called this bay "Ga-gijikensikag, the place of the little cedars".

Local Landmark

Near the lake in Beaver Bay is a large totem pole. The pole marks the site of an Indian cemetery containing burial grounds from the 1800s.

Silver Bay

Place Name

While there are many explanations regarding the city's name, the most common one comes from the captain of the ship, America, who needed a name for the shipping point at this site around 1903 and suggested the name of the bay, from which the city takes its name.

Historical Significance

The Reserve Mining Company founded the city of Silver Bay in 1856. They used the town to employ workers in the newly built taconite processing plant. This plant is one of a kind because it is the only one not built on mining grounds. It was built by Lake Superior because it needs a large amount of water to operate. The plant has the ability to produce nine million tons of iron ore per year.

Local Landmark

Rising from the waves of Lake Superior, the cliff face (of Palisade Head) serves as an awesome reminder of Minnesota's geological past. Eruptions of molten lava over a billion years ago, followed by eons of weathering and glacier scouring, created the spectacular North Shore landmark so much admired and photographed.

Palisade Head, and Shovel Point to the northeast, sometimes called the Little Palisade, are rills of igneous rhyolite overlaying softer basalt and undercut by the eroding waves of North America's largest lake. Well known by the early lake travelers and surveyors, Palisade head became a major scenic attraction when the North Shore highway, completed in 1924,

brought tourists and campers in large numbers. Today the cliff's flat face is a challenge for rock climbers, and from its top visitors have a breathtaking view of the jagged Sawtooth Range. On a clear day the Apostle Islands, 30 miles distant, can sometimes be seen.

<u>(Historical marker located on Hwy 61)</u>

Geological

Tettegouche State Park is located in Illgen City. Tettegouche means, "retreat", and the name certainly fits. The name was given to the forest by the Micman tribe. The Baptism River runs through the park too. French missionaries used to use the water to baptize converts. The truly adventurous visitor can take a 45-minute hike to the High falls on the river to admire the beauty and serenity of the Tettegouche State Park.

Place Name

Finnish immigrants were primarily responsible for settling this community around 1895, although the name was not recorded until about 1911.

General Trivia

This small community is located within George H. Crosby Manitou State Park.

General Trivia

This community is situated next to the Manitou and Caribou Rivers. The word "Manitou" comes from the Ojibwe word for "Great Spirit". The Manitou is the only river that provides a waterfall directly into Lake Superior.

The Caribou River got its name from the caribou that roamed the Northern forests in the 1800s. The caribou is closely related to the reindeer, but today they are found almost exclusively in Canada. The reason for this is that white-tailed deer began to flourish in the area. These deer carry a parasite that causes disease in caribou and moose. The caribou then had no choice but to go further north into Canada to protect themselves from the parasitic disease.

Once a logging town, Little Marais means "Little Marsh" in French.

Taconite Harbor

Place Name

Taconite Harbor was originally named Two Island River. Yet when plans for the town changed, the town's name changed too in reference to the area mining.

Taconite Harbor is home to the power plant that supplies many taconite-mining plants with electricity, and the location where the city ships taconite.

Schroeder

Place Name

The town of Schroeder originated in the late 1800s. It got its name from the Schroeder Lumber Company. The company operated in Schroeder around the turn of the century, and employed almost 1,000 people.

Prominent People

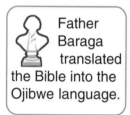

Father Baraga translated the Bible into the Ojibwe language.

Before the town was founded, the area provided refuge to Father Frederick Baraga, a catholic priest who was attempting to convert the Native Americans. Father Baraga translated the Bible into Ojibwe and wrote the first Ojibwe grammar book to help the Natives learn about Christianity.

In 1846, Father Baraga was canoeing down a river when a storm suddenly struck. Fortunately, the mouth of the river provided for him a safe haven. The Natives built a wooden cross for Father Baraga at the river's mouth where he took refuge. They also decided to name the river "Spirit of the Soul River".

Tofte

Place Name

John Tofte, his twin brother Andrew, and brother Torger; along with Hans Engleson established the town site they called Carlton for its location on the lower slope of Carlton Peak. Because there was another community with the same name, they renamed their town after their surname which was taken from their ancestral homeland of Bergen, Norway.

Historical Significance

The city of Tofte was founded in 1898 and is in close proximity to the Temperance River. The Ojibwe referred to the river as the "deep hollow". The reason for this name is that the river makes a dramatic fall of more than 150 feet in only a half mile before it drains into

Lake Superior.

Europeans renamed the river Temperance because it was the only river the European founders knew of that didn't have a bar. What they really meant by this was that the river didn't have a sandbar at its mouth. Most rivers have a sandbar-which is a mound of sand forced to the river shore by waves. Some faster moving rivers don't have a sandbar because there is not enough time for the river to build one. This river is unique in that its waters make a rapid circular motion that has caused the creation of potholes in nearby rocks.

The city of Tofte is certainly complemented by the beauty of the Temperance River. Tofte has served a variety of purposes since its origin. It was mostly involved in logging, fishing and boating in the early days. Today, some of this activity still exists.

 Carlton Peak is 1,527 feet above sea level. It is also one of the highest points on the North shore.

Place Name

Lutsen was founded in the late 1800s. It got its name from a 1632 battle site in Germany. This battle was responsible for the death of Swedish King, Gustavus Adolphus.

Historical Significance

Lutsen was originally a logging community, but now is a resort town with a booming tourism industry. As a result, the area offers a fine variety of outdoor recreational activities, including hiking, skiing, swimming, and snowmobiling.

Winter actually brings two large recreational activities to the area, the John Beargrease Sled Dog Marathon and the International 500 snowmobile race.

Local Landmark

The Cascade River State Park is near the town of Lutsen. The Cascade, along with nine other smaller streams, winds through the park before emptying into Lake Superior. The river falls 900 feet throughout the park before falling into the lake. There is one point within the park where five waterfalls can be seen at one time.

* * * *

Thomsonite is a semi-precious stone formed by gas bubbles in lava. The stone varies in color and size, but it is normally green and pink in color.

Thomsonite Beach is one of the rare areas in the world where Thomsonite is found.

Prominent People

Cynthia Nelson, a Lutsen native, has been a member of the U.S. World Cup ski team since she was fifteen years old. She won a bronze medal in Innsbruck Olympics in 1976.

Eagle Mountain

Historical Significance

The igneous rock composing Eagle Mountain is as old as the Duluth Gabbro, which geologists estimate at over a billion years in age.

When Newton Winchell, Minnesota's state geologist, and Ulysses S. Grant II (the president's son) surveyed this area in the 1890s, they concluded that a peak in the Misquah Hills was the state's highest point. Using an aneroid barometer, they set its elevation at 2,230 feet. Later comers argued that Eagle Mountain, which Winchell and Grant did not measure and which can be seen from Misquah Hills, was higher.

In 1961 a United State Department of the Interior Survey team remeasured, using aerial photographs and controlled bench marks. They found Eagle Mountain's elevation to be 2,301 feet, making it Minnesota's highest point. They also determined that the first Misquah Hills peak is surpassed by another unnamed summit 2,266 feet above sea level, located in section 19 of T63N, R1W, in the same western Cook County area. The state's lowest point is Lake Superior, which has an elevation of 602 feet. (Historical marker located 25 miles northwest of Lutsen, a 2 1/2 mile hike from the north end of county road 4)

Grand Marais

Place Name

Grand Marais got its name from French inhabitants who came to the area in the early 1800s. The name means "big marsh" in French.

Historical Significance

Early settlers relied heavily on the fur trade for an industrial base. As time went by, fur trading became practically obsolete with the introduction of commercial fishing and logging. Today, logging is still the big business in the city of Grand Marais.

Local Landmark

Grand Marais is probably most famous for the Gunflint Trail. This trail leads travelers through the Superior National Forest all the way to Lake Saganaga at the Canadian border. The trail has a distance of 58 miles.

Geological

The rocks of the North Shore of Lake Superior record the last period of volcanic activity in Minnesota. This volcanism occurred 1.1 billion years ago when the North American continent began to rupture along a great rift valley, which extended from the Lake Superior region southwest to Kansas. As this rift valley opened, basaltic lavas erupted into it

intermittently for about 20 million years, accumulating to a thickness of up to 20 kilometers in the Lake Superior region.

With each eruption, red-hot lavas fountained from kilometer-long fissures for up to decades at a time, flooding over large areas of barren landscape. Flood basalt eruptions typically followed one another in geologically rapid succession, but at times there were significant intervals (thousands to millions of years) without volcanic activity. During such intervals, streams and rivers flowing over and eroding the volcanic terrain would deposit sediments into lakes in low-lying areas. When volcanic activity resumed, these sediments could in turn be buried, heated, and compacted by lava flows and transformed into sedimentary rocks.

An example of such a geological cycle of eruption, sedimentation, and renewed volcanism appears in the cliff face across the highway from this marker. Beneath a dark-gray basalt flow is a reddish, thinly bedded siltstone, sandstone and shale formation. Beneath these sedimentary rocks is another lava flow, which is exposed in the creek bed of Cut Face Creek. The full thickness of this sedimentary rock formation is about 40 meters. This thickness indicates a prolonged lull in volcanic activity, perhaps lasting several million years. The broken-up and mineralized character of the basalt at the left side of the cliff resembles features observed when lavas explosively encounter standing water. This and the fine sediments beneath the lava suggest that a shallow lake may have existed in the area at the time of renewed volcanism.

(Historical marker located on Hwy 61)

* * * *

The harbor of Grand Marais is the result of unequal weathering or erosion of two types of rock. One of these, called diabase, resulted from the cooling of molten material which was forced between two earlier lava flows. The dark, massive diabase, being very hard and resistant to wave action, has become the outer barrier to the harbor, while the lava, which was much fractured and easily eroded, was worn away to form the harbor basin.

To the west of Grand Marais, the serrated crest of the Sawtooth Range, clearly visible from the harbor breakwater, is another example of unequal erosion. Here the relatively soft basalt and the more resistant diabase have, through the process of weathering, produced the notched profile of the hills along the coast.

Saganaga granite, is one of the oldest granites in North America.

To the east of Grand Marais rise the hills near the mouth of the Arrowhead River, while to the north, along the Gunflint Trail are older rocks. At Saganaga Lake, the Saganaga granite, one of the oldest granites in North America, marks a core of the ancient mountains of the Laurentian Highlands.

(Historical marker located on Hwy 61)

Place Name
The name was given by Anna Brunes, after her grandfather's estate in Norway.

223

Historical Significance

The town of Hovland was founded by Norwegian immigrants. An old cement dock in town tells of the town's rafting and commercial fishing background.

> 🏛 The Devil's Cauldron at Pothole Falls is a mysterious place on the river that gives the illusion of the river actually disappearing into a void, hence the name.

Local Landmark

Just southwest of Hovland is Judge Magney State Park, named in honor of Clarence R. Magney. Magney was the former Minnesota Supreme Court Justice and Mayor of Duluth. The park honors Magney because of the tremendous efforts he made to preserve the North shore.

* * * *

The Reservation River is unique in that it is one of the few in the area that does not have a waterfall. The river falls so gradually, that no waterfall ever developed. The river got its name from the Ojibwe to indicate the Western boundary of the Grand Portage Band of the Ojibwe tribe.

Pigeon River

Place Name

The city's name is in reference for the large amount of wild pigeons that used to live in the surrounding area.

General Trivia

Located on the Minnesota border, the Pigeon River marks the border between the United States and Canada in this area.

Determining, surveying, and marking Minnesota's border with Canada took 142 years and left the state with a tag end called the Northwest Angle standing isolated and alone on the Canadian side of Lake of the Woods.

At the end of the American Revolution in 1783, British and American negotiators agreed to separate Canada and the United States by a line running from the Atlantic Ocean to the Northwestern most point of Lake of the Woods in what is now western Ontario. They based their work on the mistaken assumptions that the Mississippi River would be the western border of the U.S. and that a line drawn straight west of Lake of the Woods would intersect with that river.

By the time the U.S. purchased the Louisiana Territory from France twenty years later, it was clear that the western U.S. border would not be the Mississippi River and that the river's source lay south, not northwest of Lake of the Woods. In 1818 British and American negotiators dropped the U.S.-Canadian boundary line straight south from the northwestern most point of Lake of the Woods to the 49th parallel and then straight west along the parallel to the crest of the Rocky Mountains, leaving a chimney-like projection that

included the Northwest Angle.

The eastern part of Minnesota's northern border lay along the old fur trade water routes beginning at the mouth of the Pigeon River near Grand Portage, now a national monument just a short distance from here. The routes connected Lake Superior and Lake of the Woods, but the boundary's exact demarcation had to wait until a survey in the 1920s.

(Historical marker located on Hwy 61)

Historical Significance

In early times, grand Portage consisted of a nine-mile uphill path where the Natives had to carry their canoes around the falls located on the lower Pigeon River.

Grand Portage has also been referred to as the "Oldest Settlement in Minnesota" because of its early history.

Founded by the French, Grand Portage means, "The Great Carrying Place".

The French arrived in the 1600s. They traded beaver furs along the shoreline. The French Voyageurs used the nearby Pigeon River extensively in order to journey across the border.

By 1778, the Grand Portage vicinity was transformed primarily by the Natives into the largest fur trading post in North America. The area was even involved in international trade. The Northwest Company was the culprit of this busy time in Grand Portage history. The post moved to Canada within a short period of time to avoid taxation by the American government.

The Treaty of LaPointe essentially created the city in 1854. The treaty was made between the United States government and the Ojibwe Indian Nation. The treaty created a reservation in the area for the Ojibwe tribe. The Ojibwe preferred populating the areas along the Great Lakes rather than their original home along the Atlantic coastline. The tribe found the Great Lakes environment to be much more natural, complete with forested lands and fresh water. Moreover, they had hoped that the Great Lakes region would offer wild rice plantations, since the Atlantic coastline no longer did.

Local Landmark

Circumventing 21 miles of falls and rapids, Grand Portage ran some nine miles from this vicinity to a point upstream on the Pigeon River. It was first mentioned in 1722, by a French trader named Jean Pachot. Following its use in 1732 by La Verendrye, it replaced the Kaministiquia Route as the canoe route to the West. About 1767 the Grand Portage became a rendezvous for Canadian fur traders and, after 1778, the North West Company's inland headquarters. By the Treaty of Paris, 1783, the Portage fell within American territory. In 1803 the Company moved its headquarters to Fort Kaministiquia (Fort Williams), and the Pigeon River route was then abandoned.

(Historical marker located on Hwy 61)

HIGHWAY 59

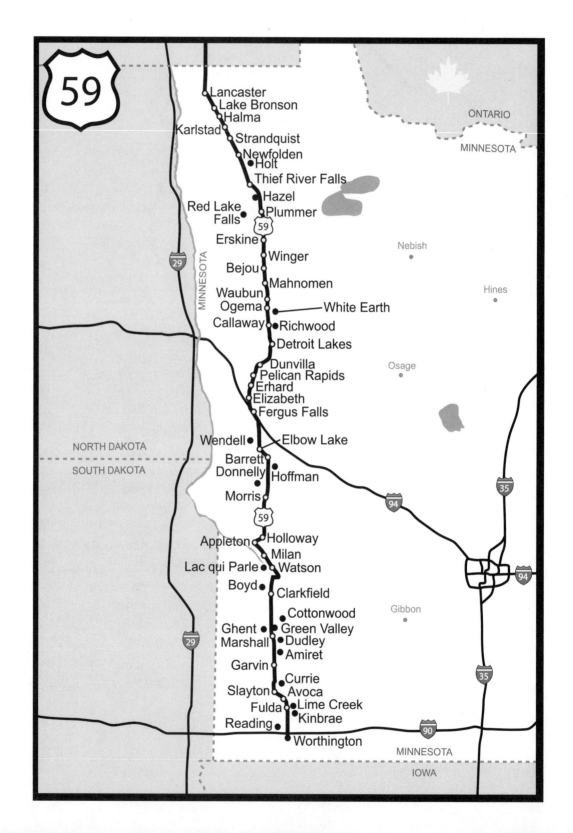

59

Lancaster
Lake Bronson
Halma
Karlstad
Strandquist
Newfolden
Holt
Thief River Falls
Hazel
Red Lake Falls
Plummer
59
Erskine
Winger
Bejou
Mahnomen
Waubun
Ogema
White Earth
Callaway
Richwood
Detroit Lakes
Dunvilla
Pelican Rapids
Erhard
Elizabeth
Fergus Falls
Wendell
Elbow Lake
Barrett
Donnelly
Hoffman
Morris
59
Appleton
Holloway
Milan
Lac qui Parle
Watson
Boyd
Clarkfield
Cottonwood
Ghent
Green Valley
Marshall
Dudley
Amiret
Garvin
Currie
Slayton
Avoca
Fulda
Lime Creek
Kinbrae
Reading
Worthington

ONTARIO
MINNESOTA
Nebish
Hines
Osage
NORTH DAKOTA
SOUTH DAKOTA
MINNESOTA
IOWA
Gibbon

29
94
35
94
35
90

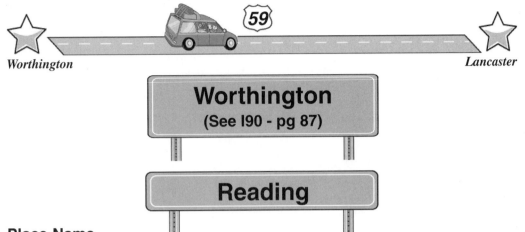

Worthington
(See I90 - pg 87)

Reading

Place Name
Henry Read, a pioneer farmer in the area is the person whose land a part of the village was developed on.

Kinbrae

Place Name
Founded by the Dundee Land Company of Scotland. The village was named Airlie, after the Earl of Airlie who was the land company president when the town site was platted.

Then for a while it was called DeForest before receiving its current Scottish name, Kimbrae, by request of the Chicago, Milwaukee and St. Paul Railroad officials.

Fulda

Place Name
Named for an ancient city on the Fulda river in central Germany, noted for its early medieval abbey and beautiful cathedral.

Lime Creek

Place Name
When Nicolaus Costello and Anton Hager founded this village, they named it after the nearby creek by the same name.

Avoca

Poet Thomas Moore called the picturesque valley the Sweet Vale of Avoca.

Place Name

This town began in 1878 and named for a river in Ireland became a key point for the sale of 50,000 acres of railroad land to Catholic colonist in Murray County through the activities of Archbishop (John) Ireland and the Catholic Colonization Bureau.

(Historical marker located on Hwy 59)

Slayton

Place Name

Originally a railway village, the township was named for its founder and chief proprietor, Charles Slayton.

Prominent People

Actor Frank Webb, who starred in numerous TV shows including Bonanza, The Virginian, Marcus Welby, M.D. and Mission Impossible died in a road accident in the Slayton area.

Currie

Place Name

This town was founded by flour mill operators Archibald Currie, a native from Argyllshire, Scotland, along with his son, Neil. Archibald Currie came with his parents to America when he was five years old, moving to Winona County. Forty six years later he came to the town which would bear his name.

Local Landmark

Lake Shetek State Monument was dedicated to the memory of those who were slain in the Lake Shetek Indian massacre of August 20, 1862 and to commemorate the privations and hardships and the heroic deeds of the surviving pioneer settlers of Murray County and vicinity.

(Historical marker located at entrance to Lake Shetek State Park)

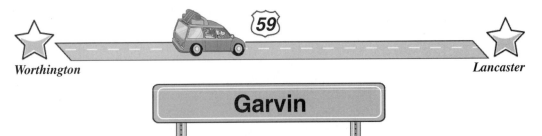

Place Name

The town was named for H.C. Garvin, a traveling freight agent of the railway.

Place Name

Originally known as Madison, the name was changed to that of the railway village in the area named for M.K. Sykes', wife Amiretta. Sykes was the vice president of the Chicago and North Western Railway company.

Place Name

Dudley was named for a town in Massachusetts.

Marshall

Place Name

Named for former Governor William Rainery Marshall who served two terms from 1866 to 1870.

Prominent People

Marvin Schwan took a one-truck, door-to-door ice cream delivery business and built it into a global company of today.

It all began with Marvin Schwan's entrepreneurial spirit. Marvin and his parents, Paul and Alma, were partners in a small dairy that was struggling due to a government price freeze on milk. Marvin learned that ice cream was selling at a higher price north of Marshall. He acted on the opportunity.

On March 18, 1952, the 23-year-old loaded 14 gallons of ice cream into a 1946 Dodge panel van and set out. By that evening, he had sold all 14 gallons, and proved the basic concept of the Schwan's Home Service system.

Schwan's Home Service now reaches millions of customers in their homes across the United States. The business Marvin established with ice cream now offers more than 300 products including appetizers, entrees, fruits, vegetables, breads, pizzas, convenience foods

> ❓❓❓ Schwan's Food Service provides a range of food including Walt Disney World and aboard Air Force One.

and juices, and the company's signature ice creams and frozen treats.

In 1969, Marvin placed an ad in the Wall Street Journal: "Wanted - One Pizza Plant". With that ad, he acquired a pizza factory in Salina, Kansas, which became the home of Tony's Pizza.

Schwans took pizza into our nation's schools in the 1970s, and now Schwan's Food Service provides a range of food solutions for schools, hospitals, institutions and businesses. Schwan's products are also served by many national chain restaurants.

Schwan's is a leader in the international frozen food industry, with manufacturing facilities in the United States, England, France and Germany.

* * * *

Steve Zahn career kicked off in his native Minnesota when he crashed the audition of a local stage production of "Biloxi Blues" and won the lead role.

He then went on to train at the American Repertory Theatre in Cambridge, MA; before moving to New York City where he won a role touring for 13 months in national company of Tommy Tune-directed version of "Bye Bye Birdie".

Back in New York, he played opposite Ethan Hawke in "Sophistry" at Playwright's Horizon where Ben Stiller noticed him and cast him, and Hawke, in Reality Bites (1994).

General Trivia

Southwest State University in Marshall is the only school in intercollegiate wheelchair basketball team in Minnesota to win three titles.

Historical Significance

On July 4th, 1875, the first Icelandic settler in Minnesota, Gunnlaugur Petursson, established a homestead on the Yellow Medicine River. The homestead was originally named in honor of Gunnlaugur's ancestral home in northeastern Iceland but in more recent years has been known as "Riverside Farm."

Later, some 800 Icelanders settled in Lyon, Lincoln, and Yellow Medicine Counties. The largest single group arrived in the town of Minnoeta (8 miles southwest of here) from northeastern Iceland in the summer of 1879. Many of these pioneers lie buried here.

The Icelanders who came to Minnesota brought with them little of this world's goods. Perhaps their most precious possessions were their sincere interest in public affairs and their traditional love of learning. Here they established schools, churches, libraries, reading societies, and the only Icelandic-language newspaper in the United States, Vinland. They also founded numerous farms and commercial enterprises including one of Minnesota's earliest consumer cooperatives, Verzlunarfelag Islendinga, a general merchandise retail store, in 1886.

(Historical marker located on Hwy 10)

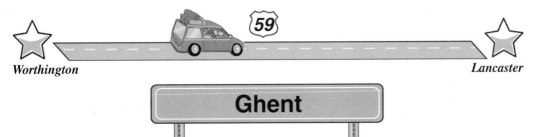

Ghent

Place Name

Bishop John Ireland led a group of Belgian colonist settling in the vicinity, who named this after the ancient city of Ghent in Belgium.

Green Valley
(See Hwy 23 - pg 273)

Cottonwood
(See Hwy 23 - pg 273)

Clarkfield

Place Name

The town was named in honor of Thomas Clark who was highly regarded by the Minneapolis and St. Louis Railroad.

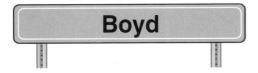

Boyd

Place Name

Boyd is another community named after officials of the Minneapolis and St. Louis Railroad.

Place Name

According to L.R. Moyer the name was selected by Cornelius Nelson, a settler from New York inspired by the wonderful view overlooking the Minnesota and Chippewa River valleys. So moved Cornelius was said to have suggested the Latin name Mount of Vision, or from the mountain I see. But actually it is believed that Nelson named the town after the capital city of Uruguay, South America.

Historical Significance

On September 26, 1862, 91 whites and about 150 mixed-blood captives, some of whom

had been prisoners of the Dakota Indians for more than a month, were returned to Colonel Henry Sibley's military camp, later joyfully known as Camp Release. In the next few days, additional captives were freed, bringing the total to 107 whites and 162 mixed-bloods, 269 in all.

When the 1862 U.S.-Dakota conflict moved into its final weeks in mid-September, attention on both sides had focused in the captives, mostly women and children, held by the Dakota. Sibley, holding a largely volunteer army, demanded that the captives be released before peace negotiations could begin. But the Dakota warriors led by Little Crow moved up the Minnesota River valley, still holding their prisoners.

Many Dakota who had not supported the war took great risks to help keep the captives alive. By late September Dakota peace factions led by Wabasha, Taopi, Red Iron, Mazomani, Standing Buffalo, and others were camped only half a mile from the war faction near the mouth of the Chippewa River. While Little Crow's men were fighting the battle of Wood Lake, the peace supporters took control of the captives, expecting to have to fight the returning war party if it were victorious against the white army. But Little Crow's men did not win at Wood Lake. The war leaders and many of their followers fled Minnesota, and the Dakota peace group sent a message to Sibley to arrange the prisoner release three days later. Many of the peace faction who surrendered to Sibley's army at Camp Release were among the Dakota exiled from Minnesota the following year.

(Historical marker located on Hwy 212)

Place Name

This community was named after the Watson Farmers Elevator. Built in 1886, it may be the first cooperative elevator in the United States. Deemed unsafe in 1993, it was removed by the Watson Fire Department with a controlled burn.

Place Name

This village was started as a Presbyterian mission located near the lake of the same name back in 1835.

Local Landmark

The Protestant Mission to the Dakota Indians established here in 1835 at the request of the trader Joseph Renville became the nucleus of one of the earliest and most colorful centers of white settlement in the Minnesota River Valley. At this remote station the valley's first school and church were founded, the state's first church bell pealed, cloth was woven for the first time in Minnesota, and the Bible was first translated into the Dakota language for

which the missionaries devised a written alphabet.

<u>(Historical marker located on west of Hwy 59 at the junction of 32 and 13)</u>

Prominent People

Joseph Renville was one of Minnesota's most prominent and influential pre-statehood citizens. The son of a Dakota woman and a French fur trader, he was born in 1779 near St. Paul. After attaining an officer's commission serving with the British in the War of 1812, he worked for the Hudson Bay Company before helping to establish the Columbia Fur Company which dominated Upper Midwest fur trade from 1822 until it merged with John Jacob Astor's American Fur Company in 1827.

In the late 1820s, Renville built a stockade log fort. At this wilderness settlement he extended hospitality to travelers and explorers, ruling, as one visitor commented, "in barbaric splendor quite like an African king". It was Renville's invitation that brought missionaries to his remote post, where they established the Lac qui Parle Mission in 1835. He helped them translate the Bible into the Dakota language, and his translation of Christian hymns are still in use today.

Crop failures in the late 1830s and the collapse of the American Fur Company in the early 1840s left Renville nearly penniless. Fort Renville began to decay, and Joseph Renville died in the spring of 1846,... "neglected by many who had profited by his generosity".

<u>(Historical marker located on west of Hwy 59 at the junction of 32 and 13)</u>

Place Name

Twelve other cities throughout the country have the same name as the great city in northern Italy.

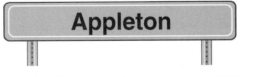

Place Name

The town was named after the city in the neighboring state of Wisconsin near Green Bay. The name commemorates Samuel Appleton one of the founders of Lawrence University located there.

Local Landmark

In the 1970s and 1980s, the town of Appleton was in serious need of jobs. The problem was so bad that residents were packing up and relocating in large numbers. The high school even shut down.

To save the town, the remaining citizens voted on building the Prairie Correctional Facility.

Appleton is located on the Pomme de Terre River. This river was named for a potato-like root that the Natives used to eat.

New York Mets and Minnesota Twins baseball pitcher, Jerry Koosman was born in Appleton.

This facility would provide jobs and help out other communities by renting it out to them based on need. The 472-bed facility gave many townspeople jobs as prison guards.

Prominent People

Local baseball pitcher, Jerry Koosman accrued two records with the Mets that he isn't exactly proud of. First, in 1962, he struck out 62 times. Second, he also pitched the ball that gave Pete Rose his 4,000 hit.

Place Name

This town was named in honor of a pioneer farmer by officers of the Great Northern Railroad.

Place Name

Charles Morris came to the United States from his native Ireland. He was associated with the engineering departments of several railroads including the Manitoba and the Northern Pacific.

Historical Significance

Established in 1864 from St. Cloud to Fort Wadsworth, later called Fort Sisseton.

The Wadsworth Trail was used by soldiers and traders who came up the Mississippi River by boat. It passed through Sauk Centre, Gager's Station, Toqua, Brown's Valley and the government agency on the Sisseton Reservation.

(Historical marker located at Seventh and California Streets)

Local Landmark

The Dormitory building is all that remains of the former Morris Industrial School for Indians. Built in 1899, it along with a classroom building, a superintendent's residence, a laundry, a bath house, and a barn were added to the Indian mission school originally established by Mother Mary Joseph Lynch and the Sisters of Mercy in 1887.

The Sisters of Mercy mission school at Morris housed Chippewa Indians from Turtle Mountain Reservation in North Dakota and Dakota Indians from Sisseton Reservation in South Dakota. The mission school was operated under a contract with the federal government, whose policy prior to 1887 had been to isolate Indians on reservations. After 1887, the Dawes Severalty Act emphasized assimilation of Indians into mainstream culture. Mission boarding schools were established to fill the need for an education system. In Minnesota, many of

these boarding schools, including the Morris school, were administered by the Bureau of Catholic Indian Missions.

In 1896 federal policy changed again, and administration of the Morris Indian mission school was transferred to the federal government. The Indian Industrial School in nearby Clontarf was closed and its students were transferred to Morris, where they were offered both industrial and academic classes. The combined school at Morris continued to operate until 1909.

Facing growing opposition to Indian boarding schools, the federal government again changed its policies and abandoned the concept. The Morris Industrial School for Indians was one of the first five federal Indian schools to be transferred to state governments for use in their general education systems. In 1909, the school was renamed the West Central School of Agriculture, and in 1960, changed to the University of Minnesota, Morris.

(Historical marker located on Cougar Circle)

Place Name

First this town was called Douglas, after Ignatius Donnelly, a distinguished farmer, politician and author in the area. Later the name was changed to Donnelly, by John Gavin Donnelly, the brother of Ignatius Donnelly, when he became the agent for the railway depot.

Place Name

The town was named for the chief engineer of the Soo Line, Robert Hoffman.

Place Name

After the Civil War, the town was renamed in honor of General Theodore Harvey Barrett, who owned and operated a large farming operation in Grand and Stevens Counties. General Barrett was captain of the Ninth Minnesota Regiment, colonel of the 62nd U.S. Colored Infantry, and brevetted brigadier general.

 Home of peace, was the Swedish meaning for Fridhem, the towns original name.

237

Elbow Lake

Place Name

Named for the lake early settlers described as being shaped like an arm bent at the elbow.

Wendell

Place Name

The town is either named for a railroad official or perhaps after Wright County judge Joseph Wendell.

Fergus Falls
(See I94 - pg 58)

Elizabeth

Place Name

The town is named after the wife of the first postmaster Rudolph Niggler.

Erhard

Place Name

This town was established as Erhards Grove, named for the postmaster Alexander Erhard.

The 15 1/2 foot concrete statue of a pelican built in 1957, is the largest in the world.

Pelican Rapids

Place Name

Pelican Rapids got its name from the river that descends in the area with rapids drifting over boulders. The Ojibwa gave the river their name for pelican, spelled Shada in the Song of Hiawatha by Henry W. Longfellow.

General Trivia

A Minnesota woman, the skeleton of a girl about fifteen years of age, was discovered at this point in 1931 by a highway repair crew. Although the skeleton has not been dated exactly, based on the site geology scientists believe it to be perhaps 10,000 years old. This would make Minnesota Woman America's oldest human skeleton.

Two artifacts, a dagger of elk horn and a conch shell, were discovered with the bones. Archaeologists believe that the girl drowned in Glacial Lake Pelican, which adjoined Glacial Lake Agassiz, a huge body of water that covered much of northwestern Minnesota during the last ice age.

(Historical marker located on Hwy 59)

Dunvilla

Place Name

First named Lake Lizzie, the name was changed to Dunvilla after a hotel owner here, Roy Emery Dunn.

Detroit Lakes
(See Hwy 10 - pg 329)

Richwood

Place Name

W.W. McLeod named this village established in 1871 after his native hometown in the province of Ontario, Canada.

Callaway

Place Name

The town is named for the general passenger agent from Minneapolis, William Callaway, when the Minneapolis, St. Paul and Sault Ste. Marie Railroad established a station here.

Ogema

Place Name

The meaning of this town's name comes from the Ojibwe meaning a chief. It is pronounced with an accent on the initial long o, g as in get, and a like ah.

White Earth

Place Name

This village is located within the White Earth Reservation, named by the Ojibwe as Ga-wababigunikag sagaiigun meaning the place of white clay lake; referring to the white clay which crops out in places along the shoreline.

Local Landmark

The first Minnesota mission to be named for Saint Columba was built by James Lloyd Breck in 1852 at Gull Lake near present-day Brainerd. It was the fourth Episcopal Church established in Minnesota.

The initial group of Chippewa Indians arrived here from Gull Lake on June 14, 1868, to begin life on the White Earth Reservation which had been created the year before. In the fall of 1868 they were joined by John Johnson or Enmegahbowh, a Canadian Indian who had served at the former mission on Gull Lake. The first religious service in Becker County was conducted that fall by Enmegahbowh, who was ordained the following year. He is said to have been the first Indian to be ordained by the Episcopal Church in the United States.

The second mission church of St. Columba, built of logs in 1868, stood several miles north of the present town of White Earth. It was replaced in 1871 by a frame church, located near the present site and consecrated by Bishop Henry Whipple in 1872. The present church was built in 1980. Enmgegahbowh is buried in the nearby cemetery.

(Historical marker located on the grounds of
St. Columba's Episcopal Church at White Earth)

Prominent People

Chief White Cloud State Monument was erected by the State of Minnesota appreciating a helpful, kindhearted, brainy man of true worth, born 1828 died October 7, 1898.

(Historical marker located in Calvary Catholic Cemetery
1 mile south of White Earth)

Place Name

Waubun is an Ojibwe word meaning "the east," "the morning," and "the twilight of the dawn". Spelled "wabun" by Longfellow in "The Song of Hiawatha," the definition means "the east wind".

Place Name

The town's and county name comes from a number of spelling of the Objiwe word for wild rice. Commonly written as manomin, the current spelling is the English interpretation for this native grain.

Place Name

This name comes from the Ojibwe salutation for greeting others, with the pronunciation and spelling similar to the French words Bon jour. Fur traders and voyageurs used this expression meaning "Good day" similar to the typical English or American greeting of "How do you do?".

> The railroad builders who came through in 1903-1904 named stations as they moved the line north, and all towns on the reservation had to be Indian names.

Place Name

Norwegian settlers named this township after a group of farms in the valley district called Gudbrandsdal in central Norway. It was changed to Winger by the Soo Line railroad.

Erskine
(See Hwy 2 - pg 345)

Plummer

Place Name

Charles Plummer for whom this town was named for, built a sawmill and gristmill on the Clearwater River in the vicinity of the town site.

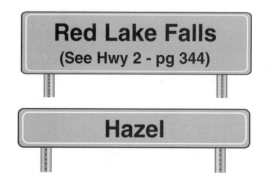

Red Lake Falls
(See Hwy 2 - pg 344)

Hazel

Place Name

Two species of Hazel trees, known for their nuts, grow in this part of the state.

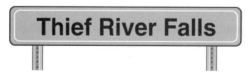

Thief River Falls

Place Name

This unusual name "Thief River" was given to the river by the Ojibwe and Dakota people. Translated from the word "Kimod akiwi zibi", the Stolen Land river or Thieving Land river.

"Falls" was added to the name of the new city in 1896 because a series of rapids in the river had been converted to a waterfall by the construction of a dam.

Industry

Artic Cat designs, engineers, manufactures and markets snowmobiles and ATVs under the Artic Cat brand.

* * * *

Digi-Key Corporation is one of the largest distributors of electronic components in the United States.

Vicki Omdahl aka Brynn Hartman was born in Thief River Falls. She starred in a few episodes of 3rd Rock from the Sun. She committed suicide after shooting her husband, Phil Hartman, dead.

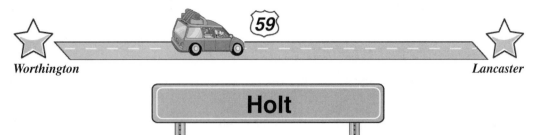

Holt

Place Name

The name with a slightly different spelling honors Norwegian pioneer Havor Holte, who came to this area in 1886. The name is an ancient Anglo-Saxon and Scandinavian word meaning "a grove" or "a wooded hill."

Newfolden

Place Name

Soo Line officials first called their station here Baltic because of the many Baltic elevators located along the line. However, since there was already a Baltic town site in the state, it was given the name of Newfolden, for the site a few miles to the south.

Strandquist

Place Name

Local merchant and area farmer John Erik Strandquist came here from Sweden in 1892. He relocated his business in the village which changed the name from Lund to honor him.

Karlstad

Place Name

In 1883, Karlstad was settled by August Carlson, for whom the town was named, with a slight various in the spelling.

Halma

Place Name

Norwegian native John Edwin Holm, moved his family to the United States, settling on a farm in the vicinity of the town site of Halma.

Place Name

The Giles Bronson family was the first settlers in the area when the town site was known as Percy, after the postmasters wife's hometown in Ontario. Later the name was changed to honor the Bronson family.

Lancaster

Place Name

It is believed that the town was named after Lancashire County, England where an official of the Soo Line railroad came from.

HIGHWAY
53

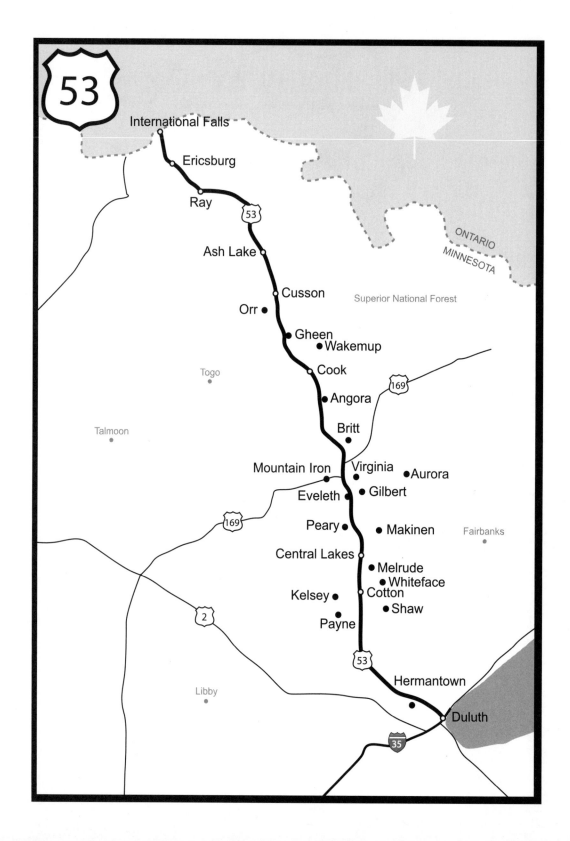

53

International Falls

Ericsburg

Ray

53

Ash Lake

Cusson

Orr

Gheen

Wakemup

Cook

Togo

Angora

Britt

Talmoon

Mountain Iron

Virginia

Aurora

Eveleth

Gilbert

169

Peary

Makinen

Fairbanks

Central Lakes

Melrude

Whiteface

Kelsey

Cotton

Shaw

2

Payne

53

Hermantown

Libby

Duluth

35

Superior National Forest

ONTARIO

MINNESOTA

169

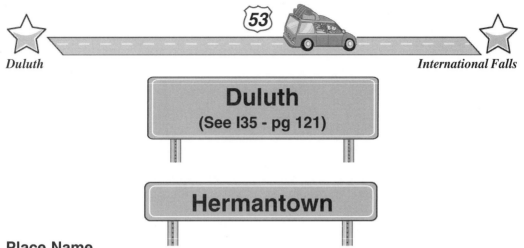
Duluth
(See I35 - pg 121)

Hermantown

Place Name

The town's name given by Germany settlers in honor of a local hero known for defeating the Roman troops in Germany during the time of Christ.

Historical Significance

Hermantown was founded in 1872. It grew slowly at first, but news of the railroad coming to the town encouraged citizens to settle within the town.

Growth, however, was set back by the great forest fire of 1918, which swept through Hermantown and 36 other townships. Almost the entire town was destroyed. The school, church, town hall, and Woodmen Hall, which was the center for all the town's events, were the only buildings that remained standing. Luckily, the town was quickly rebuilt by 1920.

In 1974, Duluth wanted to annex approximately 2/3 of the city of Herman in order to keep their population above 100,000. The residents of Herman were outraged. They didn't want to lose their sense of identity to a big city. They fought long and hard to avoid this annexation. Fortunately, the fighting worked. In 1975, the town of Herman was transformed into the city of Hermantown through the people's hard work.

Shaw

Place Name

The station was called Shan when the Duluth, Winnipeg and Pacific Railway first reached the area. Then both Shan and Shaw for awhile. The post office was referred to as Shan because there already was a Shaw in Missouri and in Mississippi. The local railroad depot was called Shaw. The town eventually took the name of the depot.

Payne

Place Name

Named for a secretary of the Duluth, Missabe and Iron Range Railroad.

Kelsey

Place Name

Kesley Chase, for whom the town is named for, came to Minnesota in 1860. During the Civil War he served in the Second Minnesota Regiment. Following the war he settled throughout the state in Rochester, Owatonna, Duluth, Crookston and Faribault establishing a mercantile business, real estate, railway and mining developments. Chase also was the president of the Duluth, Missabe and Northern Railroad company before being the president of the Chase State Bank in Faribault.

Cotton

Place Name

This town was named for Duluth lawyer, Joseph Bell Cotton. He was admitted to the bar two years after graduating from the Michigan Agricultural and Mechanical College in Lansing.

Whiteface

Place Name

The Duluth, Winnipeg and Pacific Railway station was named after the river of the same name, the Whiteface River.

Melrude

Place Name

The town's name is an anglicized form of the town in Dalsland, Sweden known as Mellerud.

Central Lakes

Giants Range, is a rare three-way continental divide.

Geological

A drop of rain water falling here in the Giants Range, a rare three-way continental divide, may flow either north into icy Hudson Bay, east into the Atlantic Ocean, or south into the warm waters of the Gulf of Mexico.

From the north slope of these very old granite ridges, streams flow into the Red River of the North, through Lake Winnipeg, and into Hudson Bay in northern Canada.

Creeks and rivers in the south slope flow into the St. Louis River, enter Lake Superior at Duluth and eventually reach the north Atlantic through the Great Lakes and the St. Lawrence River.

On a western spur of Giants Range the great watershed of the immense Mississippi River system gathers the flow from a maze of streams and swamps as the legendary river begins its winding course from Lake Itasca to the Gulf of Mexico, more than 2,500 miles away.

Lying as it does near the center of the North American continent, Minnesota marks the transition between eastern woodlands and western prairies and between northern coniferous forests and rich grain-growing lands of the mid-nation. It is a land of dramatic differences, tied to the world through three great waterways that originate in these rocks and streams.
(Historical marker located on Hwy 53 in Anchor Lake rest area)

Place Name
This town was named after their first postmaster, John Makinen.

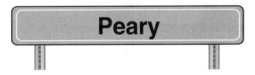

Place Name
Named in honor of Artic explorer Robert Edwin Peary. A Pennsylvania native before he traversed the inland ice of northwestern Greenland in 1891. In 1900 he traced the northern limit of the Greenland archipelago. Nine years later he reached the North Pole.

Place Name
Nicknamed "The Hill Top City," Eveleth was named for Edwin Eveleth, a Michigan lumberman.

Historical Significance
The town was slow to grow at first, but that changed after a mining boom between 1900 and 1910.

Local Landmark
Leonidas Overlook is the highest man-made point on the Iron Trail with spectacular panoramic views of the EvTac and Minntac mining operations.

Christian Brother's hockey stick measuring 107 feet, weighing over 3 tons and complete with a giant rubber puck is the world's largest.

* * * *

The U.S. Hockey Hall of Fame pays tribute to a sport with its American roots traced back to Eveleth.

Prominent People

The first United States born National Hockey League player to score five goals in a game was Eveleth native Mark Pavelich. He did it when he lead the New York Rangers to an 11 to 2 victory over the Hartford Whalers.

Pavelich was also a member of the gold medal-winning "Miracle on Ice" 1980 U.S. Olympic hockey team.

Place Name

Gilbert's beginnings can be traced to a mining location which began around 1892 and evolved into the Village of Sparta. When the town was moved to clear the way for iron ore mining in 1908, it took the name of the nearest group of mines, Gilbert. Today the mine is closed but the city remains.

Place Name

The city of Aurora was christened in 1903 by local civic leaders who were inspired by a particularly brilliant display of northern lights high above the new village.

Prominent People

Actress Francine York comes from Aurora. She has appeared in episodes of Mr. Belvedere, Beverly Hills 90210, Even Stevens as well as many made for TV movies.

Place Name

Platted in 1892 by the Virginia Improvement Company, this town is named after the home state of the company's president.

Historical Significance

This community's history is based on lumbering and mining. This is especially true after

the railroad arrived into the area.

    The Misabe Mountain Mine is one of the largest open-pit mines in the world. It shipped about 7,000 tons of ore a day.

* * * *

    A large portion of Virginia's population is Finnish. A group of them formed a Finnish Temperance Society early in the town's existence.

Geological

    The Laurentian Divide is the ride of low, rugged hills meandering through Northern Minnesota that separates the headwaters of streams which flow North and South. Streams which begin on the North slope of the Divide flow through Canada to Hudson Bay and the Arctic Ocean.

    On the opposite side of the divide, streams flow South into Lake Superior, eventually reaching the Atlantic Ocean. The Laurentian is only a remnant of a once gigantic mountain range formed more than a billion years ago.

Prominent People

    Hollywood actor Michael Goodwin, comes from the city of Virginia, MN, starred in the TV episodes of Magnum P.I., MacGyver, Jake and the Fat Man, L.A. Law, and Matlock.

Mountain Iron
(See Hwy 169 - pg 154)

Laurentian Divide

Geological

    Five miles north of Virginia the Laurentian Divide is formed by a prominent array of hills known as the Giants Range. This ridge has been a highland for over two billion years!

    The name "Laurentian" is used because the granites forming the ridges are similar to, and were once thought to be related to, granites of the Laurentide Mountains in Quebec. Although this connection is no longer made, the name has remained.

    The Giants range is made up mostly of several types of granite that formed several kilometers deep in the earth's crust about 2.7 billion years ago. Uplift and erosion slowly brought the granites to the surface; they have formed a highland throughout time because they are resistant to

> The Laurentian Divide separates the watershed of streams that flow north to the Artic Ocean from the watershed of streams that flow southeast through the Great Lakes to the Atlantic Ocean.

erosion. In the road cuts near the parking lot of the rest area, crisscrossing bodies of darker and lighter granite record several successive intrusions of molten rock. Because of the complexity of the rocks, this site is known as "Confusion Hill" to local geologists.

About two billion years ago, the lower ground south of these highlands was covered by an ocean in which sediments were deposited. These sediments formed the rocks that include the world-famous Biwabik Iron Formation of the Mesabi Range. About 80 million years ago during the Cretaceous period, sediments were again deposited in an ocean that lay south of the Giants Range.

Between two million and 10,000 years ago, glaciers that advanced and receded across this terrain removed most of the Cretaceous sedimentary rocks and scoured the older, underlying bedrock surface. Deposits of silt, sand, gravel, and boulders left behind by the glaciers now cover most of the bedrock.

(Historical marker located on Hwy 53 at the rest area five miles north of Virginia.)

Place Name

Originally the post office was known as Brittmount. When the town was incorporated it took the railway station name which was a shortened version.

Place Name

This town as well as its namesake in Turkey, celebrates their name for the long-haired goats whose wool is largely exported.

> Two quarries in the area yield granite.
>
> Note, there are only two known deposits of green granite in the world. One is in Germany, and the other is near Cook.

Place Name

This town was named in honor of a lumber dealer from Duluth, Minnesota by the name of Wirth Cook. He was also the one primarily responsible for promoting the construction of the Duluth, Winnipeg and Pacific Railroad; of which he later became president of.

Industry

There is also quite a bit of business done in the shipping of spruce and balsam for Christmas trees.

Place Name

This town borrowed the name from an Ojibwe village in the area.

Place Name

This town is named for William and Stephen Gheen, two Ojibwe mixed-blood brothers who homesteaded in the area developing a government farm and trading post at Elbow Lake. Stephen was an Indian agent for almost ten years while William was the local postmaster.

Place Name

This former Duluth, Winnipeg and Pacific Railway station was named for the areas first postmaster and owner of the general store, William Orr.

Place Name

Named for an officer of the Duluth, Winnipeg and Pacific Railway.

Place Name

This village was located on the banks of the Ash Lake when the railroad built a station in the area.

Duluth   *International Falls*

Place Name

Grand Rapids native Edwin Ray Lewis was the land surveyor and timber cruiser in the area when the town was established.

Place Name

Lou Boulin, the areas first settler, purchased land to homestead from real estate agent, Erik Franson. Swedish born Franson came to the United States in the 1890s settling in Canada before making International Falls his home.

International Falls
(See Hwy 71 - pg 195)

HIGHWAY 52

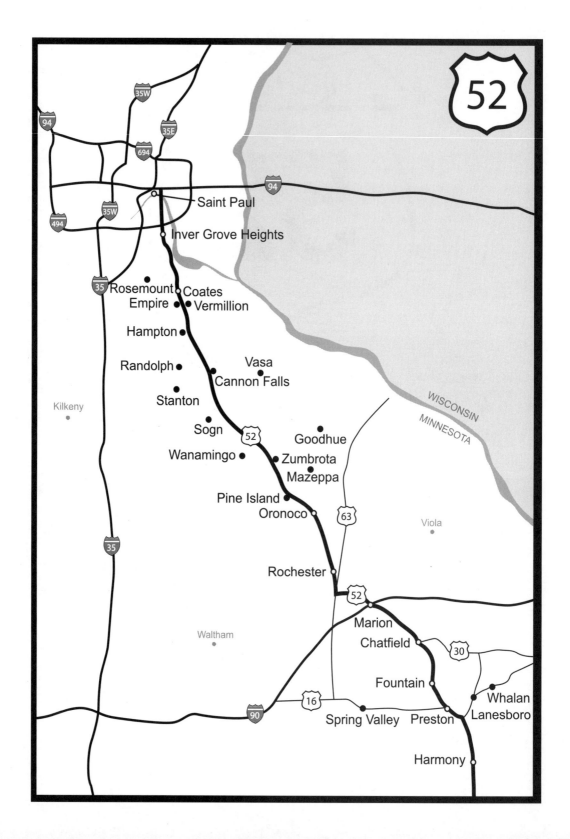

Harmony

Place Name

This town was originally known as Windom in honor of Senator William Windom.

However, legend has it when the settlers decided to make their community an incorporated village, they met to choose a name. Each group wanted the town named for its leader, and the bickering became louder. Finally the chairman banged his gavel on the table and said, "Let's have harmony here!".

Prominent People

Harmony attracted an overwhelmingly Amish culture. When traveling the bright green countryside, it is not uncommon for travelers to see horse-drawn carriages or farmers using a horse and plow.

Local Landmark

The famous Niagara cave is located only a few miles away from Harmony. This cave has a 60-foot subterranean waterfall that exists 200 feet below the Earth's surface. The falls splash into a mysterious underground river. The cave also contains a chapel and a wishing well. A labyrinth of trails and caves wind their way through the dark underground cave. The cave contains stalactites and fossils from thousands of years ago, as well.

The cave was actually discovered by accident in 1926 by a farmer who was continually losing his pigs. One day, the farmer was roaming the lands, searching for his missing pigs, when he heard grunting and squealing noises. He followed the noises to the strange underground cave where his pigs were standing, unable to get out. This resulted in the discovery of one of the most unique caves in Minnesota and in the entire Midwest.

Lanesboro

Place Name

Lanesboro is in a valley where the south branch of the Root River pierces a deep gorge. The scenic placement resulted in the town being referred to as Minnesota's "Hidden City".

Actually some believe the name was given as a result of the early settlers coming from Lanesboro Township in Berkshire County, Massachusetts. While others believe the name honors F.A. Lane, one of the stockholders in the town site company.

Historical Significance

Like immigrants from many European nations in the mid-19th century, Norwegians left their homeland to escape overpopulation, food shortages and farm foreclosures. They began arriving in Minnesota in the 1850s, drawn by rich farmland and job opportunities. Eventually they grew to become the state's third largest ethnic group, and Minnesota

became a national cultural center for Norwegian Americans.

Among the first to arrive were immigrants who had first settled in Wisconsin and then migrated into southeastern Minnesota. There they formed rural communities anchored by Lutheran churches, which were social and religious centers and visible links to the traditions of Norway.

As these farming settlements grew, newcomers moved on to the prairies of central and western Minnesota. When the railroad reached Moorhead in 1872, Norwegian immigrants poured into the Red River Valley. The earliest and most numerous group of European settlers in the valley, they quickly became leaders of business and local affairs.

Norwegian immigrants in the 1880s and 1890s found other employment as good farmland became scarce. Some pioneered commercial fishing on the North Shore of Lake Superior. Others gravitated to the cities and the iron range, where they worked in mills and mines and as domestic servants.

To serve their growing numbers around the state, Norwegians formed their own institutions such as schools, fraternal societies like the Sons of Norway, political organizations, and businesses that fostered the development of a Norwegian-American culture. Novelist like O.E. Rolvaag and Martha Ostenso wrote about Norwegian-American experiences. With an active Norwegian-American press as their forum, Norwegian-Americans rose to prominence in Minnesota politics, religion and higher education.

Immigrants' quotas, the Great Depression and World War II slowed the flow of new immigrants to the state. Yet Norwegian-Americans culture thrives thanks to an enduring interest in their heritage.

(Historical marker located on Hwy 16)

Local Landmark

The DNR fish hatchery is situated one mile west of Lanesboro. This hatchery in particular is dedicated to the preservation of rainbow trout.

* * * *

Sylvan Park contains an original 1869 stone dam that still provides hydroelectric power in Lanesboro.

Whalan

Whalan is well known for its Stand Still Parade!

General Trivia
Held in May during the area Sykkle Tur celebration, the Stand Still Parade, shown on CBS Television, features a moving audience while floats and color guard stand still.

Place Name

Plotted as a mill town, John Kaercher, its founder, named the town in honor of his millwright, Luther Preston.

Local Landmark

Take a walk through layers of rock that were once deposits of sediment on the floor of a shallow sea that covered this area 450 million years ago. Ancient marine fossils on the cave walls and ceiling reveal part of the story of life at the time. Mystery Cave is a significant feature in the local karst terrain. This terrain consists of limestone and dolostone carbonate bedrock that lies very close to the surface. The carbonate bedrock is riddled with features eroded by slightly acidic water: sinkholes, passageways, extensive underground water systems, and caves.

Mystery Cave is a significant feature in the local karst terrain.

Rainwater becomes slightly acidic by absorbing carbon dioxide in the atmosphere and, if it seeps through the soil, by absorbing the carbon dioxide given off by plant roots, bacteria, and other organisms. Over time, this water following bedrock joints, or fractures, dissolves the carbonate rock and gradually enlarges the crack. Eventually, a system of underground drainage will develop that bypasses the surface drainage pattern.

Mystery Cave is part of an active underground drainage system that captures water from the South Branch of the Root River and redirects it through a complex, three-dimensional maze of interconnecting passageways. Regionally aligned joints in the bedrock direct the water flow and gives a strong east west orientation to many cave passages. The cave ranges from 10 to 50 meters below ground and has a total of more than 20 kilometers of passageways. The underground flow finally emerges at springs 2.4 kilometers northeast of here.

Exploration reveals a variety of typical calcite speleothems (mineral deposits formed by water), including stalactites, stalagmites, flowstone, and many others. Also, some extremely rare features such as organic filaments, pool fingers, and several types of iron-cored speleothems are known only in a few other caves in the world.

It is unknown when Mystery Cave started to form. Research shows that some of its cave passages existed and were filled with silt more than 200,000 years ago, but those near the main entrance are likely to be much younger. Continually changing, Mystery Cave holds a unique record of time, sedimentation, glaciations, and karst processes that makes it an important part of Minnesota's geology.

<u>(Historical marker located Co. Rd 5)</u>

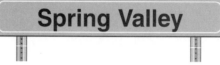

Spring Valley

Place Name
Spring Valley is a lovely town that got its name from the numerous springs in the area.

The stapler was invented in Spring Valley.

Historical Significance
Iron Ore was discovered in the Spring Valley area in 1930. It wasn't until 1942 when some five tons were mined due to the demand from the war.

Local Landmark
An old 1876 church that is now the Spring Valley Community Historical Society, is where The Laura Ingalls Wilder family once attended church here.

Fountain

Place Name
Fountain is named for the bountiful springs that lie in the region.

Geological
The surrounding area and much of southeastern Minnesota are karst landscapes. Minnesota's karst landscapes consist of limestone and dolostone bedrock that lies very close to the surface. This carbonate bedrock is often riddled with features eroded by slightly acidic water: sinkholes, passageways, extensive underground water systems and caves.

Rainwater becomes slightly acidic by absorbing carbon dioxide in the atmosphere, and if it seeps through the soil, by absorbing the carbon dioxide given off by plant roots, bacteria, and other organisms. Over time, this water following bedrock joints, or fractures, dissolves the carbonate rock and gradually enlarges the cracks. Eventually, a system of underground drainage will develop that bypasses the surface drainage pattern. Sinkholes are inlets to that system.

A sinkhole may begin to develop where joints in the bedrock intersects and the downward flow of water is more rapid. Over time, a funnel-shaped cavity often forms in the rock. Infiltrating surface water erodes the soil and moves it down the hole, thus forming a pronounced depression in the ground. When the erosion into the subsurface is slow, sinkhole formation is also a slow, gradual process. When erosion is rapid, a sudden collapse of overlying sediment can occur. Sinkholes sometimes collapse suddenly after heavy rains. A sinkhole may become temporarily closed as newly collapsed sediment clogs the passageway.

In a karst landscape, water flowing into sinkholes bypasses the natural filtering action of a lengthy percolation through thick soil and sediment layers. Once in the bedrock, water can move rapidly through a complex system of passageways at rates as high as several

kilometers per day. Using dye to color the water, scientists have shown that water entering a sinkhole emerges in about a day at the headwater springs of Trout Creek, about two kilometers north of here.

In karst terrain, bedrock aquifers, a common source for drinking water, are susceptible to rapid contamination from activities on the surface of the land. Likewise, water quality in spring-fed streams, which mark the end point of underground drainage in a karst landscape, may also be affected.

(Historical marker located on Hwy 52)

Place Name

Chatfield is named after Judge Andrew Chatfield, who served as the first judge in the county courthouse.

Local Landmark

There are 75,000 items of music housed in the Chatfield Brass Music Library, a one-of-a-kind library provided by donations that came from around the world. Not only does the library lend music, but it catalogs, repairs, and stores music as well.

The Chatfield Brass Bank Music Library is a one-of-a-kind library. It has the largest collection of brass band music in the world.

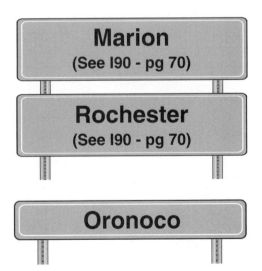

Place Name

Oronoco was established in 1854 by settlers who worked hard to develop the water-power resources of the Zumbro River. Resembling South America's Orinoco River inspired Dr. Hector Galloway to suggest the name.

Historical Significance

During the summer of 1858, gold was discovered in the bed of the Zumbro River at Rochester near Oronoco. The news created a local sensation. On July 1, 1858, the Rochester Democrat reported: "The excitement in reference to the gold discoveries in and near Rochester and near Oronoco is unabated. The diggings at Oronoco are yielding two to six dollars a day, per man... Some ninety to one hundred men are at work in the diggings". While little came of the boom in Rochester, the Oronoco Mining Company invested over $1,000 in sluices and a water wheel erected about five miles below Oronoco. The following spring, floods unceremoniously carried away the miners' handiwork. Driven on by a frenzied desire to "get rich quick," the prospectors rebuilt the installations and extracted enough gold to keep their appetites whetted. A few months later, in July, 1859, another flood demolished their works a second time. This catastrophe and the hard times lingering from the great panic of 1857 exhausted the men's determination and resources, and the boom died overnight. Perhaps someday gold will again be discovered in the river here, and Oronoco will relive its all too short moment of glory.

(Historical marker located on County Road 12)

Place Name

The Dakota Indians lived on an island in the middle of the Zumbro river, which circled the village. They lived in skin tents that used to pass the cold winter months, sheltered by the thick branches of the tall pine trees. They called it Wa-zee-wee-ta, or Pine Island.

Pine Isand is sometimes called the "Cheese Center of Minnesota".

Historical Significance

The Swiss settled the town of Pine Island establishing the cheese-making industry. In fact, in 1914, a 6,000- pound hunk of cheese was produced in Pine Island and shipped to the State Fair. This was the largest chunk of cheese ever produced from one day's whey.

Place Name

When the village was founded by Joseph Ford and his son Orville, they named it after the Cossack chief, Ivan Mazeppa, commemorated in a poem by Byron.

Zumbrota

Place Name

The town is named after the river which the Dakota called Wazi Oju, meaning Pines Planted referring to the grove of white pines at nearby Pine Island.

The French referred to the river as the Riviere des Embarras because of the substantial amount of driftwood that obstructed their navigation up and down the river.

When the English immigrants from Massachusetts came here they translated the French unrecognized name simply as the Zumbro.

At the time the village was incorporated the Dakota suffix meaning at, to, or on, was added to the name, Zumbrota.

C.C. Beck, the "Captain Marvel" cartoon creator and illustrator was born in Zumbrota.

Historical Significance

The old Dubuque Trail linked Dubuque with Saint Paul in the 1850s and was one of the major overland stage routes during the territorial period. The fare per person from Saint Paul to Zumbrota was $4.50.

Local Landmarks

The Old Covered Bridge is Zumbrota's proudest possession. This imposing 120 foot structure vividly recalls the 63 year period, 1869 to 1932, when it was located on Main Street, the gateway to the town over which hundreds of wagon loads of wheat were transported annually on their way to market and a favorite haunt for young couples until the village council ordered a kerosene lamp hung in the center.

The Old Covered Bridge is the only such bridge surviving in Minnesota.

(Historical marker located at intersection of Hwy 52 and 58)

Wanamingo

Place Name

This town takes its name from a Native American heroine popularized in a novel at that time.

Goodhue

Place Name

This town as well as the county was named in honor of James Madison Goodhue, Minnesota's first printer and editor.

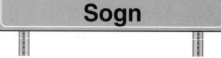

Harmony

Saint Paul

Place Name

The town is named after a district in Norway.

Place Name

This town was named for William Stanton and his sons, who together with other New England immigrants settled here in 1855. His log home was for many years the only place weary travelers could stop between Cannon Falls and places to the west. He was known for entertaining as many as fifty people in one night.

Vasa

Named for the King of Sweden, Gustavus Vasa. Known generally as Gustavus I, the Christian king and founder of the Lutheran Church.

Historical Significance

One called "the most Swedish colony in America", the town prospered as an agricultural community until its general stores, creamery, and depot office were closed in the 1950s. It has continued to serve as a religious center and its ethnic heritage has been carefully preserved.

Prominent People

Two men played major roles in Vasa's development. Mattson was one of the earliest promoters of Swedish immigration to the United States. He organized and led a company of Swedish volunteers in the Civil War and later became Minnesota's first commissioner of immigration in 1867 and its secretary of state in 1869. He later served as U.S. Consul General to India and in 1888 was named national chairman of the celebration marking the 25th anniversary of Swedish settlement in America.

Reverend Eric Norelius, who settled in Vargas in 1855, established about a dozen Lutheran congregations in southeastern Minnesota. A major force in establishing the Minnesota Conference of the Lutheran Church, the Augusta Synod, he also started the state's first Swedish newspaper and one of its first colleges, Gustavus Adolphus, now located in St. Peter. Minnesota's first private children's home and first private high school were both established in Vasa by Pastor Norelius, who was later knighted for his efforts by Swedish King Oscar.

(Historical marker located on Hwy 7)

Cannon Falls

Place Name

Cannon Falls was named for the white cascading falls of the Cannon River.

The town was originally going to be called Canoe Falls, but because the settlers misinterpreted the Native American's language, the settlement was named Cannon Falls.

Local Landmark

This was the first regiment tendered to President Lincoln at the outbreak of the Civil War; and it served three years in the Army of the Potomac, during which time it engaged in the following battles and operations.

Bull Run, Ball's Bluff, Siege of Yorktown, Construction of "Grapevine" Bridge across the Chickahominy River (over which McClelland moved reinforcements to support his left wing at Fair Oakes), Fair Oaks, Peach Orchard, Savage's Station, White Oak Swamp, Glendale, Malvern Hill, Flint Hill, Vienna, South Mountain Antietam, Fredericksburg, Chancellorsville, Haymarket, Gettysburg, Bristow Station and Mine Run.

(Historical marker located in the Cannon Falls Cemetery on state highway 19)

* * * *

Colonel William Colvill was born in Forestville, New York, April 5, 1830. He emigrated to Red Wing, Minnesota in 1854 where he opened a law office. In 1855, he established the first local newspaper, the "Sentinel", which he edited until the outbreak of the Civil War.

In 1861, he raised the Goodhue County Volunteers and was mustered in as a captain in the First Minnesota Volunteer Infantry. He was promoted to colonel of the regiment in May, 1863. During the Civil War, Colonel Colville was twice afflicted with wounds that would affect him the rest of his life. He was discharged with the regiment in 1864. He was mustered out of the service in May, 1865, with the brevet rank of brigadier general for gallant and meritorious service.

He resumed his law practice in Red Wing. Appointed editor of the "Republican", he held the position until his election to state attorney general, serving at that capacity from 1866-1868. In 1876, he entered the House of Representatives and served one term. In 1877, he was appointed registrar of the federal land office at Duluth. A student of astronomy, mineralogy and geology, Colonel Colvill was the author of a history of glaciers in the northwest.

> The William Colvill State Monument stands near Cannon Falls. Colvill was a Colonel in the Civil War that led the First Minnesota Regiment in the battle of Gettysburg in 1863.

In 1867, Colonel Colvill married Jane Morgan. Jane Morgan was born in Trenton Falls, New York on October 9, 1834. She was a direct descendant of Parson Brewster, the minister who served the little band of colonists who came to this country on the Mayflower. Highly regarded for her charity and her leadership in church work, Mrs. Colvill died in Duluth on November 13, 1894. She was laid to rest in Cannon Falls Cemetery.

Colonel Colvill died on June 12, 1905. He was buried beside his wife in the Cannon Falls Cemetery near the graves of his aunt, two sisters and their families.

The statue of Colonel Colvill, designed by Mrs. George Backus, of St. Paul, is of bronze and mounted on a pedestal of Bedford stone. A duplicate is found at the state capitol in St. Paul, Minnesota. This monument was unveiled at a ceremony in 1909. After completing ground work including the balustrade and steps to the memorial, a plaque commemorating the Colonel and the First Minnesota was unveiled at a dedication ceremony on July 29, 1928. President and Mrs. Calvin Coolidge along with Minnesota Governor Christianson were in attendance. The memorial stairway and balustrade were designed by St. Paul architect J.C. Neimeyer.

The statue is the only state monument dedicated to a Civil War Veteran.

(Historical marker located in the Cannon Falls Cemetery on state highway 19)

* * * *

At Gettysburg the loss of the Regiment on July 2nd, 1863, in its charge against the Confederate Brigades of General Barksdale and General Wilcox, was 82 per cent of the men engaged.

General Hancock says, "I ordered these men to charge because I saw that I must gain five minutes time. Reinforcements were coming on the run, but I knew that before they could reach the threatened point the Confederates, unless checked, would seize the position. The charge was necessary. I was glad to find such a gallant body of men at hand willing to make the terrible sacrifice".

Again on July 3rd, 1863, the regiment sustained a further loss of 15 per cent of the men engaged in resisting General Pickett's charge of 15,000 men against the left center of the Union line.

The regiment was successively commanded by Colonel Willis A. Groman, Colonel Napoleon J.T. Dana, Colonel Alfred Sully, Colonel George N. Morgan, and Colonel Colvill, of whom the first three, through the valor of the regiment, were made brigadier generals during the service, and the last two were brevetted brigadier generals at the close of the war. (Approved by 1907 legislature; dedicated July 29, 1928)

(Historical marker located in the Cannon Falls Cemetery on state highway 19)

Randolph

Place Name

The town was first named Richmond for John Richmond, the areas first settler. It was changed because there already was another town by the same name. When it was renamed they chose Randolph to commemorate the distinguished statesman admired from Virginia, John Randolph.

Harmony 52 *Saint Paul*

Hampton

Place Name
Connecticut native Nathaniel Martin suggested the name of his birthplace, the city of Hampton.

Empire

Place Name
Named for Empire, New York, the hometown of Mrs. Irving, the wife of one of the areas first settlers.

Vermillion

Place Name
This town gets its name from the Vermillion River which bears the name translated from the Dakota.

Coates

Place Name
Named for an early settler, G.A. Coates.

Rosemount

Place Name
Named for a picturesque city in Ireland by Andrew Keegan and Hugh Derham.

Inver Grove Heights

Place Name
Attracted by the area's rolling green hills of the countryside and the close proximity to the Mississippi River, early pioneers staked claims establishing a community.

Settlers from Germany laid claim to the wooded farmland in the northwest portion of the

community, clearing and cultivating fields from among the area lakes. Other settlers from France and England built homes along the river.

Hundreds of settlers were attracted to the township that was named after an Irish fishing village, "Iver" and commemorating the homeland of the German settlers, "Grove".

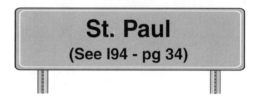

St. Paul
(See I94 - pg 34)

HIGHWAY 23

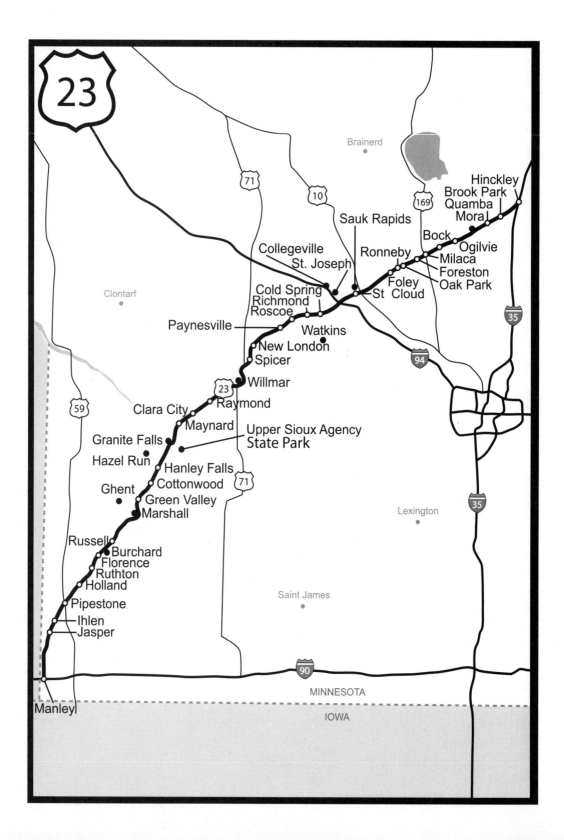

23

Brainerd

Hinckley
Brook Park
Quamba
Mora
Bock
Ogilvie
Milaca
Foreston
Oak Park
Foley
St. Cloud
Sauk Rapids
Ronneby
Collegeville
St. Joseph
Cold Spring
Richmond
Roscoe
Paynesville
Watkins
New London
Spicer
Willmar
Raymond
Clara City
Maynard
Upper Sioux Agency
State Park
Granite Falls
Hazel Run
Hanley Falls
Cottonwood
Ghent
Green Valley
Marshall
Russell
Burchard
Florence
Ruthton
Holland
Pipestone
Ihlen
Jasper
Manley

Clontarf

Lexington

Saint James

MINNESOTA

IOWA

270

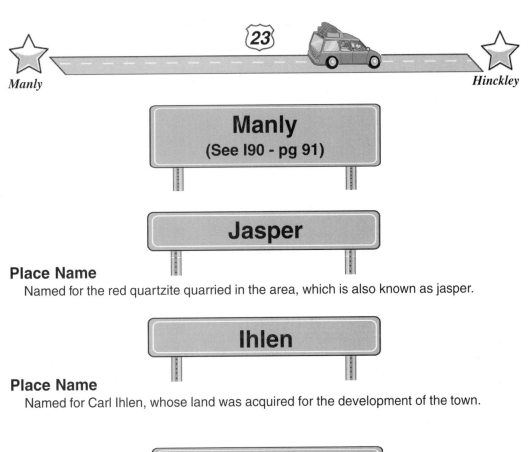

Manly

Hinckley

Manly
(See I90 - pg 91)

Jasper

Place Name

Named for the red quartzite quarried in the area, which is also known as jasper.

Ihlen

Place Name

Named for Carl Ihlen, whose land was acquired for the development of the town.

Pipestone
(See Hwy 75 - pg 161)

Holland

Place Name

Following the arrival of the Wilmar and Sioux Falls Railroad, the village was platted and named by Clara Huibregtse after the homeland of a large colony of Hollanders settling here.

Ruthton

Place Name

When the village was established by Willmar and Sioux Falls Railroad, it was named in honor of W.H. Sherman's wife.

General Trivia

In 1983, tragedy struck in this small Southern Minnesota town. James Lee Jenkins was angered over the recession, and went too far in venting. Jenkins and his son killed two bankers who had foreclosed several farmers. Jenkins and his son fled to Paducah, Texas where the elder Jenkins killed himself. The younger Jenkins turned himself in and was found guilty of first-degree murder.

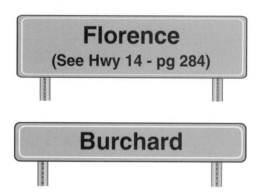

Florence
(See Hwy 14 - pg 284)

Burchard

Place Name

H.M. Burchard, a land agent for the Chicago and North Western railroad from Marshall was commemorated in the selection of the city's name.

Russell

Place Name

This town was named for, Russell Spicer, the son of a promoter responsible for building the branch of the railroad to this area.

Marshall
(See Hwy 59 - pg 231)

Ghent
(See Hwy 59 - pg 233)

Green Valley

Place Name

This name was given in reference to the green prairie along the banks of the Redwood River.

Cottonwood

Place Name

The town received its name from the lake which was called Cottonwood because of the trees growing along its shores.

Hanley Falls

Place Name

Named for John Hanley from Minneapolis, a general freight agent for the Minneapolis and St. Louis Railroad. Falls was included because of the Yellow Medicine River.

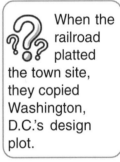
When the railroad platted the town site, they copied Washington, D.C.'s design plot.

Hazel Run

Place Name

Hazel Run gets its name from the creek in the area, which is a tributary to the Minnesota River.

Upper Sioux Agency

Historical Significance

By treaties of 1851 and 1858 the lands of the once mighty Sioux were reduced to shoestring reservations along the southern bank of the Minnesota River. The Sisseton and Wahpeton bands of the Upper Sioux held the land from lake Traverse to the Yellow Medicine River.

The Upper, or Yellow Medicine, Agency was established to serve as the government's headquarters for distributing annuity payments to the Sisseton and Wahpeton. It was also

273

the center where schools were set up and where government employees attempted to teach the Indians to farm. The agency site, selected in July, 1854, by Agent Robert Murphy, was near the missions of Dr. Thomas Williamson and the Reverend Stephen Riggs.

Like the Lower Agency thirty miles downriver, the Upper boasted sturdy homes for its physician, carpenter, farm superintendent, blacksmiths, and other employees; a two-story brick warehouse and agent's residence; a school; stables; a brick kiln; and a jail. Nearby were four traders' stores and a least a hundred houses for farmer Indians.

Here at the Upper Agency, in August 1862, the initial rumblings of the Sioux Uprising were heard. The annuity payments were late, and the Sioux were starving and restless. Although there was food in the warehouse, the Indian agent at first refused to distribute it until the annuity money arrived. When the Indians threatened a fight, the agent yielded, and the situation was temporarily quieted down.

Later that month the Sioux Uprising broke out, and the Indians looted and burned the Upper Agency. A leader of the peaceful faction of Upper Sioux, John Other Day, led many whites from the agency to safety.

(Historical marker located on Hwy 67, 8 miles southeast of Granite Falls)

Granite Falls

Geological

> ★ This town gets it name from the granite and gneiss rock outcrops and 38 foot falls of the Minnesota River.

The Minnesota River Valley is a witness to time. Rocks formed 3.8 billion years ago, some of the oldest in the world, lie exposed on the valley floor. These gray, pink and red granite rocks are memorials to a fiery young earth when molten rocks in the planet's interior pushed against the earth's crust, deforming it, creating mountains four miles high. For eons, water and ice relentlessly eroded the mountains, eventually leaving a subdued plain.

At the close of the last ice age, 12,000 years ago, mile-high glaciers melted, forming Glacial Lake Agassiz to the north of here. The outlet for the lake was Glacial Lake Warren whose torrent carved the large valley. The abrasive current streamlined the rock outcroppings which lay in its way. The roar of rushing water and tumbling boulders would have been heard for miles. Today, the gentle Minnesota River creates barely a whisper as it flows almost unnoticed in the shadow of its prehistoric glory.

Across the river, spearheads, knives, hide-scrapers, and other stone tools have been discovered in association with extinct forms of bison. These bison-butcherings have dated human occupation of the valley to 6,400 years ago.

(Historical marker located on Hwy 212 , 1 1/4 mile east of Granite Falls)

Historical Significance

In the summer of 1862 the Dakota Indians were desperate and near starvation. Confined by treaties to a narrow strip of land on the south side of the Minnesota River, they waited

for treaty money and food from the government and talked of war to regain their homeland.

On August 17, a group of young Dakota men killed five settlers in Meeker County. Many Dakota felt the die had now been cast; there was no alternative but to go to war. The next day the warring faction led by Little Crow attacked the Lower Sioux Indian Agency, and the war erupted over western Minnesota.

Settlers were killed or driven off their farms, but attacks on Fort Ridgely and New Ulm were unsuccessful. An army of volunteers was formed, led by Henry Sibley, who had been Minnesota's first state governor. Here, at Lone Tree Lake (mistaken for Wood Lake, three and a half miles to the west), Sibley's men fought a decisive battle against the Dakota on September 23, 1862. Three days later most of the Dakota surrendered. Little Crow and his most ardent followers escaped to the west and north.

White Minnesotans demanded revenge. A government tribunal sentenced more than 300 Dakota to death. President Abraham Lincoln, at the urging of Episcopal bishop Henry Whipple, greatly reduced this number. Nevertheless, on December 26, 1862, 38 Dakota were hanged in Mankato, in what has been called the largest mass execution in the United States. Some 1,700 Dakota, most having not participated in the war, were confined at Fort Snelling. Many died over the winter; the survivors were shipped to a reservation in what is now South Dakota.

(Historical marker located on Hwy 67 in Wood Lake State Wayside)

Place Name
This town was named for the superintendent of the Great Northern Railroad, John Spicer's brother-in-law.

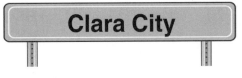

Place Name
Named for the wife of Theodor Koch, a manager for the Holland syndicate buying farmland in the area for their colony.

Place Name
John Spicer, the founder of Spicer, his son Raymond is the person this town is named after.

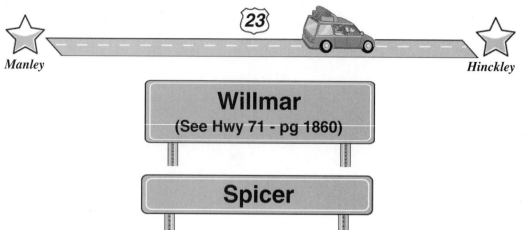

Willmar
(See Hwy 71 - pg 1860)

Spicer

Place Name

John Spicer, for whom the town is named, was the president of the railroad company and the original founder of this site.

New London

Place Name

Seeing a similarity between the prospering village of his home county, Louis Larson named this area which resembled it after New London, Wisconsin.

Local Landmark

The Lunborg-Broberg State Monument pays tribute to two families who were massacred by the Sioux Indians August 20, 1861, while on their way home from a religious meeting held at the house of Andrias Lundborg.

(Historical marker located on Hwy 9)

Paynesville

Place Name

Paynesville was named for the first settler making a homestead claim in the area, Edwin Payne.

Watkins

Place Name

This city name was given by the officers, for one of the officers, of the Minneapolis and Pacific Railroad.

Prominent People

Congressman Eugene McCarthy served for over two decades, first as a representative from 1949 to 1959 and then as a senator from 1959 to 1971. He is known for his anti-Vietnam War platform which resulted in the challenging of President Lyndon Johnson for the Democratic nomination. His stance and strong showing in New Hampshire was responsible for Johnson dropping out the race. McCarthy would eventually lose the party's nomination to fellow Minnesotan Hubert Humphrey.

> Watkins is the hometown of Eugene McCarthy.

Place Name

Originally known as Zion, the name was changed to the name of the Great Northern Railroad station.

Place Name

Rueben Richardson honors the surname for one of the areas first settlers.

Place Name

This town derives its name from the cold natural mineral springs in the area.

Local Landmark

Cold Spring is actually a warm-hearted town that embraces the Assumption Chapel. This chapel has an interesting story behind it.

In the 1850s, locusts invaded the Cold Spring area. Worried farmers vowed to the Virgin Mary that they would build a chapel in her honor if she would take the locusts away. According to legend, the locusts miraculously disappeared.

In 1877, farmers built the Gothic Revival Locust Chapel just as they promised. Yet, in 1894, nature's wrath destroyed the chapel by means of a tornado.

The people of Cold Spring have continued to be dedicated to their promise. In 1951, a replacement chapel called the Assumption was built. It still stands today in honor of the Virgin.

> The local Cold Spring Brewing Company brewed Billy Beer, made famous by President Jimmy Carter's brother.

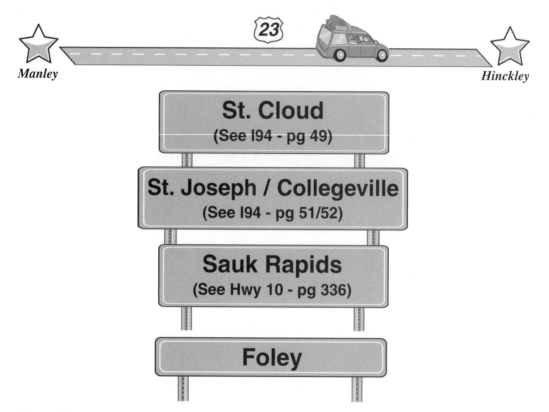

St. Cloud
(See I94 - pg 49)

St. Joseph / Collegeville
(See I94 - pg 51/52)

Sauk Rapids
(See Hwy 10 - pg 336)

Foley

Place Name

John Foley and his five brothers came to the area from Ontario, Canada as contractors with the Great Northern Railroad. After camping on this site, they acquired land that would be used when the city was platted.

Ronneby

Place Name

Named after a town in southern Sweden, near Karlskrona, located on the River Ronneby near its mouth in the Baltic Sea.

Oak Park

Place Name

This village started as a flag station for the Great Northern Railroad which received its name for the abundant oak groves in the area.

Foreston

Place Name

The town was established as Bridgman when the lumbering community was developed along the west branch Rum River. Later the name was changed to reflect on the hardwood forest that surrounded the town.

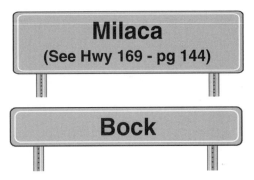

Milaca
(See Hwy 169 - pg 144)

Bock

Place Name

The officers of the Great Northern Railroad referred to the station as Tosca before renaming it for the Bock brothers of New Ulm, who were the areas first businessmen.

Ogilvie

Place Name

The Hersey Lumber Company was the original owners of the area here known first as Fisk and then later as Groundhouse. Oric Ogilvie Whited purchased the town site and renamed the town after himself.

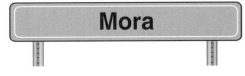

Mora

Place Name

Named by Israel Israelson hometown in Dalarna, Sweden.

Local Landmark

Mora pays tribute to its sister city in Mora, Sweden with a 20-foot high "MoraKocka" that stands in the city center has a 48" clock face and decorative painting, a design called Dala malning.

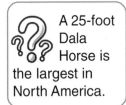

A 25-foot Dala Horse is the largest in North America.

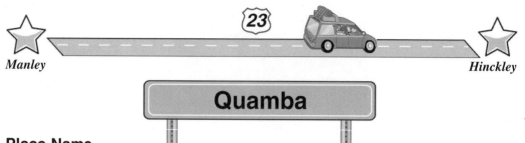

Quamba

Place Name

This town was also platted by Oric Ogilvie Whited on land adjacent to the side tracks for the Great Northern Railroad. The railroad referred to their station as Mud Creek, because of the creek where the tracks had crossed. When the depot was built, it was renamed Quamba, for the Indian word meaning mud hole.

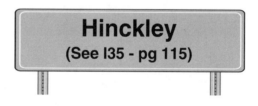

Brook Park

Place Name

When the township was established in 1894, Dr. C.A. Kelsey envisioned a lumbering camp developed in a park like setting along the Pokegama River.

Hinckley
(See I35 - pg 115)

HIGHWAY 14

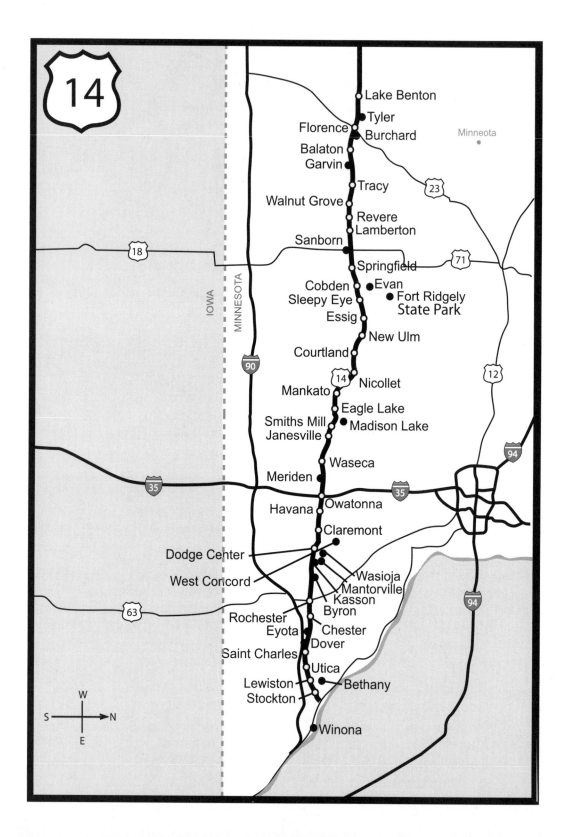

Lake Benton

Place Name

Lake Benton lies on the Southwestern shore of the lake for which the town is named.

Geological

Four miles southwest of the town is a series of towering bluffs. The Natives used to call a feature of these bluffs, "Hole in the Mountain". A cave-like hole runs through these bluffs and it used to be the channel for an ancient river.

* * * *

Buffalo Ridge marks a drainage divide separating the watersheds of the Mississippi and Missouri Rivers. Lake Benton drains east to the Mississippi River, and the Flandreau River drains west to the Missouri River.

The ridge is a moraine, a pile of sediment (silt, clay, gravel, and boulders), that was left at the edge of a glacier. The Bemis moraine was formed on the western side of an ice lobe that originated in Canada and extended south into Iowa 14,000 years ago.

Here at Lake Benton there is a break in the moraine about one to two kilometers wide. There are similar but less spectacular breaks in the moraine at Lake Hendricks and Lake Shaokatan to the north. In all these cases, a straight wide channel, now occupied by a long lake such as Lake Benton, lies on the east side of a break in the moraine. These channels, called tunnel valleys, were formed by water flowing forcefully beneath the melting glacier.

> The second highest point in southwestern Minnesota is on the Bemis moraine, locally known as Buffalo Ridge.

On the west side of the Bemis moraine, beyond the former ice margin, rivers occupy sinuous channels that vary in width. These meandering stream valleys were carved by glacial meltwater that flowed out from the tunnel valleys that cut through the moraine.

The change in character of the valleys from one side of the moraine to the other is due to a change in pressure. Water that flowed under the ice was under great pressure from the weight of the ice above. Under such high pressure, the water could flow uphill, the floor of the tunnel valley actually slopes uphill toward the moraine. Once the water flowed out from under the glacier, the pressure was released and the stream was free to meander.

(Historical marker located on Hwy 75)

Local Landmark

Lake Benton was famous for its opera. It is strange for this type of music to characterize a town of this size, but it strongly influences the community. The Lake Benton Opera House was built in 1896. The house served many entertainment purposes throughout its lifetime. It has recently been restored and is listed on the National Register of Historic Places.

Tyler

Place Name

Tyler was platted in 1879 and named in honor of C.B. Tyler, the register of the U.S. land office in New Ulm.

Florence

Place Name

The name was given for Florence Sherman, the daughter of its founder.

Burchard

Place Name

H.M. Burchard, a land agent for the Chicago and North Western railroad from Marshall was commemorated in the selection of the city's name.

Balaton

Place Name

This town takes its name from either the picturesque Lake Balaton in western Hungary or possibly after a stockholder for the Chicago and North Western Railway by the name of Balaton. Yet others say it was an adaptation of David Bell's name, called Belltown. Some even believe that the indecisiveness about selecting a name for the town resulted in a "ballot-on" election to choosing its name.

Garvin

Place Name

The town was named for H.C. Garvin, a traveling freight agent of the railway.

Tracy

Place Name

The town of Tracy was named for a former President of Chicago and Northwestern Railroad.

Local Landmark

The Wheels Across the Prairie Museum pays tribute to the settlers and the many modes of transportation they used to get to Minnesota.

Walnut Grove

Place Name

The village is characterized by rolling prairie lands and a walnut grove just outside the town for which it was named.

Prominent People

Laura Ingalls Wilder's family settled here from 1874 to 1900 except for a few years from 1876-77 when she lived briefly in Iowa.

Wilder wrote wonderful books that accurately depicted pioneer life. Her stories were transformed by Michael Landon into the hit television series, "Little House on the Prairie".

A sod-roofed home on Plum Creek was the first home of the young Wilder. Laura and her family survived a great deal of tragedy, including the grasshopper plague that struck so many regions in the state.

This community was the childhood home of author, Laura Ingalls Wilder

Revere

Place Name

Named in honor of the patriot of the American Revolution. Paul Revere is renown for his ride from Boston to Lexington to arousing the Minutemen that "the British are coming".

Lamberton

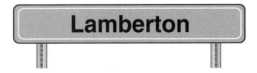

Place Name

This village commemorates the president of the Winona Deposit Bank, Henry Wilson Lamberton, who was elected president of the Winona and South Western Railway.

Historical Significance

Lamberton was a popular area for settlers to flock to in the frontier days. The reason for its popularity was that it was supposed to be rich in gold. Gold was found in some areas, but the supply was not nearly as plentiful as most believed. The gold-mining operations ceased after a short time, and the city grew from its rich agricultural industry instead.

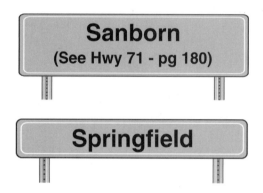

Sanborn
(See Hwy 71 - pg 180)

Springfield

Place Name

The town was originally called Burns. The name later changed to Springfield because for the large spring that connects the town to the Cottonwood River.

Cobden

Place Name

Because of its location near Sleepy Eye Creek, the principal north branch of the Cottonwood River, the original township was referred to as North Branch. The name would be changed in 1886 for the English statesman, Richard Cobden. Born in Sussex, England, Cobden entered parliament in the early 1840s and was known as an advocate of free trade and of peace. He was a supporter of the cause of the North during the Civil War.

Evan

Place Name

The original railway village was called Hanson station after Nels Hanson. Later the name was changed by the first postmaster, Martin Norseth, for his wife, Eva.

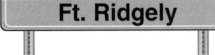

Ft. Ridgely

Local Landmark

Fort Ridgely was established in 1853 to defend the frontier and watch over the Sioux who had been moved to the Minnesota Valley two years earlier. When it was completed in 1855, the fort consisted of a large parade ground surrounded by stone and wood buildings.

From 1853-1862 the post was garrisoned first by regular U.S. army troops and then, after the outbreak of the Civil War, by volunteer regiments. When the Sioux Uprising began in 1962, Fort Ridgely assumed great importance as the only military post in the valley and a vital defense point against the Indians. Hundreds of settlers flocked here for safety, only

Fort Ridgely, Minnesota's third military post.

to encounter two Sioux offensives; these attacks were repelled mainly by the skillful use of artillery by the fort's defenders.

After the withdrawal of the military in 1872, most of the buildings deteriorated or were converted to other uses by settlers.

<u>(Historical marker located on Hwy 4)</u>

Historical Significance

Wednesday, August 29, 1862, 500 warriors assembled to capture the fort. At 1 P.M. Chief Little Crow calls out to the soldiers for a conference, but he is seated on his horse to the west of the fort and remains just out of range of the picket's guns. Suddenly the braves charge up out of the wooded ravine to the northeast. Sgt. McGrew brings his cannon out into the open to drive them back while Lt. Gene and his men route the warriors from the log buildings. Rifle fire from the barracks windows keeps the Indians on the run. The cannon fire is new to the Indians and proves to be too much for them to face. It keeps them confused and disorganizes their attack.

Little Crow and the other chiefs can not organize the warriors to get a well coordinated attack going. Finally at 3 P.M., one group charges out of the ravine to the southwest, but again the fire power of the cannon throws the warriors into a retreat. This cannon is in charge of Sgt. Jones and his infantry support from the Renville Rangers, a newly organized company of volunteers from the Upper Indian Agency near Granite Falls.

At 4 P.M. another group comes charging out of the ravine to the south, but here Sgt. Bishop's gun crew shooting across the open ground stops them before they reach the buildings.

The day ended with the young braves arguing with their chiefs over the strategy of the battle. The chiefs wanted to make a mass attack and take the fort, thus "opening the door to the Minnesota River valley," but the warriors wanted to go back to the easier task of driving the settlers from the farms and from New Ulm. The cannons at the four corners of the fort were more than they wanted to face, so off to New Ulm they rode.

Friday, August 22, 1862, 1200 warriors gathered to take the fort, but most are reluctant to start the attack. A coordinated attack is agreed on, but at 1 P.M. only the group in the wooded

ravine attack. The cannon fire from McGrew and Whipple again turn them back.

At 1:30 P.M. a large group from the west take the Sutler's store and barn, but Sgt. Jones fires red hot shells into the barn setting it afire.

Another group comes out of the ravine to the southwest and takes the barn. As the Indians build up their forces in the barn for a quick dash into the fort, Sgt. Jones maneuvers one of his cannons into position so that he can fire another red hot shell into the barn, thereby setting it on fire. This ends the threat for the time being.

By 4 P.M. the Indians seem to be getting organized for an all-out attack. A large group is gathering in the ravine to the southwest when Sgt. Jones fires several rounds from the cannon into the ravine. Women and children are also in the ravine so now the braves are furious and an attack starts anew from the wooded ravine. At the same time the Indians fire from a long distance northwest of the fort and lighted fire arrows are shot into the roofs to set the buildings on fire. Everybody within the fort is now busy putting out fires, making bullets or firing the cannons. The attack sputters, and suddenly the Indians withdraw.

For the next four days the Indians kept the fort surrounded, but did not make any mass attacks. On August 27 the relief troops under Gen. H.H. Sibley arrived to lift the siege. The Indians withdrew to the west never to again threaten the fort, but they attacked a company of these soldiers at Birch Coulee, some 18 miles west of here, and nearly succeeded in wiping out the entire party.

<u>(Historical marker located on Hwy 4)</u>

Geological

 A colossal river, called Glacial River Warren, carved it near the end of the last glacial period.

The Minnesota River valley is uncommonly wide and deep. A colossal river, called Glacial River Warren, carved it near the end of the last glacial period. Between 11,700 and 9,500 years ago, there were two separate spans of time during which this immense river flowed for a total of about 1,000 years. With its headwaters near the site of Browns Valley, it was the main outlet for Glacial Lake Agassiz, an enormous glacial meltwater lake. At its maximum, this lake uncovered the combined areas of the Red River valley, northwestern Minnesota, and much of Canada southwest of Hudson Bay. The tremendous power of Glacial Warren cut down through layers of glacial sediment (clay, silt, sand, gravel, and boulders deposited by glaciers) and clay-rich deposits of weathered bedrock to expose hard granite and gneiss bedrock in places on the valley floor. No bedrock is exposed in Fort Ridgely Park.

Possibly twice, the glacial ice receded northward enough to open lower outlets to the Great Lakes via Lake Nipigon in Ontario, and Glacial Lake Agassiz drained. Since then, the huge channels that Glacial Warren left behind has been filling in with sediment from the much smaller Minnesota River and its tributaries. The tributaries are cutting down their beds to make the riverbed slope. In the northern part of the park, one can see that Fort Ridgely Creek has cut deeply into the banks of white kaolin clay, but only forty kilometers upstream, it is a shallow upland stream. Erosion in the tributaries and sediment deposit in the channel will continue until the entire watercourse slope is uniform.

The white kaolin clay revealed by Fort Ridgely Creek is a layer of gneiss decomposed by weathering. About 100 million years ago, when Minnesota's climate was subtropical, weathering caused minerals in the gneiss to break down and form most clay minerals of the kaolin group.

In most places, the kaolin deposits are buried by tens of meters of glacial sediment, deposited during the Ice Age of the last two million years. Glacial sediment can be seen along the walls of the Minnesota River valley, and the modern river exposes more in the bottom of the valley.
(Historical marker located on Hwy 4)

Place Name
This town was named after a friendly Native American Chief, Ish-tak-ha-ba "Sleepy Eye"(s) who used to reside in the area.

The chief is supposedly buried under a granite monument. A bronze statue sculpted by Joanne Bird honors the inspirational chief.

Historical Significance
The town developed in the 1870s as a result of the railroad and milling industries. From 1883 to 1921, flour milling drew a rather large populous to the area. Today, the city lies on excellent agricultural grounds and is continuing to grow.

Local Landmark
St. Mary's gothic-style church completed in 1902 has two 170-foot high steeples plus large stain-glass windows, butternut wood altars and delicate statues.

* * * *

Situated on the shores of Sleepy Eye Lake, The Schoenstatt shrine is one of the more than 160 exact replicas of the original shrine located in Schoenstatt, Germany.

The Frank Scobie Studio was one of the first to offer film finishing by mail for people who wanted to take their own pictures.

Industry
Sleepy Eye is the nation's largest manufacturer of specialty advertising calendars.

* * * *

Del Monte has called Sleepy Eye home since 1930.

Prominent People
George Somerville was an attorney in Sleepy Eye for many years before becoming County Attorney and later serving as State Senator.

Essig

Place Name

C.C. Wheeler, an officer of the Chicago and Northwestern Railroad at the time, named the town in honor of John Essig, who built one of the first businesses in the area.

Local Landmark

The Milford State Monument is erected by the State of Minnesota in memory of the men, women and children of Milford who were massacred by the Indians August 18, 1862.
(Historical marker located on County Road 29, north of Essig)

New Ulm

Place Name

The name, New Ulm, was selected because many of the original settlers were from the Province of Wurttemberg, Germany, of which Ulm is the principal city.

Historical Significance

New Ulm, the City of "Charm and Tradition," is nestled in the heart of the scenic Minnesota River Valley.

The idea for the City of New Ulm, a settlement of German immigrants, was conceived by Frederick Beinhorn in Germany. Beinhorn came to America in 1852. By 1853, he was in Chicago where he and a group of other German immigrants formed the "Chicago Land Society". In 1854, the site of the present New Ulm was selected by the advance group.

The City of New Ulm was important in Minnesota's history. The first steamboat passed by New Ulm in 1853, going upriver with troops to lay out the site for Fort Ridgely. For the next 20 years, boats brought settlers, freight, Indian supplies and gold to the area.

* * * *

Defenders' State Monument was erected to commemorate the battles and incidents of the Sioux Indian War of 1862.

The Sioux Indians located at the Red Wood and Yellow Medicine Agencies on the upper waters of the Minnesota River, broke into open rebellion on the 18th day of August, 1862. They massacred nearly all the whites in and about the agencies. Under the leadership of Chief Little Crow, they proceeded down the river towards New Ulm, and on the 19th of August entered the settlement of Milford, about seven miles west of New Ulm, and killed many of the inhabitants. On the afternoon of the 19th of August a force of about one hundred warriors attacked the town of New Ulm, killing several of the citizens and burning a number of buildings, but did not carry the barricades, which had been hastily thrown up.

While the battle was in progress the advance of Captain Charles E.

Flandrau's company from Nicollet County, about fifteen strong under the command of L.M. Boardman, entered the town and the savages withdrew. The defense up to this time was in charge of Captain Jacob Nix. At 9 P.M. of the 19th of August, a large force, consisting of Captain Flandrau's company from Nicollet County together with a company from LeSeur County arrived and took possession of the town; reinforcements to the number of several hundred subsequently arrived. On the 20th Captain Flandrau was chosen Commander in Chief and the defenses were strengthened.

On the 23rd the Indians, six hundred and fifty strong, again attacked New Ulm at half past nine in the morning, and besieged it until noon of the 24th. The assault was vigorously executed and desperately resisted. One hundred and eighty buildings were destroyed in the contest, leaving of the town such part only as lay within the barricades. Of the defenders thirty-four were killed and about sixty wounded. Reinforcements arrived at noon of the 24th under Captain Cox of St. Peter. On the 25th the town was evacuated and the inhabitants all safely conveyed to Mankato.

(Historical marker located at Center and State Streets)

Industry

In the early 1900s, New Ulm was the 3rd largest grain milling city in America, behind Buffalo, NY and Minneapolis, MN.

* * * *

A.M.P.I. (Associated Milk Producers Incorporated) is the largest butter packing plant in North America. They make 44 different brands for various companies.

* * * *

The August Schell Brewery is the 2nd oldest family-owned brewery in the United States, starting in 1860. They make about 15 "Schell brand" beers and contract brew many more for other private labels.

By the way, the oldest brewery is the Yuengling ('ying-ling') Family in Pottsville, PA.

Note: New Ulm is the only place we have heard of, that after donating blood to the Red Cross at Turner Hall, they give you 2 free glasses of Schell's beer for your efforts. After all, you need to replenish your fluids! Schell's-made 1919 Root Beer is also served.

* * * *

The 3M Plant is the city's 2nd largest employer with over 800 people working there. They make about 17,000 different products, primarily plastic extruded connectors.

They manufacture enough wire for the computer and electronic industry in one year to go around the world 9 times!

The Kraft Foods plant in New Ulm is one of the largest processed cheese factory in the world!

They make most of the world's Velveeta and is the only place in the world where the "Cheez and Crackers" snack is made, now called "Handi Snacks".

> ❓❓❓ The Hermann Monument the 2nd largest copper-sheathed statue in the country, after the considerably larger Statue of Liberty.

Local Landmark

The Hermann Monument commemorating an early German leader who repulsed the Romans in 9 AD, is now officially "the national German-American Monument, symbolizing the contributions of German heritage to the nation".

It is also the 2nd largest copper-sheathed statue in the country, after the considerably larger Statue of Liberty. The monument and statue are 102 feet tall, sitting on one of the city's highest points.

Prominent People

Charles Eugene Flandrau, a colorful frontiersman credited with giving Minnesota the nickname of the Gopher State was born in 1828 in New York City of French and Huguenot and Irish ancestry. As a young lawyer he moved to Minnesota in 1853. After exploring the Minnesota River Valley for two years, he settled at Traverse des Sioux until 1864 and became known as the Defender of New Ulm in the Dakota War of 1862.

A lifelong Democrat, Flandrau rose rapidly in the frontier hierarchy. He became territorial legislator, Indian Agent, delegate to Minnesota's constitutional convention, and member of the territorial and state supreme courts (1857-1864). Like many of the state's male pioneers, he was an active member of the Minnesota Historical Society's executive council. He took his duties there seriously, drawing on personal experience to establish a considerable reputation as a historian of the young state. Flandrau authored numerous published speeches as well as such hefty tomes as Encyclopedia of Biography of Minnesota and The History of Minnesota and Tales of the Frontier, both published in 1900. Flandrau's published works earned him a piece of Minnesota immortality.

He was also known far and wide as a raconteur. When he died in St. Paul in 1903, one eulogy declared, "Minnesota owned Flandrau". They called upon him for addresses upon all sorts of occasions, whether to act as toastmaster or make a speech at a banquet, to celebrate an important historical event, to grave a reception, to make a memorial address, to preside at a convention, or to open a fair.

<u>(Historical marker located on Hwy 15)</u>

* * * *

John Lind, Minnesota's 14th Governor who served in the early 1900s built a beautiful home here.

* * * *

Terry Steinbach, professional baseball player with the Oakland Athletics and Minnesota Twins in the 1980s and '90s. Terry, and his brothers, Tom and Tim, were record setters in baseball at the University of Minnesota.

Brian Raabe, Larry Jensen and Jerry Gleisner were signed to other professional baseball teams but never achieved Steinbach's fame.

Stephanie Klaviter pitched in the Women's Professional Softball League.

* * * *

"Whoopee John" Wilfahrt, famous musician, is credited with popularizing "German old-time" music in the 1920s, '30s and '40s.

* * * *

Wanda Gag, a famous children's author and illustrator, whose most popular work was "Millions of Cats". The height of her fame was in the 1920s and '30s.

Her father, Anton Gag, was also regionally famous as an artist and photographer. His work is still evident in the Cathedral of the Holy Trinity in New Ulm, and at the Minnesota State Capitol.

* * * *

Willibald Bianchi is a Congressional Medal of Honor recipient for his heroism during W.W.II in the Philippines.

* * * *

Tippi Hedren is a Hollywood actress who was born in the Loretto Hospital in New Ulm, although she grew up 10 miles north in Lafayette, MN.

Her daughter, actress Melanie Griffith, had a line in a movie called "Stormy Monday," when asked where she is from and she replies, "a small town in Minnesota, called New Ulm". This is a reference to her mom's place of birth!

Tippi Hedren is most famous for her role in Alfred Hitchcock's movie, "The Birds".

* * * *

Rick Domeir has been an announcer and demonstrator for the TV shopping channel, QVC, for several years.

* * * *

Flip Schulke is a world famous photographer, especially known for his work with Cassius Clay, Martin Luther King, underwater photography pioneer and astronaut training shots.

Courtland

Place Name

When the town was first organized they called it Hilo after the town and bay in Hawaii. It was renamed after Cortland County, the county seat in New York state where many of the settlers came from.

Nicollet

Place Name

The city is named after French explorer, Joseph Nicollet.

293

General Trivia

Nicollet citizens originally called the great Mesabi Range, "Missabay Heights", although the name was quickly changed to Mesabi

Historical Significance

Mankato is a Sioux word that refers to the blue earth found in the region.

Mankato was founded in 1852 at the junction of the Blue Earth and Minnesota Rivers. Located in the Minnesota River Valley, Mankato has a rich Native American history.

Three men from St. Paul set out for the Mankato area in 1852 with hopes of finding a city. Near the completion of the journey, the three men met a group of Sioux. The chief of the Sioux refused to let the men settle in the land because of a treaty the Sioux had signed with the government. The government then basically paid the Native Americans off, which ultimately resulted in the men being able to settle on the land.

Mankato had a slow beginning, but gradually grew into a prominent frontier community. When the Sioux uprising occurred in 1862, more than 300 Sioux were condemned to death. The men were held at Mankato until the day of their execution. December 26th, 1862 was the largest legal execution that has ever taken place in the United States.

W.H. Dooley was a man whose entire family was killed by the Sioux. As a result, he got to cut the scaffold rope, which resulted in the Sioux warriors choking to death before 4,000 citizens. A granite marker commemorates the execution on the Northwest side of town. The Dakota were removed from Minnesota in 1863 by Congress as punishment for the conflict.

After all of these problems subsided, Mankato concentrated on growth and prosperity. Agriculture dominated as the prominent industry in the city's beginning days. Today the city is home to several colleges and successful corporations.

Local Landmarks

Sibley Park is the site where the three men who founded Mankato camped out in 1852. This relaxing park commemorates the town's founding fathers today. Inside there is a petting zoo, colorful gardens, and a picnic area. The Sibley park grounds are considered sacred by Native Americans.

* * * *

The National Register of Historic Places honors the Judge Lorin P. Cray's mansion. This large mansion and the land it rests on are quite breathtaking. The mansion has a Queen Anne style with towers, balconies, and brilliant stain-glass windows.

Prominent People

Biographer Walter Jackson Bate was born in Mankato. He won Pulitzer Prizes for his fine literary works on John Keats in 1963 and Samuel Johnson in 1977.

* * * *

Maud Hart Lovelace is another writer from Mankato. She was a famous children's author who created the Betsy, Tib, and Tracy stories that many children love. Lovelace patterned the young girls she wrote about after herself and her sisters.

* * * *

Enrolling in Mankato State after her children were in school, poet Cary Waterman, wrote The Salamander Migration.

* * * *

Clifford B. Fagan was also born in Mankato in 1911. He created the National Federation of High School Athletics Association and co-founded the Basketball Federation. He later became president of the Hall of Fame and was elected into it in 1983.

Geological

Lookout Drive is located near the bend of the Minnesota River directly opposite the mouth of the Blue Earth river. The abandoned channel east of it is the former course of the LeSueur before it joined the Blue Earth. Most of the broad valley of the Minnesota was carved out of bedrock prior to the last glacier which came from the northwest and partially filled this valley with debris. After the glacier melted, the river re-established itself in the old valley. The name "Glacial River Warren" is applied to the stage when it carried enormous volumes of meltwater from Glacial Lake Agassiz which for a long time occupied the Red River Valley region.

The rocks exposed in this road are cut from bottom to top, Jordan sandstone, Blue Earth siltstone, Oneota dolomite (Mankato quarry rock) and glacial drift of two ages. The lowest rock is about 500 million years old and the upper drift at least 10,000 years.

(Historical marker located on Lookout Drive)

General Trivia

The Minnesota Vikings held training camp in Mankato. This gets the citizens pumped up for the much anticipated football season.

Place Name

The town is named after the neighboring lake because of the numerous nesting bald eagles along the shores of what they called Eagle Lake.

Lake Benton

Winona

Place Name
The land and city are named by the land surveyors in honor of James Madison, the fourth president of the United States.

Place Name
Before the railroad reached the area, Peter Smith owned a mill in the area. The depot for the Chicago and North Western railroad became known as Smith's Mill.

Place Name
Originally, Janesville was founded in 1850. However, when the Winona and St. Peter Railroad was built slightly east of the town in 1870, Janesville relocated closer to the railroad.

Local Landmark
St. John's Episcopal Church is located within the confines of the town. This church was established in 1872. It was one of Bishop Whipple's, the first Bishop to preach in Minnesota, churches.

Waseca

Place Name
The railroad made its way to Waseca in 1867 and served as a hefty influence in the town's foundation and development. Waseca is a Native word meaning, "rich and fertile provider". In this case, the railroad was inevitably the rich and fertile provider. It allowed the town to thrive quickly with the construction of more than 100 buildings in one year.

General Trivia
In its early days, Waseca established the Waseca County Anti-horse Thief Detective Society. The organization served a function similar to a neighborhood watch program, except in this case, the town kept its eye open for horse thieves. The organization was extremely successful and recovered all but one stolen horse.

Prominent People

Dave and John Junst set out from Waseca in 1970 to walk around the earth. Unfortunately bandits attacked the brothers in Afghanistan, killing John and wounding Dave. Pete, Dave's brother, would join him until they reached the Indian Ocean. When Dave returned to Waseca on October 5, 1974 he became the first person to walk (14,450 miles) around the earth.

Dave Junst was the first person to walk (14,450 miles) around the earth.

Meriden

Place Name

F.J. Stephens, one of the original founders of the town, suggested the name for the city of Meriden, Connecticut which is famous for the manufacturing of silverware.

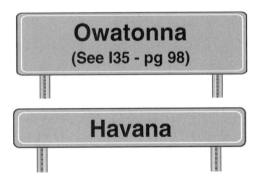

Owatonna
(See I35 - pg 98)

Havana

Place Name

This town has had many different names over the years including Lafayette, Freeman, and Dover. The name was changed at the request of Elijah Easter for Havana, the county seat of Mason County, Illinois.

This Spanish word means "a haven, a harbor," and is appropriate for its location on Rice Lake.

Claremont

Place Name

Claremont was settled in the 1850s by New Englanders. These settlers built a road to Wasioja, then planted elm trees on both sides of the street. They called the road Claremont Street, which is how the town got its name.

West Concord

Place Name

West Concord was settled in the 1880s and was established because of its proximity to the railroad. It gets it name from Concord Township which was named for the capitol city of Concord, New Hampshire.

Dodge Center

Place Name

D.C. Fairbank suggested the name for its location in the center of the county.

Historical Significance

The town is an agricultural center. The local canning factory is kept busy by the abundance of pea and corn crops supplied through the fertile soil in the area.

The First National Soil Conservation District Field Day and Plow Matches were held here on September 6, 1952. Over 125,000 spectators saw demonstrations of new methods and new techniques for soil conservation during the event. The presidential candidate for the 1952 election spoke here on the importance of agriculture. Both Adlai Stevenson and Dwight D. Eisenhower acknowledged that the future of the country depended on the preservation of soil and water resources.

This event was held because of actions begun in the 1930s. The U.S. Congress had enacted the Soil Conservation Act in 1935, in response to the dust storms and floods that ravaged the country because of drought and poor land management practices. The legislation led to the creation of a partnership between government agencies, states, and individuals to address a broad range of resource concerns. They ranged from erosion control, contour plowing, flood prevention, water quality, wetlands, and wildlife to recreation and community development.

Today there are over three thousand conservation districts covering 98% of the privately owned land in the 50 states, and, Puerto Rico, the Virgin Islands, the District of Columbia, the Northern Mariana Islands and Guam.

Within Minnesota there are 91 Soil and Water Conservation Districts that generally follow the borders of the county in which they are located.

(Historical marker located on County Road 34)

Wasioja

Place Name

Translated from the Dakota word for the Zumbro River, Wasi Oju, meaning pine clad; the village name is in reference to the large white pines that grew along the banks of the river.

Local Landmark

The role of buildings in the development of a community and their significance in history is amply pointed out by the history of the Wasioja Seminary. Anxious to promote the growth of the newly formed town, the citizens agreed to provide the Free Will Baptists with a building for a seminary. A structure of native limestone was completed in 1860, and the Minnesota Seminary opened in November of that year with an enrollment of more than 300 students. By 1861 the school had been renamed Northwestern College and offered classes on all levels from primary to collegiate. In 1862 Wasiouja had a dozen stores, a hotel, a flour mill, and was surrounded by farms and quarries that promised a great future.

Then the course of history was changed. The Civil War had begun and men from Minnesota were on the battlefields. Captain James George, who had served in the Mexican War, asked the students to volunteer. Led by Professor Clinton A. Cilly, the young men marched down to Captain George's law office and enlisted. Organized as Company C of the 2nd Minnesota, they marched off to war. Just over a year later at Snodgrass Hill near Chickamauga, they stopped the Confederates' advance at a high cost. Of the eighty young men that left Wasioja, only 25 returned with life and limb intact. The town never recovered from the great loss.

The school continued to operate, although its enrollment had been cut in half, and in 1868 the Free Will Baptists ceased their sponsorship. It was reopened as the Groveland Seminary, closing in 1872 and was re-opened again in 1873 by the Wesleyan Methodist Conference. The school finally closed in 1894, and in 1905 a fire destroyed the building, leaving the ruins that stand today.

<u>(Historical marker located on Hwy 16)</u>

Place Name

The town of Kasson was named for Jabez Hyde Kasson. Jabez was of Irish descent and was one of the three men who platted the village and secured a railroad depot in town.

Place Name

This village adopted the name of the three founding brothers, Peter, Riley and Frank Mantor, who came from here in 1854 from Pennsylvania.

Local Landmark

The town is relatively old, and some of its most prominent buildings were built in the 1850s. Surprisingly, these Mantorville stone buildings are still in excellent condition today. The city is unique in that it was given the rare honor of being placed on the National

Register of Historic Places as an entire city.

The Grand Old Mansion is just one of the reasons why the city was given this tremendous honor. Constructed in 1899, this building is a fine example of the durability of Mantorville limestone.

Industry

Mantorville is home to several quarries that have provided materials for many of the buildings in the Rochester area.

General Trivia

Mantorville is home to Minnesota's oldest farmer's organization, the Dodge County Historical Society. The Society was organized in 1857.

Frank B. Kellogg spent his childhood days in Mantorville and had a lifelong dream of bringing peace to the world.

Prominent People

Frank B. Kellogg's impressive resume includes U.S. Senator in 1917, U.S. Ambassador to Great Britain in 1923, and Secretary of State for President Calvin Coolidge.

Kellogg, along with French explorer, Aristide Briand developed an agreement signed by many nations that made a pact not to go to war ever again. Unfortunately, the agreement was not legally binding. Kellogg's effort was awarded with the Nobel Peace Prize in 1929.

Byron

Place Name

G.W. Van Dusen, a local grain buyer, suggested the name of his hometown of Port Byron, New York as the name for this town.

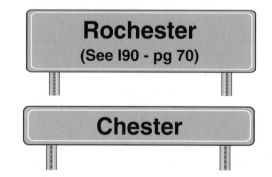

Rochester
(See I90 - pg 70)

Chester

Place Name

This town was established as a branch station of the Chicago and North Western Railway. The town's name is an abbreviation for the town to its east, Rochester.

Eyota

Place Name

Taken from the Dakota word, iyotan, meaning greatest or most.

Dover

Place Name

The town and nearby river were named after Dover, New Hampshire, where many of its early settlers came from.

Saint Charles

Historical Significance

St. Charles was founded in an interesting way. When the founders surveyed the area in 1854, they wanted to strategize a way to develop the town quickly. Their final decision was to give a free one-acre lot to every Christian democrat that agreed to settle here. This proved to be an attractive deal that was accepted by many settlers.

This town is named in honor of St. Charles of Italy, who became cardinal of Milan and secretary to Pope Pius IV.

Utica

Place Name

This township derives its name from the ancient city of Utica, founded by the Phoenicians in North Africa.

Bethany

Place Name

This town was established by the Winona Southwestern Improvement Company which in turn named the village after the Bethanian Moravian Church.

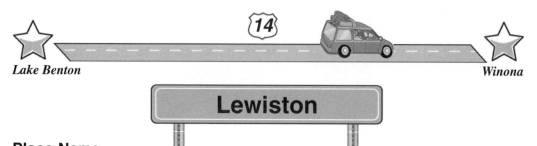

Lewiston

Place Name

S. J. Lewis, the area's first settler gives his name to the town.

Local Landmark

Lewiston was the first stagecoach stop in the Winona-Rochester area. Worn out travelers took a break from their journeys here and took complete advantage of the tasty food and warm atmosphere for which the old town was famous.

Stockton

Place Name

Stockton was founded as one of many gristmill towns in this region. It rests on a peaceful creek that winds its way towards the mighty Mississippi. It's named for J.B. Stockton, one of the town's first proprietors.

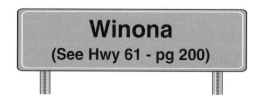

Winona
(See Hwy 61 - pg 200)

302

HIGHWAY

12

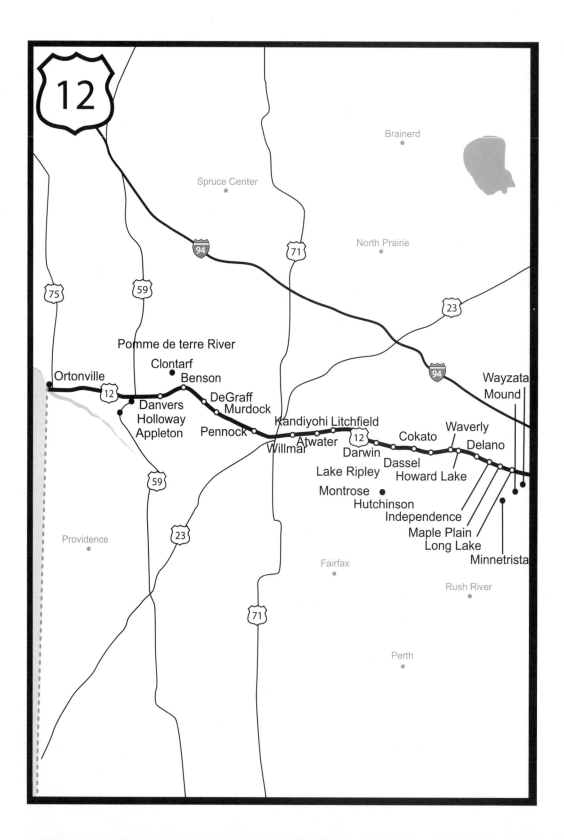

U.S. 12

Brainerd

Spruce Center

I-94

71

North Prairie

75

59

23

I-94

Pomme de terre River

Wayzata
Mound

Ortonville

Clontarf

12

Benson

DeGraff

Danvers

Murdock

Waverly

Holloway

Kandiyohi Litchfield

Cokato

Delano

Pennock

12

Appleton

Atwater

Willmar

Darwin

Dassel

Howard Lake

Lake Ripley

59

Montrose

Independence

Hutchinson

Maple Plain

23

Long Lake

Providence

Minnetrista

Fairfax

Rush River

71

Perth

Ortonville

Place Name

Ortonville was named after C.K. Orton. This man settled in the area in 1872. In 1873, he laid the town out and established a trading post with the Sioux. This fueled the town's development and soon the agricultural industry took over.

Industry

The town is known for its granite quarries. The colorful ruby-red granite is quarried here.

Geological

Of all the geological agents which have played a part in shaping the face of Minnesota, the most overwhelming and powerful one is glacial ice. At least four times during the last million years, continental glaciers have spread over the state during long periods of cold climate, each advance being followed by widespread retreat.

The last glacier that invaded Minnesota from Canada came by the low valley of the Red River of the North, pushed its way southward across Minnesota and advanced as far as Des Moines. During its slow retreat, 11,000 years ago, the largest glacial river of them all, the Glacial River Warren, formed the valley in which the Minnesota River now flows. This valley is an impressive reminder of the volume of water it once carried.

Big Stone Lake, now the headwaters of the Minnesota River was formed behind a delta-like barrier of sand and silt deposited across this ancient drainage channel by the Whetstone River of South Dakota.

(Historical marker located on Hwy 12)

Local Landmark

Ortonville is located on the Southern shore of Big Stone Lake. Just west of town lies the Big Stone Lake Dam and nearby dike. These two structures raise the level of the Big Stone Lake three to six feet.

> The Big Stone Canning Company was one of the largest corn canneries in the U.S. Their canning plant originated and patented the equipment used in canning whole kernal corn.

> G.F. Kaercher of Ortonville was the first woman to be elected Clerk of a State Supreme Court in 1922.

Holloway
(See Hwy 59 - pg 236)

Pomme de terre River

Place Name

The Pomme de Terre River is named for the prairie turnip with eyes like a potato, which explains why the French called it by the word meaning potato.

The river gets it start about 100 miles north, winding its way south to the Lac Qui Parle Wildlife Area.

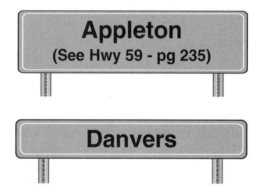

Appleton
(See Hwy 59 - pg 235)

Danvers

Place Name

When the town was incorporated in 1900, it was given the same name as towns in Massachusetts and Illinois.

Clontarf

Place Name

Clontarf was largely founded and established by Archbishop Ireland. He led a group of Irish Catholics from the east coast to Benson. This group of people were fed up with the crowded and poverty-stricken areas on the Atlantic. From Benson, the adventurous group made their way up to Clontarf. The people decided to name the town "Clontarf" for an Irish watering place near Dublin.

Historical Significance

In the first year that the people were here, they were hit with a grasshopper plague. Although they were disappointed, they took it in stride and believed the grasshoppers were sent from God to punish the people for their sins.

The archbishop built a school shortly after the plague ended. The purpose of the school was to instruct young Native boys on the Roman Catholic religion as well as to teach them to be "kind husbands". Because of low attendance, the government decided to take the school over in 1897.

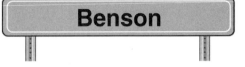

Benson

Place Name

There are two explanations on who this town is named after. The first says the name was given in honor of Ben Benseon, who was born in Norway before coming to the United States in 1861, eventually settled in the area establishing a mercantile business.

The second credits Jared Benson, a prominent citizen and political leader from Anoka. He farmed in the area raising cattle before becoming a member of the House of Representatives in the state legislature.

Historical Significance

Benson was settled in 1870. At first, Benson was established as an agricultural center. Unfortunately, a two-year grasshopper plague devastated the crop. After this misfortune, farmers took up wheat farming and the village began shipping hundreds of thousands of bushels as early as 1875.

Benson used to be the far western terminal of the great Northern Railway which enabled its early growth spurt.

De Graff

Place Name

Born near Amsterdam, New York, Andrew De Graff came to the state building many of the railroads including the Great Northern line through the county here.

Murdock

Place Name

Samuel Sabin Murdock was the former manager of the St. Paul Harvester Works who owned 3,000 acres of land in the area.

Pennock

Place Name

St. John's township as the railway station was originally called, was changed in honor of George Pennock from Willmar, a superintendent of the Great Northern Railway.

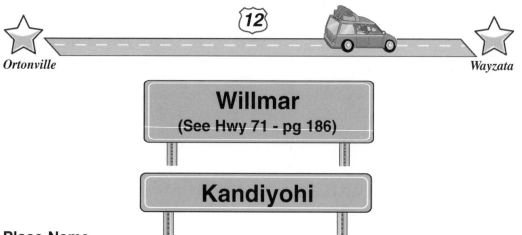

Willmar
(See Hwy 71 - pg 186)

(See Hwy 71 - pg 186)

Kandiyohi

Place Name

This town was named for the Kandiyohi Lakes which the Dakota referred to as Kahn-Dee-O-He meaning abounding in buffalo fish. The fish swam upstream each spring from the rivers and streams to spawn in the lake.

Historical Significance

In 1869, both houses of the Minnesota state Legislature voted to move the capitol to a town near here. Unfortunately the town no longer exist as the governor vetoed the proposed bill.

Atwater

Place Name

Named to commemorate the secretary of the land department of the St. Paul and Pacific Railroad, Mr. E.D. Atwater.

Litchfield

Place Name

Litchfield was platted in 1869. It was named after three brothers with the last name Litchfield. These men helped finance and construct the St. Paul and Pacific Railroad. Litchfield is the proud seat of Meeker County.

Local Landmark

The Grand Army of the Republic was an organization established in 1866 by Union veterans of the Civil War to preserve friendships, honor fallen comrades, and aid widows and the handicapped. It was wielded great political influence in the years just after the war. The G.A.R. last met in 1949 for its 83rd encampment; today there are no survivors of this organization.

One of the finest examples of the architecture inspired by this movement is Litchfield's

Frank Dagget Post, No. 35, organized in 1883 and named to honor the founder of the G.A.R. association in Meeker County. Dedicated on Memorial Day, 1885, the Memorial Hall was designed to resemble a fort and included a public library and reading and museum rooms. A "neat tin box" placed in the building's cornerstone contains a Bible, the names of post members and community leaders, and such memorabilia as postage stamps, coins, and battlefield relics.

<u>(Historical marker located at 320 N. Marshall Avenue)</u>

* * * *

The Rosemary Home in Litchfield is a Victorian mansion. Litchfield resident, Dorothea Kopplin passed away in 1970. Her last will and testament was a request to create a memorial to Rosemary, who was her six-year old daughter that died of leukemia. Her last wish was established in 1972.

Lake Ripley

Place Name

It is told that Dr. Ripley along with John McClelland were almost out of supplies around March. So they headed out to seek assistance from John Huy who lived in a cabin north of them. The area which would later became Forest City. During their trip a blizzard developed, forcing them to seek shelter in a snow bank. The next morning slightly disorientated they backtracked through the deep snow to their own cabin. Unfortunately they couldn't start a fire because their matches became wet. Having no other choice, they were forced to go back out seeking shelter. When Dr. Ripley became too weak to continue he pleaded with McClelland to proceed on, leaving him to freeze to death. His body never found until the next spring. McClelland survived, but in an attempt to save his life, both of his legs were amputated.

This lake name commemorates Dr. Frederick Ripley who froze to death here in the winter of 1855-56.

Darwin

Place Name

This town's name honors E. Darwin Litchfield of London, England. He was one of the principal stockholders and promoters of the St. Paul and Pacific Railroad. (now the Great Northern)

Local Landmarks

People come from all over the country to see an attraction in this small town. A gazebo in the town park contains the world's largest ball of twine.

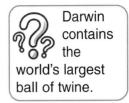

Darwin contains the world's largest ball of twine.

The Guinness Book of World Records claims that the mighty ball of twine was created by Francis Johnson, a local farmer who couldn't bear to throw anything away, not even old used scraps of twine.

In 1950, the farmer began to roll all of the twine he collected together into a ball that kept growing and growing. In 1979, he put the giant ball on display. Today, the twine ball rests at 11 feet tall, 13 feet in diameter, and it weighs a whopping 11 tons. The great twine ball resulted in a song called, "The Biggest Ball of Twine in Minnesota".

The Ball of Twine Inn contains another Francis Johnson invention. This invention is an eight-foot pliers that keeps opening into smaller and smaller pliers until 27 are opened. Johnson was indeed a clever man.

Place Name

Hutchinson was established in 1855 by three brothers. Asa, Judson, and John Hutchinson were these three happy brothers. They came from a family of popular singers. The Hutchinson brothers gave concerts throughout the United States from 1841 until the 1870s.

Historical Significance

Hutchinson is unique in that when it was incorporated, the village charter allowed women to vote on local questions. Their early support of abolition, temperance, and women's suffrage was a precursor to the significant legislation in the 20th century.

* * * *

The Sioux uprisings in 1862 caused the death of Little Crow.

A fire in its early days burned a considerable portion of the town. During this fire, the Pendergast Academy was destroyed. This was one of the first schools ever built in the state.

* * * *

Little Crow was a significant leader of the Sioux. Apparently, he and his son were picking berries near Hutchinson when a white man by the name of Nathan Lamson approached them while hunting. The two exchanged shots, resulting in the Sioux leader's death.

Prominent People

Hutchinson native, Les Kouba, was an avid wildlife artist.

* * * *

On January 26, 1942, Private Milburn Henke from Hutchinson, was the first enlisted man to land with the first American Expeditionary Force in Europe in World War I

Place Name

Dassel is named after a lake that was named after Bernard Dassel. This man was the secretary of the St. Paul and Pacific Railway in 1869.

Historical Significance

There is a fun story about an interesting rivalry between Dassel and the neighboring town of Hutchinson.

In 1887, the community baseball team in Dassel won the first game of the season-ending doubleheader against Hutchinson.

Hutchinson wasn't going to let Dassel get away with the victory so easily though, especially when Hutchinson got a secret tip from an informant that Dassel hired professionals in order to win. They also hired a professional umpire that called the game in favor of Dassel.

Hutchinson was downright angry, but transformed their anger into confidence for the second game. The odds were 4 to 1 against Hutchinson.

Even when Hutchinson was down 6-3 in the bottom of the 9th, they didn't give up. Moreover, the "professional umpire" must have decided he wanted a split. Jack Bennett refused to call strikes against Hutchinson.

They ended up pulling off the victory by three runs and the bragging rights that went with it.

Place Name

Cokato was founded in the late 1800s by the Swedes. As time went by, the Finns began to flock to the scenic town conveniently located on Cokato Lake. The town now largely inhabited by Finnish descendents, name means, "out the middle" or "stopping place".

Place Name

Howard Lake was established in 1879. The village and the lake were both named for John Howard who was an English philanthropist and prison reformist.

Historical Significance

In 1878, right before the town was founded, it experienced a surge of locusts in the area. The farmers throughout the region were desperate for help because the little pests were

destroying their crop and eating their clothing. Their last resort was an organized prayer, which resulted in the immediate disappearance of the locusts. Perhaps it was an act of God, or it could have just been a coincidence. No one knows for sure.

Place Name

One of the first pioneer settlers came from Waverly, New York, which gives this town its name.

General Trivia

Hubert H. Humphrey used to live in Waverly. During his vice presidential years the town would be overrun with the press when he returned home.

Place Name

This town was named after a royal burgh and seaport in Scotland.

> **???** Known by the Dakota as Wak-pah-Kahn-ghe-toka the River of the Crows, Crow River flows 20 miles north emptying in to the Mississippi River.

Place Name

Delano was named for Frances Delano. He came as a pioneer to Minnesota and quickly succeeded as a railroad superintendent and lumberman.

Industry

The town is one of the largest granite monument memorial retail manufacturers in the Northwest.

Place Name

Nearby Lake Independence, for which the town was also named, was named during a party on the lake over the Fourth of July.

Maple Plain

Place Name

Like Maple Grove, a community to the north, this town was named for the abundance of maple trees, both hard and sugar, in the forested area around the vicinity.

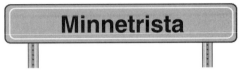

Minnetrista

Place Name

Several names were suggested for this community. The name selected (Minne meanning water and trista meaning crooked) was given in reference to the irregular shaped lakes in the area, especially that of the zigzagging outline of Whale Tail Lake.

Mound

Historical Significance

In May, 1822, a Fort Snelling drummer boy named Joseph R. Brown and his friend, William Snelling, son of the fort's commander, canoed up what is now called Minnehaha Creek to discover a lake long sacred to the Indian people who built burial mounds along its shores. Thirty years later, the 23-square-mile natural lake with 110 miles of indented shoreline was named "Minnetonka," Dakota for "Great Piece of Water," by Governor Alexander Ramsey.

By the early 1880s Lake Minnetonka had become a favorite summer resort for the rich and famous of the United States and Europe, including Presidents Ulysses S. Grant and Chester A. Arthur. The 300-foot "Belle of Minnetonka" and other excursion boats nearly as large carried thousands of visitors enjoying the holidays at comfortable summer homes or elegant hotels like the Chapman House on Cook's Bay and the prestigious Hotel Lafayette on Crystal Bay.

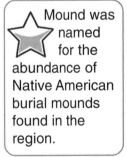

Mound was named for the abundance of Native American burial mounds found in the region.

With the arrival of the automobile, the great hotel era faded and the summer cottages evolved into permanent homes. Lake Minnetonka is still known for its beauty and its many recreational opportunities.

(Historical marker located on Hwy 15)

Prominent People

Native Kevin David Sorbo spent 3 years traveling around the world, modeling for print ads

and appearing in over 150 commercials.

At the end of 1986 he settled in Los Angeles. Kevin began to make guest appearances on such popular shows as "Murder, She Wrote". At 6' 3" and very muscular, Kevin was a natural for the title role in what would become his signature series "Hercules: the Legendary Journeys".

He was runner-up in 1993 to Dean Cain for the role of Superman on TV's "Lois & Clark: The New Adventures of Superman".

Place Name

The town takes its name from the adjoining lake of the same name.

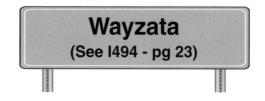

(See I494 - pg 23)

HIGHWAY

11

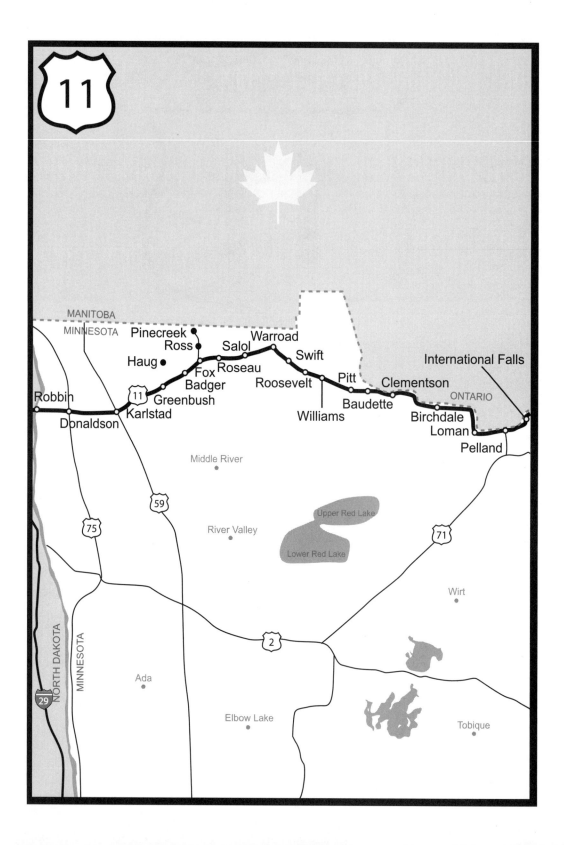

11

MANITOBA
MINNESOTA

Pinecreek
Ross
Haug
Fox
Badger
Greenbush
Karlstad
Robbin
Donaldson

Salol
Roseau

Warroad
Swift
Roosevelt

Williams

Pitt
Baudette

International Falls

Clementson
ONTARIO

Birchdale
Loman
Pelland

Middle River

Upper Red Lake

River Valley

Lower Red Lake

Wirt

71

NORTH DAKOTA
MINNESOTA

29

75

59

2

Ada

Elbow Lake

Tobique

Robbin

Place Name

The town was originally called Teien Township, in honor of Andreas C. Teien. His brother George immigrated to the area from Drammen, Norway to open a general store. He also became the first postmaster and named the post office for the bird with a slight change in the spelling.

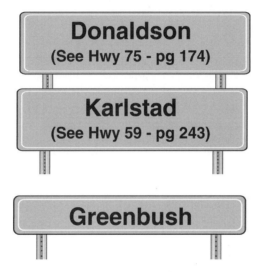

Donaldson
(See Hwy 75 - pg 174)

Karlstad
(See Hwy 59 - pg 243)

Greenbush

Place Name

In 1904, Greenbush began to develop because of the Great Northern Railway. As a result, in 1905, the town was incorporated because of a population surge.

The name "Greenbush" comes from the eastern part of the township, which houses numerous evergreens. This massive accumulation of evergreen trees became a meeting place for settlers traveling along the route

Haug

Place Name

Named for a homestead farmer from Norway, Theodore Haug, whose land the first post office was built on.

Place Name

The town and the flowing creek in the area take their names from the burrowing animal that frequented Minnesota and the neighboring state of Wisconsin, which is called the Badger State.

Place Name

Like the town west of here, the town's name was given for an animal. This time, obviously the fox.

Place Name

The town of Ross was settled by Norwegians in the late 1800s and given the same name as a county in Ohio.

Local Landmark

The Jesse Nelson Farm is located in the area. It rests on an old Native American village. The farm is supposedly haunted with the Windego and the Roseau Lake ghost. This apparition has frightened people for generations.

Whenever the Windego makes an appearance, someone in the community has died. For this reason, the Windego is seen by residents as a Grim Reaper.

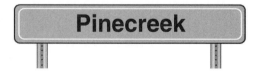

Local Landmark

The first church in Roseau County was built in Pinecreek. When it was first built in 1891, it was constructed of logs and was intended to serve as a fort. However, the citizen's dedication to their religion prompted the establishment's change to a church.

Roseau

Place Name

Roseau is the county seat of Roseau County and it is named for Roseau Lake. Roseau developed from the French phrase, "Riviere aux Rouseaux", which means "River of the Rushes" in reference to the nearby river rapids.

Historical Significance

Two historic artifacts have been found in the Roseau region. First, a round stone that displays inscriptions within a circle carved in the stone is believed by some to be from prehistoric times. Also, an ivory fish spear dated back to the 16th century was unearthed early in the 20th century.

Industry

Edgar and Allan Hateen and David Johnson from Roseau formed Polaris Industries. Originally, this company made mostly farming equipment.

David and Allan put their minds together to develop another contraption to add to their line. This machine was a motorized vehicle on skis, or what is now called a "snowmobile".

Edgar didn't believe that the snowmobiles would be successful, so he sold them just to help pay the company's bills. Eventually, the product gained popularity.

> In 1954, three intuitive entrepreneurs formed Polaris Industries.

Prominent People

Neal LaMoy Broten was born in Roseau. He was the first hockey player in America to score 100 points in one season.

Salol

Place Name

The origin of this town's name is quite interesting. The traditional story behind the name is that three Swedes were chosen to ask nearby Roseau's elite residents to assist them in selecting a name for the new town.

When the Swedes arrived in Roseau, they began to socialize with the leading citizens so much that they lost track of time. Once the sun rose in the wee hours of the morning, the men were so fatigued that they could barely even think about their city's name.

Their solution: the men walked into a local drugstore and picked the name out of a drawer that was "labels". The name had a ring to it and ended up sticking.

Place Name

The Warroad region exists at the end of a trail, which stretches northeast from the Red River to the Lake of the Woods. When the Chippewa and Dakota battled one another, they often times used this natural trail to wage their battles on. At first, the Chippewa called the trading post in Warroad, "Kabeckanungi", which means, "dark and bloody end of the trail". When the French began to inhabit the area in the early part of the 19th century, they began to call the post "the road of war". As Warroad grew, largely because of the logging and farming industries, resident started calling the city Warroad in honor of the city's history.

Local Landmark

The mysterious Gull Rock can be seen when people look out towards the crisp lake waters. Natives regard this island as highly spiritual.

Natives dare not set foot on the island because of a long-lasting legend that has been passed down from the earliest Native Americans that inhabited the area.

In the early days of Lake of the Woods history, the Assiniboine, Chippewa and Cree fought one another until almost all of their bravest men were dead. This lack of dominance caused the Dakota to want to come in and try to take over the area.

 Gull Rock Island has always been regarded as a sign of unity given to the Natives by the Great Spirit.

In the midst of all the bloodshed, the Great Spirit descended to the land one day and spoke to the children. He explained to them that he was unhappy and angry because the environment became so hostile.

Consequently, the Great Spirit brought the land a plague of arid, dreadful heat. All of the people in the land and even all of the wildlife bathed in the Lake of the Woods to cool themselves from the unbearable heat.

As the people mourned over their own discomfort in the lake, a sudden flash of light glistened in the heavens, followed by the voice of the Great Spirit. The Spirit commanded the people to get along with one another.

He explained that the consequence would be the Dakota coming in to take all of the land from everyone. The Spirit offered the people an ultimatum; either get along as brothers and thrive in the land, or to be driven out of the land forever, as a divided people.

After the Spirit spoke, the sun's rays ceased and a calm wind filled the land. The people lifted their bowed heads from the ground in an attempt to see the Spirit ascent into the heavens. The Natives saw the Spirit leave the Earth from the "Rock of the Gods" in the Lake, otherwise known today as Gull Rock.

Before the Spirit came, the small island was supposedly blanketed with trees and grass. After the Spirit left, the rock was completely bare. Since the Spirit's appearance, the three tribes united and ended up defeating the Dakota.

* * * *

Just north of the mouth of Warroad River, stood a post of the American Fur Company,

built about 1820.

The French explorer, La Verendrye, and his party probably visited the region in 1732 en route to build Fort St. Charles in the present Northwest Angle.

<u>(Historical marker located on Hwy 11)</u>

* * * *

Pierre Gaultier de Varennes, Sieur de la Verendrye, established Fort St. Charles on Lake of the Woods in 1732. A daring soldier, fur trader and explorer, La Verendrye had the ambitious dream of the fabled "Western Sea" and sought to establish French outposts along the way. On Magnusons Island (then connected to the mainland) he built a palisaded fort which he named in honor of Charles de Beauharnois, governor of New France.

Fort St. Charles became the western capital of the French empire in the Northwest. From it, expeditions were launched and supplies dispatched to newer posts around Lake Winnipeg. Indians brought furs to trade for white men's goods and these pelts were sent by canoe to Montreal. The scarcity of food and Indian warfare made life precarious. In 1736 La Verendrye's oldest son, Jean-Baptiste, nineteen voyageurs, and Father Jean-Pierre Aulneau, a Jesuit priest, were sent on an expedition to the east for supplies. They were massacred by a Sioux war party on a nearby island.

Abandoned after 1760, the fort was rediscovered and marked by a group of Jesuit fathers in 1908. The site was acquired and the buildings reconstructed by the Minnesota 4th Degree Knights of Columbus some forty years later.

<u>(Historical marker located at the end of Lake Street)</u>

General Trivia

Warroad is nestled on the Warroad River at the point where it flows into Muskeg Bay. Warroad is unique in that it is the only United States port on the Lake of the Woods.

Prominent People

1984 Hockey Hall of Fame inductee, Bill Christian was born in Warroad in 1959.

* * * *

In 1995 another Warroad native, Henry Charles Boucha would also be inducted into the U.S. Hockey Hall of Fame. Boucha, an Ojibwa Indian, played for the Detroit Red Wings and Minnesota North Stars.

 Christian Brothers Factory is one of the only companies in the United States that manufactures hockey sticks.

Swift

Place Name

The Canadian National Railroad come through the area stopping at a station known as Muirhead Siding for Harry Muirhead, pioneer settler. When Harry, Carl Carlquist the first

postmaster and others were watching the train come in one day, they all commented on how "swift" it traveled; thus giving the station a new name.

Place Name

Eminent author and statesman, Theodore Roosevelt is the person to honor with this towns name. Besides being President of the United States, Roosevelt served as a colonel in the Spanish-American War, and as Governor of New York.

Place Name

George Williams and William Mason, for whom the town is named, followed the Minnesota and Manitoba Railroad track roadbed back in 1901, to state claims in the site established as a shipping center for the timber products.

Place Name

The name of this town does have some significance, even though at first glance, it seems to be a bit strange. Where the town sits now, there used to be a large pit that was dug to supply materials for the Canadian National Railway. There is also a ridge in the town that is composed entirely of gravel. The reason for this material's presence is that the Lake of the Woods shoreline used to rest there. These pits that were created resulted in the unique name.

Place Name

This community began as a steamboat landing and lumber town with a sawmill following the arrival of the railroad in the area in 1901.

The town was called Port Hyland, after postmaster Daniel Hyland, but renamed, Baudette for local trapper Joseph Baudette who resided in the area since the early 1880s.

Historical Significance

Northern Minnesota forests were tinder dry during the fall of 1910. Marshes and streams shriveled. Small fires smoldered here and there in the peat bogs and underbrush.

On October 4, a forest fire consumed the communities of Williams, Cedar Spur, and Graceton. The flames, bed by loggers' slashing, crackled onward and three days later completely destroyed all the buildings in the little town of Pitt except the depot.

The fire approached Baudette and Spooner on the evening of October 7. As the towns rapidly became furnaces of flames, the citizens gathered at the depot for safety. Victims of a typhoid epidemic were evacuated by train before a whirlwind of flame swept away the two towns and the bridge over the Baudette River that connected them.

Before morning almost everything at Baudette was leveled, leaving what one survivor called "a desolate plain" covered by charred ruins. Only a sawmill at Spooner remained standing.

Forty-two persons lost their lives in the great fire of 1910. About 300,000 acres were burned in ten townships, including much valuable timber and many homesteads and livestock.

(Historical marker located off state highway 72)

* * * *

Tradition is woven of fact and fiction. Two islands in the Lake of the Woods are named "Massacre", one on the Canadian, one on the American side of the boundary. The Canadian island, the larger of the two, is heavily wooded. The American island is small, rocky and barren. These islands were so named because of the following events.

In 1732, Pierre Galtier de Varennes de la Verendrye, French-Canadian explorer and trader, built Fort St. Charles at Northwest Angle Inlet on Lake of the Woods. From this base he traded with the Cree and Assiniboine for furs to finance explorations for a passage to the Western Sea.

Early in June, 1736, La Verendrye sent his son, Jean-Baptiste, with the priest, Father Pierre Aulneau, and nineteen voyageurs eastward for supplies. At their first campsite, a small rocky island "seven leagues" from the Fort, they were attacked and killed by a Sioux war party. The bodies were decapitated and placed in a row. The heads of the voyageurs were wrapped in beaver pelts and left near the bodies. Those of Jean-Baptiste and Father Aulneau may have been carried off as trophies.

Several weeks after the massacre, a party of Chippewa passed a small island and discovered the victims of the massacre. Out of reverence for the priest, and because they could not dig a grave on the rocky island, they raised a stone cairn over his body.

> Weighing in at 2 1/2 tons and measuring 40 feet long, Willie Walleye is definitely the biggest lunker ever to be produced in the Lake of the Woods. It is believed to be the most photographed Walleye in the world.

When he learned of the tragedy, the elder La Verendrye had the remains of the men taken to Fort St. Charles and buried near the chapel. They were found there in 1908 by an archaeological party from St. Boniface College, Manitoba, Canada.

The island where the massacre occurred has never been satisfactorily identified.

(Historical marker located off state highway 72)

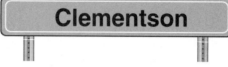

Clementson

Place Name

Helec Clementson was the owner of the local sawmill for whom this town was named after. Helec was also a former county commissioner.

Birchdale

Place Name

The abundant number of birch trees and its moraine hills and dales gives this town its name.

Loman

Place Name

This town is named for the Canadian homesteaders, George and Mary Loman.

Local Landmark

Loman is located on the Northeastern tip of the Pine Island State Forest. The Black River, the Big Fork River, and the Little Fork River wind through the forest and naturally add to its beauty. Within this state forest is the Red Lake Indian Reservation.

Pelland
(See Hwy 71 - pg 194)

International Falls
(See Hwy 71 - pg 195)

HIGHWAY 10

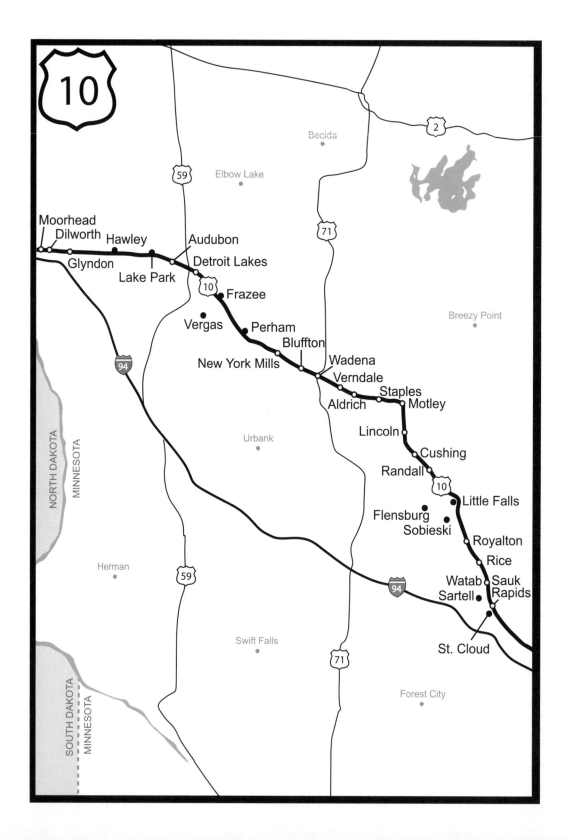

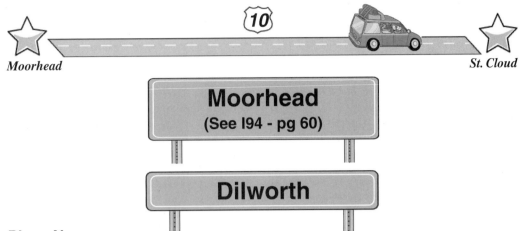

Moorhead
(See I94 - pg 60)

Dilworth

Place Name

The town first known as Richardson would change its name to honor Joseph Dilworth, a coffee importer. He was one of the original stockholders of the Northern Pacific Railroad. While residing as the director in Pittsburg, Pennsylvania, he purchased 4,000 acres in this vicinity, making him one of the largest landholders along the route.

Glyndon

Place Name

Named by the officers of the Northern Pacific Railroad, the town, like many others in Pennsylvania and Maryland, it was named for a popular writer. Laura Catherine Redden Searing, who used the name Howard Glyndon as a non de plume with the Atlantic Hearth and Home.

Hawley

Place Name

Named in honor of General Joseph Hawley of Connecticut, one of the original stockholders of the Northern Pacific Railroad company.

Geological

Toward the close of the last or Wisconsin stage of glaciation about 10,000 years ago, the ice front receded from central Iowa toward the north and, in the latitude of Browns Valley, crossed the continental divide between the Mississippi River and the drainage to Hudson Bay. After the glacier had retreated north of this divide the meltwaters, unable to follow the natural drainage northward, were confined between the ice and the divide to the south.

Thus Glacial Lake Agassiz was created. At its maximum it was 600 feet deep and larger than the combined areas of the five Great Lakes today.

The outlet of the lake was at Browns Valley. There, the Glacial River

> General Hawley served as commander in the Union army during the Civil War, later becoming a member of Congress and U.S. Senator.

Warren had its source and carried the overflow from the lake through the valley of the present Minnesota River. When the northern ice eventually melted away the impounded water escaped to Hudson Bay and left behind on the floor of Lake Agassiz the lake sediments which are now rich soils in the Red River Valley region.

(Historical marker located on Hwy 10)

> Robert Asp spent 10 years building a full-scale replica of a Viking ship in an old potato warehouse.

General Trivia

The last herds of bison to roam the state of Minnesota did so here in the 1850s. According to Alex Henry, the great herds drowned when they attempted to cross the thin ice of the Red River.

* * * *

The building where Robert Asp built his Viking ship would have to be torn down to get the 76 foot ship out in order to take it on Lake Superior for its maiden voyage. Although Asp died in 1980, his children fullfilled his dream by sailing to Norway aboard the "Hjemkomst." Norwegian for "homecoming" they returned from Norway in the summer of 1982.

Lake Park

Place Name

Lake Park was settled in 1870. The name is actually the result of a collection of Ojibwe words translating by Gilfillan to mean, "the lakes where there are streams, groves, prairies, and a beautiful diversified park country".

General Trivia

The Cormorant Lake lies near the town. Three so-called "anchor stones" rest on the lake. The "stones" are actually massive boulders. They are believed to have been used by Norse explorers to tie up their boats. The theory is arguable, but it makes the town unique.

Audubon

Place Name

This towns name was in remembrance of the great American ornithologist, John James Audubon, celebrated for his pictures of birds.

The name was suggested by his niece when she was camping near the area with a group of friends. She was impressed with the natural beauty of the area and said that if a railway station ever was built here, it should be called Audubon.

Detroit Lakes

The Tamarac National Wildlife Refuge stands just north of Detroit Lakes.

Place Name

A French priest named the seat of Becker County in the late 18th century. A "Detroit" is a strait or narrows. "Lakes" was added to the name because they clearly characterize the region with some 500 lakes in the vicinity.

Local Landmark

Through woodland and prairie, along riverbanks and through sloughs, the mixed-blood American and Canadian buffalo hunter called Metis blazed trails with their oxen and squeaky-wheeled wooden carts. They carried buffalo robes and pemmican from their homes along the Red River of the North to market in St. Paul, and then carried supplies back again. The heyday of the complex network of Red River trails lasted from about 1820 to 1872, when the first railroad reached the Red River at Moorhead.

The northernmost of the Red River trails ran through forested stretches along a portion of the 400 mile route. It was known as the Woods Trail and passed right through this area. This name was an exaggeration, since only the section from Detroit lakes to Crow Wing was wooded. South from Pembina the trail crossed the Red and ran along the east bank through low savannah dotted with willow and onto a high and treeless prairie. It followed beach ridges of glacial Lake Agassiz on the eastern border of the Red River Valley, entering the forest at Detroit Lakes. The trail proceeded along the Otter Trail and then the Leaf and Crow Trail made its way over sandy prairie on the east bank of the Mississippi to Sauk Rapids, where it merged with the Middle Trail, which took a more southerly route toward the Mississippi River, for the rest of the distance to St. Paul.

<u>(Historical marker located on U.S. Hwy 10)</u>

Geological

The great ice ages that began about one million years ago, were characterized by the advance and recession of huge ice sheets over vast areas of North America. These continental glaciers, originating in Canada, moved southward, scraping up mantle rock and soil which was dropped in central and southern Minnesota to produce plains and irregular belts of hills. Most of Minnesota's 10,000 lakes lie in such deposits and trace their origin directly or indirectly to glaciation.

In the rugged surface that extends from Detroit Lakes to Alexandria, where glacial action was particularly vigorous, the lakes are irregular in outline. Elsewhere they may be round, long, wide, narrow, big, little, sun-warmed or ice-cold; shallow and sandy or rocky and or without islands, inlets, bays, sand bars, beaches, or cliffs. Taken together they give Minnesota a water area greater than that of any other state.

<u>(Historical marker located on U.S. Hwy 10)</u>

Prominent People

Basketball Hall of Fame Coach, George E. Keogan was born in Detroit Lakes in 1890.

* * * *

Hollywood Editor Skip Craig was born in Detroit Lakes. His professional work includes 1001 Arabian Nights, the Bullwinkle Show, George of the Jungle and others.

Place Name

Randolph Frazee was the owner of a lumber and flour mill, and store which housed the post office which bears his name. Frazee would become a representative in the legislature.

Place Name

The Soo Line that operated between Minneapolis and Winnipeg designated the sleeping cars as the "V" series. Vergas was one of the four, the others being Viking, Venus and Venlo.

Local Landmark

The 20-foot Vergas Loon overlooking Loon Lake was dedicated in memory of Edward Krueger in 1963. He was the community's third postmaster who served from 1933 until his death in 1962.

Place Name

Josiah Perham, for whom the town was named, was known for his enthusiastic efforts for the construction of the transcontinental railway line when he was president of the Northern Pacific Railroad.

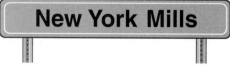

Place Name

New York Mills was founded in 1884 by a group from New York who came to town to establish lumbering mills; hence the name.

Prominent People

1970s girl's basketball star, Janet Karvonen is from New York Mills. She led her high school to three state championships. She scored more points than any other male or female

in state history. She received over 150 college scholarships. She decided to go to Old Dominion, and later to Louisiana Tech.

Place Name

The appearance of the high bank of bluffs of the Leaf River, along its course south of town, gives the town its name.

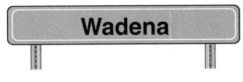

Place Name

Wadena is a Native word meaning "a little round hill". The bluffs along the Crow Wing River probably explain how the town got its name.

Place Name

Named in honor of Lucas W. Smith's, one of the first settlers, granddaughter; Helen Vernette "Vernie" Smith.

Historical Significance

In 1887, Verndale made a strong attempt to become the county seat, but unfortunately, the attempt didn't work to its advantage. Constant fighting went on between Wadena and Verndale until 1886. The fighting was so serious that women were warned to stay off the streets. In 1887, Wadena finally won the battle.

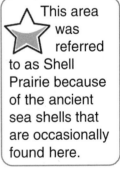

This area was referred to as Shell Prairie because of the ancient sea shells that are occasionally found here.

Industry

Early settlers relied on wheat growing throughout the area, and as many as 30 wagons would wind their way down the road. For many years, wagons unloaded both day and night with the golden grain that was grown throughout the region. However, the farmers knew little about preserving the soil nutrients which resulted in smaller yields. The pine forest eventually crept across the prairie replacing the road once known as the "Wheat Trail."

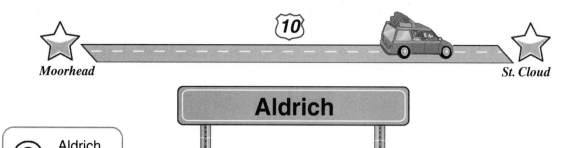

Aldrich

Aldrich Cheese has been sent to 15 out of the 16 NATO countries.

Place Name

This small village grew up as a station along the Northern Pacific Railroad tracks which was given the name by officers in honor of Cyrus Aldrich, a representative in Congress.

Staples

Place Name

The name of this town commemorates the Staple family (Samuel and Isaac) from Stillwater who were instrumental in the development of lumbering and manufacturing in the area.

Historical Significance

Staples was settled in the 1870s. Lumbering dominated the area at the time. When the Northern Pacific Railway came to the town in the 1880s, the town continued to flourish and grow. Staples became known as "The Rail Hub of the Northwest".

Motley

The Motley Castle is a four story, 18-room, moorish onion-shaped dome built in 1905 by Alfred Wilson as a boarding house for those seeking the solitude of the north power.

Place Name

Motley is named for the village established by the Northern Pacific Railroad company.

Lincoln

Place Name

Like many towns across the country, this community was named after the 16th President of the United States, Abraham Lincoln.

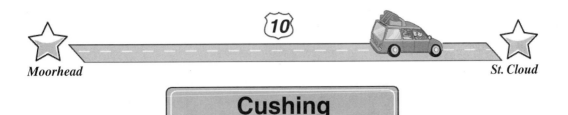

Place Name

The town was named for Massachusetts Congressman, Caleb Cushing. Joined by Franklin Steele and others, they founded St. Anthony and the lumbering industry of the upper Mississippi.

Historical Significance

Three years after its founding, fire engulfed the town of Cushing. Unfortunately, before help from nearby Little Falls could arrive, the village was virtually destroyed.

Place Name

Roxbury, Massachusetts native John Randall, for whom the town is named, came to Minnesota in 1856 working for the St. Paul and Pacific Railroad.

Prominent People

When the town was incorporated in 1900, Charles Lindbergh Sr. was the special attorney.

Industry

Cuyler Adams was joined by his faithful companion, Una, on the western edge of the range known as the Cuyuna Iron Range. The name combines the name of the prospectors and his dog's.

Iron ore was discovered in 1913 by prospector Cuyler Adams.

Thirty seven years later the Fontelle Brothers from Ironton would pile 55,000 tons of ore along the highway. For the next few years, strip mining shipped ore to Ohio and Georgia for processing. Eventually the shipping cost became too expensive for the success of the operation.

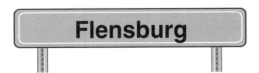

Place Name

Originally the town was platted and named after a seaport and fjord in the province of Prussian, adjoining Denmark, called Schleswig.

The village would later be known as Flen's Landing or Flynn's Siding when the Little Falls and Dakota Railroad completed the sidetrack to the local mill. The name was given in honor of a Little Falls schoolteacher, J.C. Flynn, who became an inspector for the Northern Pacific Railroad. Later Flynn became a representative in the state legislature.

Little Falls

Place Name

Little Falls developed on both banks of the Mississippi River. Little Falls is the seat of Morrison County and is named for some nearby falls by French Voyageurs.

Prominent People

Charles A. Lindbergh, Jr., who became world famous in 1927 when he flew nonstop and alone from New York to Paris in the Spirit of St. Louis, spent his boyhood summers here.

"I never deserted the farm as the ultimate goal of my return, and there is my home when I am home, for the farm unquestionably is the best of all places to live, and it affords the most independence". Thus wrote Congressman Charles Lindbergh, Sr., about his home in Little Falls on the banks of the Mississippi River.

C.A. Lingbergh was born in Sweden in 1959. One year later, his father August Lindbergh, a former member of the Swedish Parliament, brought his wife and infant son to a farm near Melrose, Minnesota, where C.A. grew up. He came to Little Falls as a young lawyer and became a prominent member of the community, and served five terms as a United States Congressman from 1907 until 1917.

Charles A. Lindbergh, Jr., who became world famous in 1927 when he flew nonstop and alone from New York to Paris in the Spirit of St. Louis, spent his boyhood summers here in the house built by his father in 1907. In the years following his landmark achievement in aviation he had an active career in exploration, scientific research, writing, and conservation.

In 1931, the Lindbergh family gave his house and 110 acres to the state of Minnesota as a memorial to Charles A. Lindbergh, Sr.

(Historical marker located at 1620 Lindbergh Drive in Lindbergh State Park)

* * * *

Little Falls is also home to Jim Langer. After becoming a football standout at South Dakota State, Langer played professional ball for the Cleveland Browns and the Miami Dolphins. He was often times referred to as the best center to ever play the game. Langer was named to the Pro Football Hall of Fame in 1987.

Geological

An esker is a landform built of sand and gravel deposited by a meltwater stream that flowed beneath a glacier. The Ripley esker is a classic esker; it stands 3 to 18 meters above the surrounding plain, and is about 68 to 76 meters wide. Although the Ripley esker is broken into several segments, it has an overall length of about 11 kilometers.

The narrow, sinuous, steep-sided ridge of sand and gravel that forms the esker is flanked on both sides by a row of small lakes and depressions. The ice that surrounded the stream was under pressure from the glacier's weight. When the stream's flow diminished, the ice squeezed inward to form a narrower tunnel. The smaller, slower stream in the smaller ice

tunnel could not carry as much sediment, and it began to deposit it on the streambed. As the sediments accumulated, they raised the level of the streambed and along with it the stream, which continually melted the ice above it and kept an open passage. This narrow, raised streambed grew to a height that became the ridge one sees today about the surrounding plain. The esker slopes down from the ridge along its length because the sediment slumped after the glacier melted away.

The Ripley esker was formed beneath a tongue-shaped lobe of ice called the Superior lobe, which flowed into this area from the northeast about 20,000 to 15,000 years ago. The esker was deposited as the Superior lobe receded. The sands and gravels of the esker were derived from the Lake Superior basin and include reddish volcanic and sedimentary rocks as well as Lake Superior agate. The pile of glacial sediment (silt, sand, gravel, and boulders) left at the edge of the Superior lobe at the point of its furthest advance is the St. Croix moraine. It is the broad swath of high hills that lies to the east of the esker.

From this point the best views of the esker are in the spring and fall, when the trees have no leaves and the prairie grasses are the dominate feature on the top of the esker.

(Historical marker located north of Little Falls on Hwy 282)

Place Name
The town of Swan River which was known throughout its history as Ledoux, Green's Ferry and Aitkinsville changed its name to honor a Polish hero, Prince

Place Name
Royal Gray one of the areas first farmers is given the honor by selection of the town's name.

Place Name
George T. Rice, the man whose name was given to the town, was the person responsible for maintaining a rest stop for the stages that traveled between St. Paul and Little Falls.

With its start 45 miles to the northeast of Royalton, the Platte River, which is French for "flat, dull, or shallow" flows through town before emptying into the Mississippi River a short distance away.

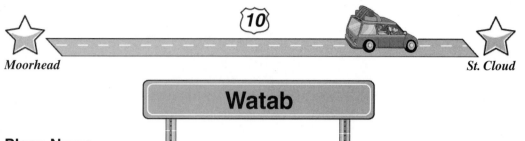

Watab

Place Name

Watab is located between Little Rock Lake and the Mississippi River. It was established in 1858 and is named for the Watab River. "Watab" is a Chippewa word referring to the long roots of the tamarack and pine trees. These roots were used by the Natives as threads to sew their birch bark canoes together.

General Trivia

The first bridge to be built across the Mississippi River north of St. Anthony Falls was in Watab. This 1855 structure collapsed after a strong wind blew it down, shortly after it was built. The bridge was never replaced.

Sartell

Place Name

Joseph Sartell, was one of the areas first farmers settling here in 1854.

Historical Significance

Sartell holds a great deal of Native American history. One example is the Indian boundary established by the Prairie du Chien Treaty of 1825, which crosses the Mississippi River in Sartell. There is a sign at the point at which it crosses that marks the boundaries. The Sioux were restricted to the southern part of the line, while the property to the north of the line was designated as Chippewa territory.

Sauk Rapids

Place Name

Sauk Rapids was originally a chunk of land sought after by the Native American Sac tribe. The Sac took refuge on this land after being forced to leave Wisconsin for attacking white settlers.

Historical Significance

Sauk Rapids served an important function in the early days of its existence. Since the town was the meeting point for rail and ox-cart traffic via the Northern Pacific and Great Northern Railways, the city of Sauk Rapids was significant to transporting goods.

However, in 1886, a tornado destroyed the city and killed 79 people. The only structure left from the town's boom days is the foundation of an old sawmill. Consequently, flour milling

Moorhead   St. Cloud

replaced transportation as the primary industry.

General Trivia

The town also supplies some high-grade rock from its quarries. Probably the most famous function its granite has served was to construct the Civic Opera Building in Chicago.

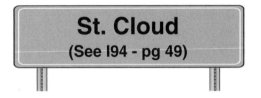

St. Cloud
(See I94 - pg 49)

HIGHWAY 2

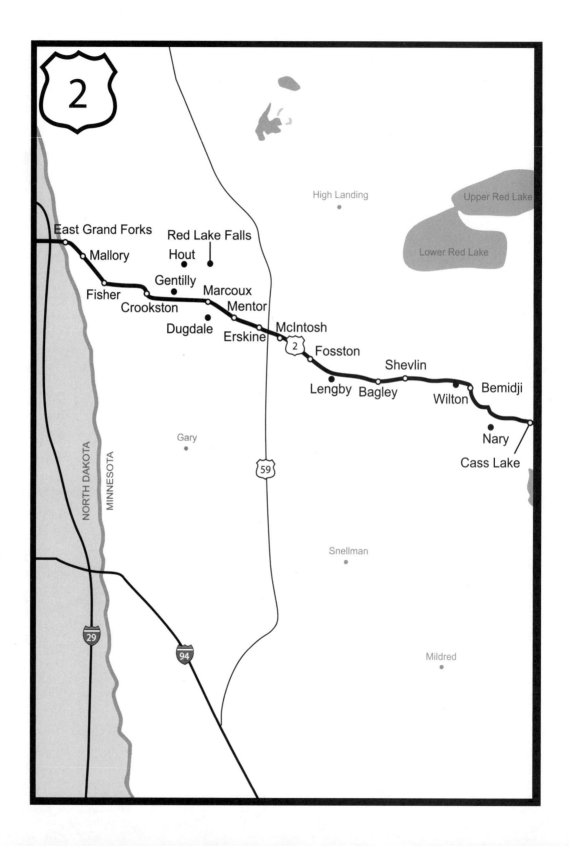

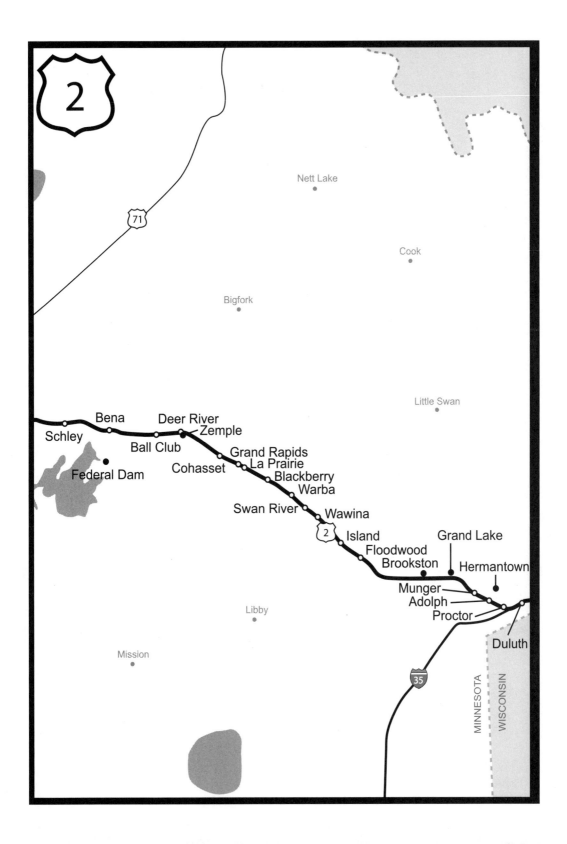

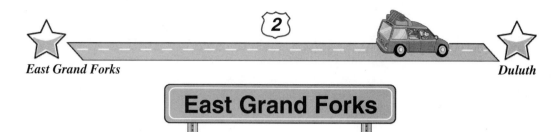

East Grand Forks

Place Name

East Grand Forks is the sisterly city to Grand Forks, North Dakota. The cordial community of East Grand Forks lies on the Red River, which separates Minnesota from North Dakota.

The first settlers arrived in the area slightly before 1800. When they arrived they set up a trading post. The population was sparse and the business was slow until 1880, when the settlement's history officially began. Sugar beet farming became popularized in the early 20th century. But later, it was potato farming that really caught on. Perhaps this is why it is known as "The Potato Capital of the World".

Mallory

Place Name

This village was named for in honor of a local lumber merchant by the name of Charles Mallory; who came from Quebec and settled in nearby Fisher.

Fisher

Place Name

First known as Shirt-tail Bend because of the shirt that was tied to a pole was used to warn the steamboats of the bend in the river ahead.

Later it was renamed Fisher's Landing after William Fisher who was engaged in the railroad business. His name eventually was adopted.

Historical Significance

Fisher is located on the Red River. Since it was the head of navigation on the river, Fisher was an extremely important frontier center. As a result of industrial change, steamboat navigation on the Red River declined, which eventually caused the entire village to relocate due to a lack of employment in the area.

A gradual shift occurred in the village, which caused its revival thanks to the American Crystal Sugar Company and sugar beet farming in the countryside.

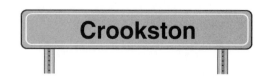
Crookston

Place Name

The city of Crookston was originally going to be called Hawley. However, a post office

already existed with that name. Thus, the postmaster ordered a new name. Ames, Aetna, Davis, and Crookston were the only suggestions that resulted from the order. The name "Crookston" was finally decided upon after a series of coin flips.

Crookston was named for Colonel William Crooks, the chief engineer of the first railway that reached the city.

Geological

The topography of the city and the surrounding area is exceptional. Like many towns in Northern Minnesota the land surrounding Crookston was once covered by glacial Lake Agassiz. This feature created a broad valley with several levels of beaches that show the historical development and eventual deterioration of the lake.

Industry

Wheat farming in the Crookston vicinity was popularized by the fine, dark, fertile soil. Polk County alone is responsible for producing two million bushels of wheat, annually. That is twice as much wheat as any other county in Minnesota produces.

Potatoes, barley, and flax are among the other crops that are grown in Crookston. Raising birds and livestock has also become popular among farmers in the Crookston region.

General Trivia

The famous Petrified Man was discovered in 1896. He was dead when he was discovered, but everyone thought that the body was that of a 17th century French voyageur.

Crookston is home to the thrilling story of Minnesota's "Petrified Man".

The famous Petrified Man was sold for $175 to Peter Bergo. He displayed this body for its fame until he basically got bored with it and sold it for $1,000. Eventually, everyone wanted a piece of the Petrified Man. The key to the Petrified Man's origin was soon found in Crookston. He was a hoax. A plasterer essentially "made" him during a slow business period.

Needless to say, the widespread interest in the famous Petrified Man deteriorated almost immediately after the information on his real origin was released.

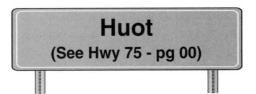

Huot
(See Hwy 75 - pg 00)

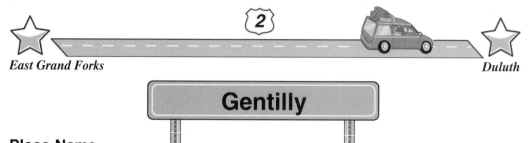

Gentilly

Place Name

The city received its name from a village on the St. Lawrence River in the Province of Quebec, which was named for the town of Gentilly in France, a southern suburb of Paris.

Historical Significance

The village of Gentilly was founded in 1895. After it was founded, Father Eli Theilon, who was born in Limoges, France, practically begged his congregation to organize a cooperative to make Limoges cheese based on a recipe the priest obtained in France. His idea turned out to be an industrial revolution for the small town.

The town organized the Gentilly Dairy Association in 1895 and produced 15,000 pounds of cheese in the first year. By 1927, the cooperative was producing 150,000 pounds a year. The cheese was sold primarily on the east coast. Father Theilon served as president for the successful cooperative that brought the first signs of prosperity to the town. As a result of his unbridled success, his thankful parishioners built a cathedral that rests just outside the village in honor of the intuitive priest.

Red Lake Falls

Place Name

Both the Red Lake and Clearwater Rivers provide a valuable supply of waterpower to the community which is named for the rapids and falls located within the area.

Historical Significance

The Northwest Company established yet another fur trading post in this town in 1798. It was in this year that Jean Baptiste Cadotte explored the area and lured other French settlers to the scenic falls.

Sculptor Carl C. Mose's monument represents a Chippewa Indian with a pipe of peace.

Local Landmark

Within the area comprising of Old Crossing Memorial Park, in the fall of 1863, negotiations were conducted with the Pemina and Red Lake bands of Chippewa Indians by which they ceded to the United States about three million acres of land in northwestern Minnesota and northeastern Dakota. This cession made possible the settlement of the Red River Valley. Here stood the great cottonwood tree which served the early settlers as a post office and here also the ox-cart trains which carried furs and supplies between St. Paul and Pembina, by way of St. Cloud or Crow Wing, forded the Red Lake River.

(Historical marker located on Hwy 11)

Place Name

This village began in 1927 with just a cafe and service station by Edward Marcoux. Eleven years later he moved to California.

Place Name

This Great Northern and Northern Pacific railway station was first called Albert before being changed to Dugdale.

Historical Significance

The Native American's would come to the area on the northwest side of Maple Lake each spring to collect syrup. The early settlers were attracted to the area because of the abundance of trees that could be cut for fuel.

Mentor was given the name for a town in Ohio where President Garfield purchased a farm and lived in the country home the last three years of his life.

Place Name

The town is named in honor of George Erskine, the person who originally platted the townsite. He came here from Racine, Wisconsin and was president of the First National Bank of Crookston.

Place Name

The original owner of part of the village site was Angus J. McIntosh. He owned a store and hotel about one and a half miles east of the present townsite, as well as some land in town. He would later move to Detroit Lakes.

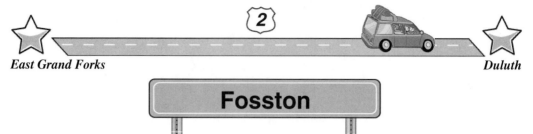
Fosston

Place Name

One of the earliest merchants in the area was Louis Foss. He was told that if he opened a general store here, the town would bear his name. Shortly after opening his store, he was wounded in an attempted robbery. Disenchanted with everything, he left the area. Arriving in the state of Washington, he would become a politician.

Lengby

Place Name

When the Swedish settlers established the town site in 1883 it was supposed to be named in honor of a local settler named Lindahl, with the addition of the "by", meaning village in Swedish. However, when the post office registered the name, they altered it slightly to Lengby rather than Lindby.

Bagley

Place Name

Sumner Bagley is the person honored by the name of this village. He was an early lumberman in the Clearwater River area, just north of here.

Shevlin

Place Name

Thomas Henry Shelvin, a former president of several logging and manufacturing companies, is the person honored in the name of this township.

Wilton

Place Name

The town's name was chosen after the town of Wiltshire, England, which was famous for the manufacturing of carpets.

Bemidji

Place Name

The city is named after Chippewa Chief Bemidji. Bemidji is a Chippewa word that means "lake with a river flowing through", or "cross lake".

Historical Significance

Bemidji was one of the last city's to settle along the Mississippi River. The city was found almost by accident. In 1894, explorers found shiny pebbles along the lakeshore. Thinking they were diamonds, the happy, presumably rich explorers purchased several acres of land in the vicinity. What started as a boom in 1894, resulted in a total collapse just one year later.

Knowing that the land could be used for something besides trying to mine for diamonds, lumberjacks started to inhabit the area. Fourteen sawmills sprang up and together, the employees that worked in these sawmills cut a million feet of lumber a day. Twenty years later, all the lumber was used and Bemidji was back to the drawing board.

Dairying and woodworking kept the town alive, and today it has even more to offer. Because of its strong lumbering background, legends of lumbering in Bemidji still exist today.

The legend of Paul Bunyan has been passed down from generation to generation in Bemidji and throughout the United States. You may hear that it took 10 storks to deliver the big boy to his parents.

You may also hear that Babe, who was Bunyan's giant, blue pet ox, created all of the tiny "footprint" lakes in the region. Supposedly, Babe was so big that every where she stepped, a new lake was formed.

Local Landmarks

Library Park contains a statue of Chief Bemidji carved from a log. The story of its construction has two conflicting origins. Some believe a lumberjack that was aided by the chief made it. Others believe a man who was honoring the chief for saving his life during a massacre made it. Either way, it is a good example of someone being very skillful at woodworking.

Prominent People

While it is extremely unusual for statues dedicated to the memory of common soldiers to be of specific individuals, a statue unveiled in Periers, Normandy, France commemorates two Minnesotans.

Virgil Tangorn of Bemidji and Richard Richtman of Minneapolis were two of the four American soldiers who died trying to free the town from the Germans during World War II.

> Chief Bemidji's band of about 50 Natives once occupied the area where the city now lies on the southern end of Lake Bemidji.

> As a result of legends, massive statues of Paul Bunyan and his pet blue ox, Babe, were constructed on the lake. The Bunyan statue weighs two tons and stands 18 feet tall.

* * * *

Ernestine Jane Geraldine Russell's father was an US Army lieutenant and her mother had been a student of drama and an actress with a traveling troupe. Once her father was out of the service he lived in Canada before finally residing in California.

Actress Jane Russell was born in Bemidji in 1921.

Jane was ultimately signed by Howard Hughes for his production of The Outlaw, the film that was to make Jane famous. Probably the pinnacle of her career was in 1953s Gentlemen Prefer Blondes as Dorothy Shaw, with Marilyn Monroe.

Her last appearance before the public was in the 1970s when Jane was a spokesperson for Playtex bras. Incidently 'Howard Hughes', in addition to designing airplanes, is said to have designed a "cantilever bra" to take care of Miss Russell's physical endowments.

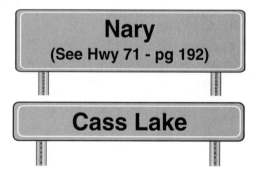

Nary
(See Hwy 71 - pg 192)

Cass Lake

Place Name

The Chippewa originally called this area "the place of red cedars". It was renamed in honor of Lewis Cass who explored the region in 1820.

The Chippewa weren't forgotten though, because the Cass Lake region is still known as "the capital of the Chippewa nation".

Historical Significance

Bishop Whipple, the first Bishop of Minnesota, led a religious mission in this area aimed at the Chippewa.

Local Landmark

The Chippewa National Forest Headquarters Building is situated in Cass Lake. The headquarters is constructed of red pine logs. It is one of the largest log structures in the world.

Prominent People

Known as Wrinkled Meat, Ga-Be-Nah-Gwen-Wonce, an Ojibwe man reportedly died in Cass Lake at the age of 137 years old.

Schley

Place Name

The Great Northern Railway station here was named in honor of a rear admiral of the U.S. Navy. Winfield Scott Schley, a graduate of the U.S. Naval Academy was an instructor there after the Civil War. During the Spanish-American War he commanded the "Flying Squadron", and led the naval battle off Santiago, Cuba.

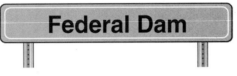

Federal Dam

Place Name

Federal Dam is situated on Leech Lake, whose name comes in reference to the reservoir dam built by the U.S. government.

Local Landmark

The town is also located next to Chippewa National Forest, which was established as a national forest in 1902.

The forest rangers in the Chippewa National Forest are particularly concerned with forest fire prevention. After all, human beings cause 90 percent of all forest fires. The forest service provides several lookouts, water tanks, tools, and telephone lines to prevent dreadful fires from destroying the land. An extensive replanting mission began in 1911 to preserve the forest.

General Trivia

On February 9th, 1899, the Federal Dam area recorded a chilling temperature of 59 degrees below zero!

Bena

Place Name

The Ojibwe word meaning "a partridge", is spelled bine, which is the word the town's name comes from. This game bird species, sometimes known also as ruffled grouse or pheasant are common to the area.

Historical Significance

Just south of Bena is Leech Lake. This lake is where the last Native American uprising in the state took place. The United States Indian Service keeps its tribal headquarters at this historic site.

The city of Bena has been called the "City Where the Partridge Finds a Refuge".

★ ★ ★ ★

The 1880s brought work to this lake region when headwater dams were constructed in each lake. These dams were constructed to control the water flowing in the lower Mississippi River.

These dams resulted in several hundred men being employed, the construction of sawmills, and thus, population growth in the region.

The dams were finally finished in 1883. However, because they were made of white pine, they were incredibly unstable, and therefore, unable to deal with the strength of the waters. As a result, they collapsed.

All that hard work went for nothing but a valuable lesson to never build a dam out of wood. Consequently, in 1898, the dams were reconstructed out of steel and concrete. These materials have enabled the dams to last much longer.

Local Landmark

Bena is located at the foot of Lake Winnibigoshish, which is a Chippewa word meaning, "miserable, dirty, water". The lake is extremely shallow with an average depth of 20 to 25 feet. It has a muddy bottom that when strong winds form waves it contributes to the dirty, mucky look.

The town takes its name from the nearby lake which was given the name by the Ojibwe because of the shape of the lake.

Historical Significance

The Native American's enjoyed playing their game using bats and balls. This game was known as La Crosse by the French.

Note: Because this name given to a town in the adjoining state of Wisconsin, the post office kept the name of the lake.

Place Name

This town is named for the person who owned most of the land, R.T. Zemple, who would become the first president of the village.

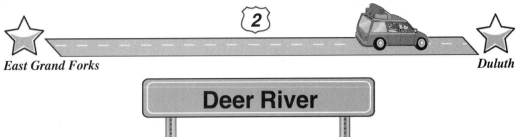

Deer River

Place Name

Deer River is a small town named for its hefty deer population. When the Ojibwe hunted along the banks of the river, they referred to it as "Wawashkeshiwi," which meant Deer River.

Historical Significance

The Deer River would plan a substantial role in the development of the area. Lumbering companies were established in the 1870s, cutting white pine to float down to the nearby mills. As the forest was depleted near the lake, the Itasca Lumber Company would build a railroad to transport the logs out of the woods. Houses sprang up near this railroad spur, which was known as Itasaca City and eventually would become Deer River.

Cohasset

Place Name

Cohasset, an Indian word, meaning "place of pines" or "fishing promontory", was named for the town of the same name on the east coast of Massachusetts.

Grand Rapids

Place Name

Grand Rapids is the seat of Itasca County and is situated at the Western end of the Mesabi Iron Range. Grand Rapids became a city in 1877 and it is named for the turbulent river rapids in the region.

Prominent People

Garland was born as Frances Ethel Gumm on June 10, 1922. The family moved to California when Frances was 12 and consequently, changed her name to Judy Garland.

Garland beat out Shirley Temple for the part of Dorothy in "The Wizard of Oz". When she was just 17 years old, she picked up her first special Oscar. However, it wasn't the real thing. Children weren't given actual Oscar's until years later. Judy was also nominated for Oscars in "A Star is Born" and "Judgment at Nuremberg". She won a Grammy for "Judy at Carnegie Hall".

Judy Garland's birthplace can be seen in Grand Rapids.

* * * *

Lois Hall was also born in Grand Rapids. She moved with her family to Long Beach, CA where she had her first experience with theatre as a set designer, stage manager and head electrician, was given a scholarship at the Pasadena Playhouse and became bitten by the "acting bug". Her career includes such tv episodes on The Lone Ranger, Father Murphy, Marcus Welby, M.D., Star Trek the Next Generation, and The Practice.

Place Name

Named in honor of an Ojibwe leader, Scotty La Prairie.

Historical Significance

This town would get its start as developers in the area promoted it as the head of navigation on the Mississippi River. However, the steamboats traveling north from Aitkin, passed through the area enroute to the true head of navigation which is at the falls of Grand Rapids. Being overlooked the town eventually faded off to sleep to become a bedroom community for Grand Rapids.

Place Name

Peter Larsen gave the name of this town in reference to the abundance of blackberry briers in the area.

Place Name

First known as Dickson's Spur after a lumberman by the name of Dickson. The name of the logging site would be changed to Verna. Located side by side with the village named for Thomas Feeley, the sawmill owner, it would be known as Feeley.

Anyways, when the post office was established it thought the name Feeley resembled the name Foley. When they suggested renaming the village, they held a contest. The winner A.A. Hall suggested the word warbasibi, an Indian word interpreted as "resting place" or "white swan". Eventually both Verna and Feeley would become Warba.

Swan River

Place Name

In 1855, the Chippewa ceded the land between the Red and Swan rivers. The town got its name from the river located due west of town.

Wawina

Place Name

According to the Baraga's Dictionary, this town's name comes from an Ojibwe word meaning "I name him often, or mention him frequently".

Island

Place Name

A tract of dry farming land was surrounded by a very extensive swamp region with the exception of a higher ground of land which gave the appearance of an island.

Floodwood

Historical Significance

This community was established at the junction of the St. Louis, Savanna and Floodwood rivers. It was a trading post area for the fur traders and explorers traveling from Lake Superior to the Mississippi River. With the arrival of the railroad so did the first settlers. Staking their claims they started lumbering, harvesting the large amounts of white pine from the surrounding forest. This lasted until the final log had gone down stream in 1923. With the lumbering companies leaving the area, it would develop into a dairy farm area.

> Floodwood was named for the large pieces of driftwood that obstructed the nearby stream.

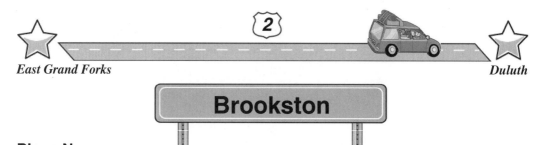

Place Name

This station located on the Duluth, Missabe and Iron Range Railroad was first called Stoney Brook Junction. After it was destroyed by fire in 1918, it was rebuilt, with the name slightly altered.

Place Name

The name comes in reference to the nearby lake which was much larger or grander than those of the surrounding area.

Place Name

The town is named for a Connecticut native. Roger Munger relocated to Duluth from the Twin City area where he was a partner in a music store with his brother, Russell. Once here, he started a lumber company. A few years later he and others established the Munger, Markell and Company which built grain elevators. Their efforts made the city a great grain-buying and shipping market. He would become the president of the Imperial Mill Company, the Duluth, Missabe and Iron Range Railroad and the Duluth, Winnipeg and Pacific Railway.

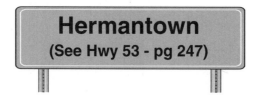

Place Name

Derived from the old German language, this town has a personal name meaning "noble hero".

Hermantown
(See Hwy 53 - pg 247)

354

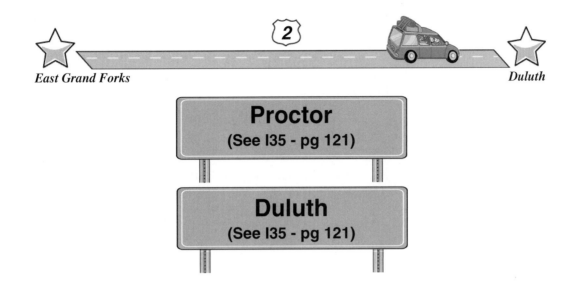

Proctor
(See I35 - pg 121)

Duluth
(See I35 - pg 121)

Index

Note: Since some cities are located on more than one route (highway and/or interstate), and because trip trivia information is included on only one, see the **bolded** listing for more detailed information

Breckenridge	168	Hwy 75	Clarissa	188	Hwy 71
Brickton	143	Hwy 169	Clarks Grove	96	I-35
Britt	252	Hwy 53	Clearwater	48	I-94
Brook Park	280	Hwy 23	Clements	181	Hwy 71
Brooklyn Center	**9**	**I-694**	Clementson	324	Hwy 11
	45	I-94	Climax	171	Hwy 75
	138	Hwy 169	Clinton	166	Hwy 75
Brooklyn Park	**10**	**I-694**	Clinton Falls	99	I-35
	45	I-94	Clontarf	306	Hwy 12
	139	Hwy 169	Coates	267	Hwy 52
Brookston	354	Hwy 2	Cobden	286	Hwy 14
Brownsdale	75	I-90	Cohasset	351	Hwy 2
Brush Creek	80	I-90	Cokato	311	Hwy 12
Brushvale	168	Hwy 75	Cold Spring	277	Hwy 23
Buffalo	46	I-94	Coleraine	148	Hwy 169
Buhl	154	Hwy 169	Collegeville	**52**	**I-94**
Burchard	**272**	**Hwy 23**		278	Hwy 23
	284	Hwy 14	Comstock	169	Hwy 75
Burnsville	16	I-494	Cook	252	Hwy 53
	105	**I-35**	Coon Rapids	9	I-694
Byron	300	Hwy 14		**139**	**Hwy 169**
Callaway	239	Hwy 59	Cottage Grove	213	Hwy 61
Calumet	149	Hwy 169	Cotton	248	Hwy 53
Cambridge	113	I-35	Cottonwood	233	Hwy 59
Canby	164	Hwy 75		**273**	**Hwy 23**
Cannon City	102	I-35	Courtland	293	Hwy 14
Cannon Falls	265	Hwy 52	Crookston	172	Hwy 75
Carlisle	58	I-94		**342**	**Hwy 2**
Carlton	120	I-35	Currie	230	Hwy 59
Carver	136	Hwy 169	Cushing	333	Hwy 10
Cass Lake	348	Hwy 2	Cusson	253	Hwy 53
Castle Danger	216	Hwy 61	Dakota	**67**	**I-90**
Castle Rock	104	I-35		199	Hwy 61
Cazenovia	163	Hwy 75	Dalton	58	I-94
Central Lakes	248	Hwy 53	Danube	185	Hwy 71
Ceylon	85	I-90	Danvers	306	Hwy 12
Champlin	139	Hwy 169	Darwin	309	Hwy 12
Chanhassen	**19**	**I-494**	Dassel	311	Hwy 12
	137	Hwy 169	Dawson	165	Hwy 75
Chaska	136	Hwy 169	Deer River	351	Hwy 2
Chatfield	69	I-90	DeGraff	307	Hwy 12
	261	**Hwy 52**	Delano	312	Hwy 12
Chester	300	Hwy 14	Delft	179	Hwy 71
Chisago City	110	I-35	Detroit Lakes	239	Hwy 59
Chisholm	153	Hwy 169		**329**	**Hwy 10**
Circle Pines	107	I-35	Dexter	74	I-90
Clara City	275	Hwy 23	Dilworth	327	Hwy 10
Claremont	297	Hwy 14	Dodge Center	298	Hwy 14

Donaldson	**174**	**Hwy 75**	Fairfax	184	Hwy 71
	317	Hwy 11	Fairmont	84	I-90
Donnelly	237	Hwy 59	Faribault	100	I-35
Doran	167	Hwy 75	Farmington	104	I-35
Dover	**69**	**I-90**	Federal Dam	349	Hwy 2
	301	Hwy 14	Fergus Falls	**58**	**I-94**
Dresbach	66	I-90		238	Hwy 59
Dudley	231	Hwy 59	Finland	219	Hwy 61
Dugdale	345	Hwy 2	Finlayson	117	I-35
Duluth	**121**	**I-35**	Fisher	342	Hwy 2
	214	Hwy 61	Flensburg	333	Hwy 10
	247	Hwy 53	Floodwood	353	Hwy 2
	355	Hwy 2	Florence	272	Hwy 23
Dumont	167	Hwy 75		**284**	**Hwy 14**
Dundas	102	I-35	Foley	278	Hwy 23
Dunville	239	Hwy 59	Forest Lake	109	I-35
Eagan	**14**	**I-494**	Foreston	279	Hwy 23
	108	I-35	Fort Ridgely	184	Hwy 71
Eagle Bend	189	Hwy 71		**287**	**Hwy 14**
Eagle Lake	295	Hwy 14	Fosston	345	Hwy 2
Eagle Mountain	222	Hwy 61	Fountain	260	Hwy 52
East Grand Forks	342	Hwy 2	Fox	318	Hwy 11
Eden Prairie	**19**	**I-494**	Fox Lake	85	I-90
	137	Hwy 169	Frazee	330	Hwy 10
Edgerton	161	Hwy 75	Freeport	53	I-94
Edina	**18**	**I-494**	Fridley	8	I-694
	137	Hwy 169	Friesland	115	I-35
Elbow Lake	238	Hwy 59	Frontenac	208	Hwy 61
Eldred	172	Hwy 75	Frost	81	I-90
Elizabeth	238	Hwy 59	Fulda	229	Hwy 59
Elk River	141	Hwy 169	Funkley	193	Hwy 71
Ellendale	96	I-35	Garden City	130	Hwy 169
Elmore	81	I-90	Garfield	57	I-94
Ely	157	Hwy 169	Garrison	146	Hwy 169
Empire	267	Hwy 52	Garvin	231	Hwy 59
Erhard	238	Hwy 59		**284**	**Hwy 14**
Ericsburg	254	Hwy 53	Geneva	96	I-35
Erskine	241	Hwy 59	Gentilly	344	Hwy 2
	345	**Hwy 2**	Georgetown	170	Hwy 75
Esko	120	I-35	Gheen	253	Hwy 53
Essig	290	Hwy 14	Ghent	**233**	**Hwy 59**
Euclid	171	Hwy 75		272	Hwy 23
Evan	286	Hwy 14	Gilbert	250	Hwy 53
Evansville	57	I-94	Glyndon	327	Hwy 10
Eveleth	249	Hwy 53	Golden Valley	**138**	**I-494**
Excelsior	20	I-494		138	Hwy 169
Eyota	**69**	**I-90**	Goodhue	263	Hwy 52
	301	Hwy 14	Gooseberry Falls	216	Hwy 61

Gotha	136	Hwy 169	Holt	243	Hwy 59
Graceville	167	Hwy 75	Homer	199	Hwy 61
Granada	83	I-90	Hopkins	**21**	**I-494**
Grand Falls	194	Hwy 71		138	Hwy 169
Grand Lake	354	Hwy 2	Houston	67	I-90
Grand Marais	222	Hwy 61	Hout	343	Hwy 2
Grand Meadows	74	I-90	Hovland	233	Hwy 61
Grand Portage	225	Hwy 61	Howard Lake	311	Hwy 12
Grand Rapids	148	Hwy 169	Hubbard	190	Hwy 71
	351	**Hwy 2**	Humboldt	175	Hwy 75
Granite Falls	274	Hwy 23	Huot	172	Hwy 75
Green Valley	233	Hwy 59	Hutchinson	310	Hwy 12
	273	**Hwy 23**	Ilhlen	271	Hwy 23
Greenbush	317	Hwy 11	Illgen City	219	Hwy 61
Groningen	116	I-35	Imogene	83	I-90
Guckeen	83	I-90	Independence	312	Hwy 12
Hallock	174	Hwy 75	International Falls	**195**	**Hwy 71**
Halma	243	Hwy 59		254	Hwy 53
Halstad	171	Hwy 75		324	Hwy 11
Hampton	267	Hwy 52	Inver Grove Heights	**14**	**I-494**
Hanley Falls	273	Hwy 23		267	Hwy 52
Hardwick	161	Hwy 75	Island	353	Hwy 2
Harmony	257	Hwy 169	Ivanhoe	164	Hwy 75
Hassman	147	Hwy 169	Jackson	**86**	**I-90**
Hastings	211	Hwy 61		179	Hwy 71
Hasty	48	I-94	Janesville	296	Hwy 14
Haug	317	Hwy 11	Jasper	271	Hwy 23
Havana	297	Hwy 14	Jeffers	180	Hwy 71
Hawley	327	Hwy 10	Jordan	136	Hwy 169
Hayward	77	I-90	Kandiyohi	308	Hwy 12
Hazel	242	Hwy 59	Karlstad	**243**	**Hwy 59**
Hazel Run	273	Hwy 23		317	Hwy 11
Henderson	135	Hwy 169	Kasota	131	Hwy 169
Hendricks	164	Hwy 75	Kasson	299	Hwy 14
Hendrum	170	Hwy 75	Keewatin	151	Hwy 169
Hermantown	**247**	**Hwy 53**	Kellogg	204	Hwy 61
	354	Hwy 2	Kelsey	248	Hwy 53
Hewitt	189	Hwy 71	Kennedy	174	Hwy 75
Hibbin	151	Hwy 169	Kent	168	Hwy 75
High Forest	74	I-90	Kinbrae	229	Hwy 59
Hill City	147	Hwy 169	Kinney	154	Hwy 169
Hinckley	**115**	**I-35**	Knife River	214	Hwy 61
	280	Hwy 23	Kragnes	169	Hwy 75
Hoffman	237	Hwy 59	Lac gui Parle	**234**	**Hwy 59**
Holland	271	Hwy 23		165	Hwy 75
Hollandale	96	I-35	LaCrescent	**66**	**I-90**
Holloway	**236**	**Hwy 59**		199	Hwy 61
	305	Hwy 12	Lake Benton	163	Hwy 75

Place	No.	Highway	Place	No.	Highway
Lake Benton	**283**	**Hwy 14**	Mahnomen	241	Hwy 59
Lake Bronson	244	Hwy 59	Mahtowa	120	I-35
Lake City	207	Hwy 61	Makinen	249	Hwy 53
Lake George	192	Hwy 71	Mallory	342	Hwy 2
Lake Itasca	191	Hwy 71	Manchester	80	I-90
Lake Park	328	Hwy 10	Mankato	130	Hwy 169
Lake Ripley	309	Hwy 12		**294**	**Hwy 14**
Lakefield	86	I-90	Manley	**91**	**I-90**
Lakeville	104	I-35		271	Hwy 23
Lamberton	180	Hwy 71	Mantorville	299	Hwy 14
	285	**Hwy 14**	Maple Grove	10	I-694
Lamoille	199	Hwy 61		25	I-494
Lancaster	244	Hwy 59		**45**	**I-94**
Landfall	**3**	**I-694**	Maple Plain	313	Hwy 12
	13	I-494	Mapleview	75	I-90
	34	I-94	Maplewood	3	I-694
Lanesboro	257	Hwy 52	Marble	149	Hwy 169
LaPrairie	148	Hwy 169	Marcoux	345	Hwy 2
	352	**Hwy 2**	Margie	194	Hwy 71
Laurentian Divide	155	Hwy 169	Marion	**70**	**I-90**
	251	**Hwy 53**		261	Hwy 52
Leaf River	189	Hwy 71	Marshall	**231**	**Hwy 59**
Lengby	346	Hwy 2		272	Hwy 23
LeSueur	133	Hwy 169	Maynard	275	Hwy 23
Lewiston	**68**	**I-90**	Mazeppa	262	Hwy 52
	302	Hwy 14	McIntosh	345	Hwy 2
Lilydale	108	I-35	Medford	100	I-35
Lime Creek	229	Hwy 59	Medicine Lake	**23**	**I-494**
Lincoln	332	Hwy 10		138	Hwy 169
Lindstrom	112	I-35	Melrose	54	I-54
Litchfield	308	Hwy 12	Melrude	248	Hwy 53
Little Canada	**4**	**I-694**	Menahga	190	Hwy 71
	109	I-35	Mendota	**15**	**I-494**
Little Falls	334	Hwy 10		108	I-35
Little Marais	219	Hwy 61	Mentor	345	Hwy 2
Little Sauk	187	Hwy 71	Meriden	297	Hwy 14
Loman	324	Hwy 11	Mesabi Range	151	Hwy 169
Long Lake	314	Hwy 12	Milaca	**144**	**Hwy 169**
Long Prairie	188	Hwy 71		279	Hwy 23
Long Siding	143	Hwy 169	Milan	235	Hwy 59
Louisburg	166	Hwy 75	Millersburg	102	I-35
Lutsen	221	Hwy 61	Minneapolis	8	I-694
Luverne	**90**	**I-90**		23	I-494
	161	Hwy 75		**38**	**I-94**
Luxemburg	49	I-94		106	I-35
Madison	165	Hwy 75		138	Hwy 169
Madison Lake	296	Hwy 14	Minneiska	204	Hwy 61
Magnolia	89	I-90	Minnesota City	203	Hwy 61

Minnetonka	21	I-494		Northfield	103	I-35
Minnetrista	313	Hwy 12		Oak Park	278	Hwy 23
Mizpah	194	Hwy 71		Oakdale	3	I-694
Money Creek	67	I-90		Odessa	166	Hwy 75
Monticello	47	I-94		Ogema	240	Hwy 59
Montrose	312	Hwy 12		Ogilvie	279	Hwy 23
Moorhead	**60**	**I-94**		Okabena	86	I-90
	169	Hwy 75		Olivia	185	Hwy 71
	327	Hwy 10		Onamia	145	Hwy 169
Moose Lake	119	I-35		Oronoco	261	Hwy 52
Mora	279	Hwy 23		Orr	253	Hwy 53
Morris	236	Hwy 59		Orrock	47	I-94
Morristown	100	I-35		Ortonville	166	Hwy 75
Morton	183	Hwy 71			**305**	**Hwy 12**
Moscow	77	I-90		Osakis	55	I-94
Motley	332	Hwy 10		Osseo	10	I-694
Mound	313	Hwy 12			45	I-94
Mounds View	**7**	**I-694**			**138**	**Hwy 169**
	106	I-35		Ottawa	133	Hwy 169
Mountain Iron	**154**	**Hwy 169**		Owatonna	**98**	**I-35**
	250	Hwy 53			297	Hwy 14
Mountain Lake	179	Hwy 71		Park Rapids	190	Hwy 71
Munger	354	Hwy 2		Payne	247	Hwy 53
Murdock	307	Hwy 12		Paynesville	276	Hwy 23
Murray	157	Hwy 169		Peary	249	Hwy 53
Nary	**192**	**Hwy 71**		Pease	143	Hwy 169
	348	Hwy 2		Pelican Rapids	**59**	**I-94**
Nashwauke	150	Hwy 169			238	Hwy 59
Nevis	190	Hwy 71		Pelland	**194**	**Hwy 71**
New Brighton	**6**	**I-694**			324	Hwy 11
	106	I-35		Pennock	307	Hwy 12
New London	187	Hwy 71		Perham	330	Hwy 10
	276	**Hwy 23**		Perley	170	Hwy 75
New Munich	53	I-94		Pickwick	199	Hwy 61
New Prague	135	Hwy 169		Pigeon River	224	Hwy 61
New Ulm	131	Hwy 169		Pine City	114	I-35
	290	**Hwy 14**		Pine Island	262	Hwy 52
New York Mills	330	Hwy 10		Pinecreek	318	Hwy 11
Newfolden	243	Hwy 59		Pipestone	**161**	**Hwy 75**
Newport	**14**	**I-494**			271	Hwy 23
	213	Hwy 61		Pitt	322	Hwy 11
Nichols	147	Hwy 169		Pleasant Grove	73	I-90
Nicollet	**293**	**Hwy 14**		Plummer	242	Hwy 59
	130	Hwy 169		Plymouth	**24**	**I-494**
Nielsville	171	Hwy 75			138	Hwy 169
Nodine	67	I-90		Ponsford	191	Hwy 71
North Branch	112	I-35		Predmore	70	I-90
Northcote	175	Hwy 75		Preston	259	Hwy 52

Shoreview	5	I-694	
Silver Bay	218	Hwy 61	
Silver Creek	48	I-94	
Simpson	70	I-90	
Slayton	230	Hwy 59	
Sleepy Eye	289	Hwy 14	
Smiths Mill	296	Hwy 14	
Sobieski	335	Hwy 10	
Sogn	264	Hwy 52	
Soudan	156	Hwy 169	
Spafford	86	I-90	
Spicer	187	Hwy 71	
	276	**Hwy 23**	
Spring Valley	260	Hwy 52	
Springfield	180	Hwy 71	
	286	Hwy 14	
Stacy	112	I-35	
Stanton	264	Hwy 52	
Staples	332	Hwy 10	
Stark	113	I-35	
Steele Center	97	I-35	
Stephen	174	Hwy 75	
Stewartville	73	I-90	
Stillwater	31	I-94	
Stockton	302	Hwy 14	
Strandquist	243	Hwy 59	
Sturgeon Lake	118	I-35	
Sunrise	112	I-35	
Swan River	353	Hwy 2	
Swift	321	Hwy 11	
Taconite	149	Hwy 169	
Taconite Harbor	220	Hwy 61	
Taylors Falls	110	I-35	
Tenney	167	Hwy 75	
Tenstrike	193	Hwy 71	
Thief River Falls	242	Hwy 59	
Tofte	220	Hwy 61	
Tower	155	Hwy 169	
Tracy	285	Hwy 14	
Traverse	132	Hwy 169	
Trosky	161	Hwy 75	
Turtle River	193	Hwy 71	
Two Harbors	214	Hwy 61	
Two Inlets	191	Hwy 71	
Tyler	284	Hwy 14	
Upper Sioux Agency	273	Hwy 23	
Utica	**69**	**I-90**	
	301	Hwy 14	

Vadnais Heights	4	I-694	
	109	I-35	
Vasa	264	Hwy 52	
Verdi	163	Hwy 75	
Vergas	330	Hwy 10	
Vermillion	267	Hwy 52	
Verndale	331	Hwy 10	
Vernon Center	130	Hwy 169	
Vineland	146	Hwy 169	
Virginia	155	Hwy 169	
	250	**Hwy 53**	
Wabasha	205	Hwy 61	
Wabasso	181	Hwy 71	
Wadena	189	Hwy 71	
	331	**Hwy 10**	
Wakemup	253	Hwy 53	
Walnut Grove	285	Hwy 14	
Wanamingo	263	Hwy 52	
Wanda	181	Hwy 71	
Warba	352	Hwy 2	
Warren	173	Hwy 75	
Warroad	320	Hwy 11	
Waseca	296	Hwy 14	
Wasioja	298	Hwy 14	
Watab	335	Hwy 10	
Watkins	276	Hwy 23	
Watson	234	Hwy 59	
Waubun	241	Hwy 59	
Waukenabo	147	Hwy 169	
Waverly	312	Hwy 12	
Wawina	353	Hwy 2	
Wayzata	**23**	**I-494**	
	314	Hwy 12	
Weaver	204	Hwy 61	
Webster	104	I-35	
Welcome	85	I-90	
Wells	80	I-90	
Wendell	238	Hwy 59	
West Concord	298	Hwy 14	
Whalan	258	Hwy 52	
Wheaton	167	Hwy 75	
White Bear Lake	**3**	**I-694**	
	109	I-35	
White Earth	240	Hwy 59	
Whiteface	248	Hwy 53	
Williams	322	Hwy 11	
Willmar	**186**	**Hwy 71**	
	276	Hwy 23	

Willmar	308	Hwy 12
Willow River	118	I-35
Wilno	164	Hwy 75
Wilson	68	I-90
Wilton	346	Hwy 2
Windom	179	Hwy 79
Winger	241	Hwy 59
Winnebago	129	Hwy 169
Winona	**200**	**Hwy 61**
	302	Hwy 14
Witoka	68	I-90
Wolverton	169	Hwy 75
Woodbury	**13**	**I-494**
	33	I-94
Worthington	**87**	**I-90**
	229	Hwy 59
Wyattville	68	I-90
Wyoming	110	I-35
Zemple	350	Hwy 2
Zimmerman	143	Hwy 169
Zumbrota	263	Hwy 52